THE TORAH IN THE TALMUD

SOUTH FLORIDA STUDIES IN THE HISTORY OF JUDAISM

Edited by
Jacob Neusner
William Scott Green, James Strange
Darrell J. Fasching, Sara Mandell

Number 69

THE TORAH IN THE TALMUD
A Taxonomy of the Uses of Scripture in the Talmud
Volume I

by
Jacob Neusner

THE TORAH IN THE TALMUD

A Taxonomy of the Uses of Scripture in the Talmud

Tractate Qiddushin
in the Talmud of Babylonia
and the Talmud of the Land of Israel

Volume I

Bavli Qiddushin
Chapter One

by

Jacob Neusner

Scholars Press
Atlanta, Georgia

THE TORAH IN THE TALMUD
A Taxonomy of the Uses of Scripture in the Talmud
Volume I

©1993
University of South Florida

Publication of this book was made possible by a grant from the Tisch Family Foundation, New York City. The University of South Florida acknowledges with thanks this important support for its scholarly projects.

Library of Congress Cataloging in Publication Data
Neusner, Jacob, 1932-
    The Torah in the Talmud: a taxonomy of the uses of Scripture in the Talmud: Tractate Qiddushin in the Talmud of Babylonia and the Talmud of the land of Israel / by Jacob Neusner.
    p. cm. — (South Florida studies in the history of Judaism; no. 69-no. 70)
    Includes bibliographical references and indexes.
    Contents: 1. Bavli Qiddushin chapter one — 2. Yerushalmi Qiddushin chapter one and a comparison of the uses of Scripture by the two Talmuds.
    ISBN 1-55540-828-1 (v. 1). — ISBN 1-55540-829-X (v. 2)
    1. Talmud. Kiddushin I—Criticism, interpretation, etc.
2. Talmud Yerushalmi. Kiddushin I—Criticism, interpretation, etc.
3. Bible. O.T.—Quotations in rabbinical literature.   I. Title.
II. Series: South Florida studies in the history of Judaism; 69-70.
BM506.K53N48   1993
296.1'2406—dc20   92-46278
                                       CIP

Printed in the United States of America
on acid-free paper

Table of Contents

Preface

This monograph stands on its own and also relates to its successor. On its own, it deals with the role of Scripture in the Talmud of Babylonia, thus: "the Torah in the Talmud." I believe the results of this systematic analysis present some surprises and raise puzzling questions, which I propose to solve in Chapter Three. At the same time, I set the stage for a comparison between the two Talmuds, the one of Babylonia, the other of the Land of Israel, within a single framework: how Scripture makes its way in each of the two. In Chapter One I explain the first of these two purposes, and here, briefly, the second.

Through my analytical translation of the Talmud of Babylonia and also my (to date: seventeen) associated monographs,[1] I have been

---

[1] *The Bavli and Its Sources: The Question of Tradition in the Case of Tractate Sukkah* (Atlanta, 1987: Scholars Press for Brown Judaic Studies).

Making the Classics in Judaism: The Three Stages of Literary Formation (Atlanta, 1990: Scholars Press for Brown Judaic Studies).

Tradition as Selectivity: Scripture, Mishnah, Tosefta, and Midrash in the Talmud of Babylonia. The Case of Tractate Arakhin (Atlanta, 1990: Scholars Press for South Florida Studies in the History of Judaism).

Language as Taxonomy. The Rules for Using Hebrew and Aramaic in the Babylonian Talmud (Atlanta, 1990: Scholars Press for South Florida Studies in the History of Judaism).

The Bavli That Might Have Been: The Tosefta's Theory of Mishnah Commentary Compared with That of the Babylonian Talmud (Atlanta, 1990: Scholars Press for South Florida Studies in the History of Judaism).

The Rules of Composition of the Talmud of Babylonia. The Cogency of the Bavli's Composite (Atlanta, 1991: Scholars Press for South Florida Studies in the History of Judaism).

The Bavli's One Voice: Types and Forms of Analytical Discourse and Their Fixed Order of Appearance (Atlanta, 1991: Scholars Press for South Florida Studies in the History of Judaism).

The Bavli's One Statement. The Metapropositional Program of Babylonian Talmud. Tractate Zebahim. Chapters One and Five (Atlanta, 1991: Scholars Press for South Florida Studies in the History of Judaism).

engaged in the systematic description of the Talmud. The present exercise continues that work. The importance of the project requires no considerable explanation. It is the simple fact that the Talmud of Babylonia defined Judaism from the age of its closure to our own day. Represented as the record of a tradition that began with God's revelation of the Torah to Moses at Sinai, the document demands analysis in its own terms. It is my analytical translation that makes possible the study that has been too long postponed: just what is this document, how does it work, in what ways do its authors convey their message and make their statement? The analytical translation forms the foundation because it identifies the smallest whole units of discourse and defines the relationships of one to the next, and of groups to other groups. Without such a clear, visual re-presentation of the document, we simply do not have a grasp of the Talmud's building blocks, in our terms, its sentences, paragraphs, chapters, and therefore we cannot set forth and test a theory of how these components combine to form the whole: an analytical account of the writing. Like the inventor of the first telescope, as these pages will show, I find myself puzzled by what I am seeing; all the received categories fail as I attempt to frame an account of what is there.

My question here is a very specific one. It concerns what happens to the Torah (a.k.a., Hebrew Scriptures, "Old Testament," "Written Torah")

How the Bavli Shaped Rabbinic Discourse (Atlanta, 1991: Scholars Press for South Florida Studies in the History of Judaism).

The Bavli's Massive Miscellanies. The Problem of Agglutinative Discourse in the Talmud of Babylonia (Atlanta, 1992: Scholars Press for South Florida Studies in the History of Judaism).

Sources and Traditions. Types of Composition in the Talmud of Babylonia (Atlanta, 1992: Scholars Press for South Florida Studies in the History of Judaism).

The Law Behind the Laws. The Bavli's Essential Discourse (Atlanta, 1992: Scholars Press for South Florida Studies in the History of Judaism).

The Bavli's Primary Discourse. Mishnah Commentary, Its Rhetorical Paradigms and Their Theological Implications in the Talmud of Babylonia Tractate Moed Qatan (Atlanta, 1992: Scholars Press for South Florida Studies in the History of Judaism).

The Discourse of the Bavli: Language, Literature, and Symbolism. Five Recent Findings (Atlanta, 1991: Scholars Press for South Florida Studies in the History of Judaism).

How to Study the Bavli: The Languages, Literatures, and Lessons of the Talmud of Babylonia (Atlanta, 1992: Scholars Press for South Florida Studies in the History of Judaism).

The Bavli's Intellectual Character. The Generative Problematic in Bavli Bava Qamma Chapter One and Bavli Shabbat Chapter One (Atlanta, 1992: Scholars Press for South Florida Studies in the History of Judaism).

Decoding the Talmud's Exegetical Program: From Detail to Principle in the Bavli's Quest for Generalization. Tractate Shabbat (Atlanta, 1992: Scholars Press for South Florida Studies in the History of Judaism).

in the Talmud, and how the Talmud is shaped by the Torah. The premise, of course, is that we distinguish the Torah from the Talmud, and the puzzling outcome will be that that premise is dubious and misleading. But it will take a considerable effort to explain why, in detail, in the context of a complete chapter of the Bavli. The premise is universally held by both theology and history of religions, that the Hebrew Scriptures form a critical component of the Talmud of Babylonia, and I am hardly to be faulted from asking, if so, then how? In the opening chapter I spell out the question at hand and why I think the question deserves considerable attention. Scriptural authority in Judaism, as much as in Christianity, forms a principal source of theological formation. Not only so, but all literary study of the Talmud proceeds from the assmption that Scripture forms a principal constitutive component. So now it is time to move beyond generalization and toward the particularization of the matter: what purpose does the Written Torah serve, and how in the canon of the Judaism of the Dual Torah that reaches its climax in the Talmud does Scripture make its definitive contribution? Knowing the answer to those questions materially advances our work of description of the Talmud.

In Volume II, I undertake the parallel analysis of the same chapter in the Talmud of the Land of Israel (a.k.a., Yerushalmi, Palestinian Talmud). The reason for a second volume presents no mystery to anyone who understands that there is no describing one writing without comparing it and contrasting it with another of its genre; that is the sole position from which we gain perspective. He who knows one book knows none. Since I need also to know how the Talmud of Babylonia relates to, compares with, other writings of its genre, and this, of course, means to and with the Talmud of the Land of Israel, I need to find bases for comparison. These bases will define terms to be addressed in the same way, invoking the same category, in both documents. One reliable basis for comparison is how two documents deal with a third, which they have in common. Both Talmuds, of course, form commentaries to the Mishnah, and in a separate study I shall compare how each reads the document read by the other as well. But there is another basis for comparison. Scripture, too, forms a shared document, to which each responds, and I am able to compare the one to the other by appeal to that trait common to them both. In this comparative part of the study (presented in Volume II of the present work), what I want to find out, through various probes, is whether it sets forth a statement of its own or reworks received materials.

So much for the work at hand. But let me also place it into the context of the next phase in this rather single-minded program of mine, which began with my book, *A Life of Yohanan ben Zakkai* (Leiden, 1962: E. J. Brill) and has continued, on a continuous and quite straight path, for thirty years since then. I have now published more than four hundred books, all but one of them dealing with only one thing: Judaism, mainly in its formative age. Standing on its own terms, this inquiry also marks the beginning of the next stage in my work, which has returned to its starting point, the study of the Talmud of Babylonia. Now, as is clear, I reach the comparative stage. I have described the document, as best I can, in its own terms and framework. Nearly a score of monographs have now come forth as byproducts of my systematic, analytical translation of the document. I have come as far as I can presently imagine in the description of the document out of its own evidence, phenomenologically analyzed. The comparison to the other Talmud affords not only perspective, but also addresses a very specific claim that is commonly set forth about the Talmud's character. The regnant theory of its literary character, framed in the myth of tradition, means to insist that the document forms a link in a great chain of tradition. That remains to be not only asserted, as has been done for the entire history of the reception of the writing, but also demonstrated. Or the opposite characterization of the document requires not merely assertion but verification through sustained and systematic inquiry. It is that inquiry that commences in these monographs. The work begins because a massive preparatory project is now complete. Specifically, to define the document, I had first to translate it in an analytical manner, identifying its components and their relationships. That project made possible the exact and accurate comparison of one thing to some other, and since I had already translated the Talmud of the Land of Israel in precisely the same analytical mode, the analysis and comparison of both Talmuds is now possible. This work of analytical translation I have now done for twenty-seven of the thirty-seven tractates, and co-workers have done most of the other tractates in the same way. So we now know what the document says and how it delivers its message,[2] and therefore may now proceed to ask about that for which it stands.

Accordingly, it is time to find out whether the Bavli stands on its own and makes a statement in behalf of its framers or authorship, or whether it continues the work of other writing of its class, the Talmud of

---

[2]With the proviso that there is always room for improvement on episodic problems of philology and on-site exegesis, and I never claim to have done full justice to the profundity of speculative and abstract thought of many passages, on the one side, or the mystery of some words and phrases, on the other. But I find the unsolved problems of philology and exegesis no material obstacle in the way of analysis of another order altogether, just as I am unimpressed by the complaints of those who maintain that, until we know the meaning of every word in its historical context, we can say nothing about the structure and program of the document overall.

the Land of Israel or Yerushalmi. The first comparison concerns how each of the two writings responds to a document common to them both, that is, the Written Torah. The second, which will follow in sequence, addresses the issue of how each responds to another document common to them both, the Oral Torah contained in the Mishnah. These comparisons of the two Talmuds to the two documents they have in common will tell me whether the writings relate to one another directly, or only through a common, prior document, Scripture and the Mishnah, respectively.[3]

I mean systematically to propose solutions to a variety of long-standing problems in the study of the formation of Judaism culminating in the Talmud of Babylonia. Now a variety of further studies, hitherto impossible because of the absence of an analytical system and structure, get underway, leading, I anticipate, to "from religion to theology," the movement from the Yerushalmi and its associated Midrash compilations to the Bavli and its associated Midrash compilations. The works I plan in succession to my Bavli translation and the present work are the following eight monographs:

The Bavli and the Yerushalmi. A Systematic Comparison. A Preliminary Probe: Bavli and Yerushalmi to Mishnah-tractate Qiddushin. I. Chapter One (Atlanta, 1994: Scholars Press for South Florida Studies in the History of Judaism).

The Bavli and the Yerushalmi. A Systematic Comparison. A Preliminary Probe: Bavli and Yerushalmi to Mishnah-tractate Qiddushin. II. Chapter Two (Atlanta, 1994: Scholars Press for South Florida Studies in the History of Judaism).

The Bavli and the Yerushalmi. A Systematic Comparison. A Preliminary Probe: Bavli and Yerushalmi to Mishnah-tractate Qiddushin. III. Chapter Three (Atlanta, 1994: Scholars Press for South Florida Studies in the History of Judaism).

---

[3]I have already compared the Bavli's and Tosefta's address to the Mishnah in *The Bavli That Might Have Been: The Tosefta's Theory of Mishnah Commentary Compared with That of the Babylonian Talmud* (Atlanta, 1990: Scholars Press for South Florida Studies in the History of Judaism). Compared from that perspective, the two documents showed no sustained or consistent relationship to one another, only to the Mishnah.

The Bavli and the Yerushalmi. A Systematic Comparison. A Preliminary Probe: Bavli and Yerushalmi to Mishnah-tractate Qiddushin. IV. Chapter Four (Atlanta, 1994: Scholars Press for South Florida Studies in the History of Judaism).

The Bavli's Unique Voice. A Systematic Comparison of the Talmud of Babylonia and the Talmud of the Land of Israel. I. Bavli and Yerushalmi Qiddushin Chapter One Compared and Contrasted (Atlanta, 1994: Scholars Press for South Florida Studies in the History of Judaism).

The Bavli's Unique Voice. A Systematic Comparison of the Talmud of Babylonia and the Talmud of the Land of Israel. II. Yerushalmi's, Bavli's, and Other Canonical Documents' Treatment of the Program of Mishnah-Tractate Sukkah Chapters One, Two, and Four Compared and Contrasted. A Reprise and Revision of The Bavli and Its Sources (Atlanta, 1994: Scholars Press for South Florida Studies in the History of Judaism).

The Bavli's Unique Voice. A Systematic Comparison of the Talmud of Babylonia and the Talmud of the Land of Israel. III. Bavli and Yerushalmi to Selected Mishnah Chapters in the Division of Moed. Erubin Chapter One, and Moed Qatan Chapter Three (Atlanta, 1994: Scholars Press for South Florida Studies in the History of Judaism).

The Bavli's Unique Voice. A Systematic Comparison of the Talmud of Babylonia and the Talmud of the Land of Israel. IV. Bavli and Yerushalmi to Selected Mishnah Chapters in the Division of Nashim: Gittin Chapter Five, Nedarim Chapter One, and Niddah Chapter One (Atlanta, 1994: Scholars Press for South Florida Studies in the History of Judaism).

The results of the foregoing, rather painstaking and detailed analyses, will shape the principal project, which presently looks this way:

The Definition of Judaism. From the Yerushalmi's Religion to the Bavli's Theology. The Autonomous Discourse of the Bavli and Its Associated Midrash Compilations. The Traits and Program of the Normative, Dual Torah in Conclusion.

The Bavli and the Denkart. A Comparison of the Systemic Statements of Judaism and Zoroastrianism.

From Old Order to New: Judaism, Zoroastrianism, Islam at the End of Antiquity.

My present expectation is that, on the other side of the work outlined here, I shall be able to set forth the theology of the Judaic canon, as that canon had come to conclusion (never to closure!) at the end of ancient times. That is to say, I hope to find out what in the Judaism of the Dual Torah it means to have access to God's mind, through our mind: what it means to love and serve and know God in intellect, as our sages of blessed memory did (and do) through the Torah. For others know and serve and love God through other media: God incarnate, for example. But as to the Judaism of the Dual Torah, we know God through the Torah and only through the Torah. Then what does that knowing know? And what is knowing? At the closing lines of my *Uniting the Dual Torah*[4] I point to some lines of inquiry, but, of course, until the Bavli is truly and accurately described, until we have access to its statement, whole and cogent, we can only stand on the hither side of that particular mountain, the one before Sinai, I suppose. The stakes, for the understanding of the formative history of Judaism, are formidable.

JACOB NEUSNER

Distinguished Research Professor of Religious Studies
UNIVERSITY OF SOUTH FLORIDA
Tampa, FL 33620-5550 USA

---

[4]*Uniting the Dual Torah: Sifra and the Problem of the Mishnah* (Cambridge and New York, 1989: Cambridge University Press).

1

The Torah in the Talmud

The pages of the Talmud of Babylonia are studded with citations of verses of Scripture. I want to know why and how the Hebrew Scriptures or "Written Torah" serve in the writing of that Talmud. So by "the Torah in the Talmud" I refer to the uses of Scripture, or the Written Torah, in the two Talmuds, the Yerushalmi and the Bavli, the latter being the principal document of the Oral Torah. Though the ramifications are many, the inquiry is simple. It is to classify the kinds of compositions and composites in the Talmud (in this volume: of Babylonia) that contain verses of Scripture ("the Written Torah"), in each case asking a few simple questions about the form and purpose of the composition. When I find a clear citation of a verse or clause of Scripture, I want to know why that citation is introduced, what it is assumed to demonstrate, and how it serves the plan of the framer of the composition in which it occurs. Sample questions include these: Is a verse of Scripture determinative of the structure of a passage or is it instrumental and subordinate? Does a clause of Scripture undergo sustained, consistent analysis, in the way in which a clause of the Mishnah does, or is it treated in a casual way, for example, as a mere illustration or a touch of literary artifice? Are coherent, analytical, hermeneutical principles brought to bear upon the reading of Scripture in the context of the Talmudic inquiry, or are readings haphazard and episodic? These and similar questions have not yet been answered, so far as I know, and I see no evidence that they engage many others. And yet, they seem to me critical to an understanding of both the document and the category formation upon which it rests (a matter that will engage us when data are in hand).

Let me now define what seem at the moment to be entirely valid categories: "Torah," meaning, the Pentateuch, or the entirety of the Hebrew Scriptures, and "the Talmud," in this case, as I said, the Talmud of Babylonia. (In the present context, the mythic category, "Oral Torah," plays no role; this study is narrowly phenomenological, as are all of my monographs in this series.) At the moment, after all, these distinct pieces of writing – the Torah, the Talmud – surely stand on their own, and everyone knows what this one is and what that one is; only at the end shall we find reason to wonder. But now, within the established categories, the abstract issue before us concerns the standing in, and uses and authority of, the Torah for the Talmud. An account of scriptural authority in the formative Judaism of late antiquity will hardly puzzle those familiar with the scriptural religions of the age, the Judaisms and most of the Christianities of that time. For the case of Judaism, we all know, of course, that all parties to Judaism accord to the (Written) Torah's ultimate authority, not only in abstract, but in concrete and detailed terms.

But it does not suffice to say at the outset, Scripture formed the court of final appeal, settling all questions, solving all problems. That may be so, but it does not account very well for the character of all the evidence or even very much of it: all the many ways in which a verse of Scripture, or a fact imputed to Scripture, contributes to a variety of compositions and even composites. It is true, too, as we all know, that Scripture, for Judaism the Written Torah, was and is inerrant, the precise statement of God's will in God's words. That allegation, too, while true, obscures all the interesting problems, for all parties to the heritage of the Torah, in diverse Judaisms as well as Christianities, affirmed that authority and did so in terms easily rendered in the language just now used; no one in the Judaic and Orthodox and Catholic Christian worlds of antiquity (excluding, therefore, only Marcion and those of his classification) would have argued about that point so far as the Hebrew Scriptures of ancient Israel are concerned.

In fact, we shall soon see, matters prove far more complex and turn out indeed to define their own problematic. We shall see that Scripture plays an active and a passive role; it dictates the shape of inquiry and its logic, and it merely contributes inert facts to an inquiry framed in other terms altogether. Consider, furthermore: Scripture forms the principal locus of discourse and takes up a merely tangential position. Verses of Scripture are accorded probative value and may be manipulated in an essentially formal manner. Make sense, if you can, of the fact that disputes may take shape on the principles by which a verse is to be read and its evidence as to fact to be uncovered, and verses may be read as if we all know precisely how to read them and what, of course, everyone knows they mean. Scripture determines the structure and program of a composition and even of large composites, and Scripture plays scarcely any more than an illustrative, formal role in a great many others. Passages of Mishnah exegesis claim that what the Mishnah says derives from Scripture, alongside passages of Mishnah exegesis that make no such pretense. In some contexts the issue proves urgent, in others, the same question attracts slight interest.   That body of contradictory evidence, when fully appreciated by the reader, will explain why what we all know – which is, Scripture forms a principal component of the Talmud – raises more questions than it settles. We really do not know whether it is true that Scripture forms a principal component of this document, and, if it does, how it does and why: Is Scripture read in the same way in which the Mishnah is, in other ways, or perhaps, is Scripture read at all? All of these questions flow in the wake of our simple question: How does the Torah makes its way into the Talmud?

This catalogue of questions is not meant to intimidate the reader, but only to explain why our task is to ask whether what everybody knows is true is true. For the one sure result is that, by whatever criterion of analysis we introduce, we find in the Talmud everything and its opposite. That simple fact turns the issue of the Torah in the Talmud into a question of more than routine and commonplace interest – much more. What we shall see, indeed, is that in the Talmud the Torah plays a role as formative, determinative, and definitive, as does the Mishnah. But it does so in its own way, which is different from that of the way of the Mishnah; it is the simple fact that the Mishnah defines the main frame of the Talmud, and not Scripture; and where Scripture dictates the structure of a composition or even of a composite, it does so in a position well subordinated to the task of Mishnah exegesis and amplification that, for this Talmud, defines the task at hand.

Still, what we are going to see is that Scripture is read in the same way as the Mishnah, and, apart from its subordinate structural position, Scripture is as formative for the Talmud as is the Mishnah. Or, to put it differently, Scripture forms a far more central presence in the Talmud than my original impression – Scripture as a source of prooftexts – suggested. And, it is clear, a quite different theory of how matters should be set forth, one that appealed to Scripture instead of to the Mishnah, or to Scripture as much as to the Mishnah, was rejected by the framers of the Talmud in favor of their own structural preference: everything formed, or reformed, into Mishnah commentary. That there was a different, and I think, clearly prior, stage in the formation of an account of the Torah, one in which commentary on Scripture predominated, presents no surprises; everyone knows about Sifra and the two Sifrés. That, in the shift to Mishnah commentary as the main frame of sustained discourse, Scripture, as much as the Mishnah, would demand, and receive, sustained and rigorous reading, in the manner and in the model of the reading of the Mishnah, is not something that is to be gainsaid; but it is so. And, yet, that fact, which we shall rapidly find instantiated in what follows, in no way solves the puzzle of the Torah in the Talmud. But for a full statement of what that puzzle is and why it is troubling, readers will want to wait until the survey of Chapter Two and the first part of Chapter Three is in hand.

As I have already hinted, that is not a result I had anticipated, but, by the end of this monograph, ample evidence will have made its impression on the reader, so that, beyond the confusion of our analytical findings, the main point will indeed emerge: the Torah as much as the Mishnah proves definitive of the Talmud: structure, problematic, and form alike. But, too, as I have already signaled, at the end of our analytical survey of the writing, that conclusion will appear rather beside the point.

What makes the inquiry engaging to those for whom the Talmud does not prove self-evidently important in its own terms is a simple fact. The place of Scripture in the Judaisms and Christianities that inherited the writings of ancient Israel never appealed for definition to Scripture, while always adducing from Scripture proof for whatever those Judaisms and Christianities determined they wished to say. That self-evident fact has now to be placed into juxtaposition and contrast with a second. It is not enough to say that Judaisms and Christianities manipulated Scripture for their own purposes. The Torah, for its part, made its impact upon Judaisms and Christianities, more or less in its own terms (whatever they can have been). While all Judaisms and most Christianities accorded to the Written Torah ultimate authority, each Judaism and Christianity reached conclusions of its own, citing verses of Scripture – to its entire satisfaction – to validate those conclusions.[1] As a matter of fact, even in formal and aesthetic terms, as much as in substantive and intellectual ones, each Judaic and Christian system through its canon found in Scripture ample evidence for propositions critical to itself (and therefore also inimical to all other systems subject to that same court of final appeal).

But, on the other side, the Torah stood supreme, placing certain limits on systemic formulation and extension, always serving as ultimate arbiter, forbidding as much as it permitted: Christianities and Judaisms in the end did form biblical religious systems, though hardly systems that cohered or proved materially congruent to one another. That underlines the complexity of our problem, and that explains why it

---

[1]That simple fact renders moot, indeed, irrelevant to all heuristic work, the conclusion urged by Judaic theologians that the Midrash reading of Scripture presented the plain sense of Scripture, so that Judaism in its successor documents states the simple truth of the Torah, while Christianity does not. Debates with critics, most recently, Hyam Maccoby, in my "Mr. Maccoby's Red Cow," *Journal for the Study of Judaism* (1991), prove that I am not beating a dead horse.

hardly settles any question to know that the framers of the Talmud cited the Torah. When we know that they settled questions through verses of Scripture, we know very little more than we did before we produced that unsurprising observation. Issues are more complicated once we turn to the writing of a particular Judaism (or Christianity), and that is what I propose to do in this exercise.

Let us start back now with an elementary question: What do we mean by the uses of Scripture? The very meaning of "use" of course is rich, the appeal to Scripture ubiquitous and compelling, in that Talmud. Clearly, the framers of the Talmud acknowledge the inerrant and verbal accuracy of the Written Torah: God's dictated, word-for-word message to Moses, our lord, at Mount Sinai. But that uniform conviction, which governs throughout, encompasses more than a single dimension of discourse, and propels us through many and profound layers of meaning. But how are we to discern in allusions to verses of the Torah the third and fourth and fifth dimensions of discourse, and in what we are we to uncover the successive layers of meaning and intent? Let me set forth one of the questions that helps us respond to the challenge.

When the author of an analytical passage appeals to Scripture, at what point in the argument he is framing, and for what compelling purpose does he invoke a verse of the Torah? Why here, not there? What is Scripture asked to contribute to discourse – a fact? a principle? a precedent? How does Scripture settle questions, and what questions does Scripture not settle? Where does Scripture form the main frame of argument, and when is a verse of Scripture tangential and merely formal? We find in the Talmud rich and sustained, indeed rather overwhelming, discussions of how components of a given verse are to be read to mean one thing, rather than some other; are left open to prove this, rather than that; or are so preoccupied in proving this that they cannot prove that. So Scripture is divided, as the Mishnah is, into its component parts, and each part is given a presence and a probative value of its own – so all are deprived of that original meaning that they had in the verse in which they stood together to say some one thing. Just how does this sleight of hand work, so as to recast Scripture into words and phrases and clauses, standing on their own, saying each what it wishes to say out of all relationship with all other words or phrases or clauses or even particles of words? To ask, then, about "the uses of Scripture" is to introduce a complex set of questions, which I think may be restated in one sizable one: Precisely what happens to Scripture, and to verses of Scripture, and to parts of those verses, down to the words, down to the letters – what happens to the Torah in the Talmud? And, more urgent still, precisely how does the Torah impart shape and structure to the Talmud, as does the Mishnah?

These questions prove schematic and at best suggestive. In fact, without analyzing a sizable corpus of data, we cannot ask a well-crafted question. So, if somewhat clumsily, having framed the question in all its diversity, I of course leave myself no option on how to proceed. We have to turn to a detailed analysis of a sustained and sizable body of writing, for there alone answers will be found – always, and only, in the details, sifted with great care and accuracy, beginning to end. For, as is now clear, to answer questions such as these, it is not enough merely to know that the author of a composition or framer of a composite deems Scripture, the Written Torah, to convey God's will in God's exact wording. That fact stands only at the threshold of inquiry; it in no way serves to differentiate data or to clarify what is at stake, or what various stakes may be at hand, when a verse or clause or word or particle of Scripture is adduced in evidence or in argument. We want also to know how a verse of Scripture accomplishes a particular purpose, why one verse rather than another is invoked, and how a repertoire of Scriptures has dictated the form and flow of his argument – if it does – or how that available store of verses has proved incidental to that argument, if it has. Not only so, but we ask, what formal or verbal signals accompany one function served by the citation of Scripture, and how do authors tell us the probative purpose – within a range of such purposes – that citing a verse of Scripture in one way, rather than in some other, is meant to accomplish?

In this context, it must be obvious, the question of how Scripture is used addresses not the technology of exegesis at all. Some find acute interest in uncovering in a given verse of Scripture the peculiar detail, for example, in wording or in context, that led an exegete to reach one conclusion rather than some other. The premise of that inquiry, of course, reveals its own apologetic: what our sages of blessed memory say is what Scripture "really" meant; and that is beyond argument – to them. But that apologetic program, sometimes disguised in literary-critical language, conveys no analytical insight; we know no more about the uses of the Torah in the Talmud than we did before, after we have been assured that the Torah was used by the Talmud in a manner wholly in accord with the Torah's intent. Nor do we require further proof of what everybody rightly knows, which is that our sages of blessed memory knew how to read Scripture and quote it for their own purposes.

The range of questions I raised just now underline that I have a different question in mind altogether. What I want to know is how framers of compositions and composites in the Bavli turned to Scripture, at what point in the writing, for what purpose, with what result – both for their writing and for Scripture: what happens to the Torah, and what happens to the Talmud, when the two meet and fuse. The traits of

Scripture in this context are of no interest at all, the traits of Talmudic thought and argument, of critical concern. For verses of Scripture, as we shall see, served a sizable repertoire of purposes, would be introduced with a range of verbal or formal signals, would dictate a choice of secondary analytical procedures. Scripture was there to be used, to be sure, but our sages of blessed memory knew how to use verses of Scripture because a variety of rules told them precisely what to expect in Scripture and what to do with Scripture. So I want to know what those rules were, what choices they identified for themselves, how they knew they were to do one thing, rather than some other, with this verse, rather than that one – the answers to these questions form an account of the Torah in the Talmud. Since the uses and authority of Scripture prove various, each defined use, each specific mode of authority, proves particular to its context until proven otherwise.

In this sustained exercise, we sift the data of a long and important tractate, identifying the types of uses of Scripture – the forms those uses take, the place in an unfolding argument accorded to them, the result, for analysis and argument, of the introduction of a verse of Scripture. My goal, therefore, is to differentiate among the numerous instances in which the Talmud appeals to the (Written) Torah, to find out what various purposes Scripture is asked to serve, how appeals to Scripture are given a particular form, and what kinds of sustained dialectical arguments are framed around the Torah in the Talmud. It is this third type of discourse involving Scripture that strikes me as the most complex and that demands the greatest attention. I accomplish that goal in the concluding chapter, which presents a systematic taxonomy of the ways in which Scripture occurs in the tractate at hand, and which also shows what happens to Scripture in that tractate: the results of that fusion that turned Scripture into a component of a distinct discourse, just as much as the Talmud turned the Mishnah into a component of a discourse entirely different from that defined by the Mishnah's own statement. The way in which, out of Scripture and the Mishnah, the Talmud made its own statement – written with Scripture, written with the Mishnah – is set forth through the details analyzed here.

As is my way, I choose a sample text and work my way through its elements. I know no more reliable way of answering questions than systematically, in dialogue with a sustained and representative part of the document under study. In this way I find pertinent data and form of them a single coherent theory of matters. I have chosen Mishnah-tractate Qiddushin, as it is expounded in the Talmud of Babylonia (and in the companion study, in the Talmud of the Land of Israel), because that tractate is rich, interesting, and a mixture of scripturally generated facts and free-standing issues and problems. A Mishnah tractate such as

Yoma, wholly dependent on Leviticus Chapter Sixteen for its program, seemed to me less suggestive than one that incorporates a variety of topics and issues, many of them autonomous of verses of Scripture. But a Mishnah tractate such as Bava Batra, with its vast conceptual and factual heritage but paltry corpus of verses of Scripture, would not serve our purpose, since the data vastly overspreads our particular problem. Qiddushin strikes me as a middling document, not too close to, nor too far from, a scriptural foundation.

Even here, let me signal what we shall see at the end: my question proves incomprehensible. The reason is that I appear to have raised a question that the framers of this writing will not have grasped. And the reason is that their categories do not permit them to answer our question – and therefore, I have framed the wrong question. What that simple observation means will be explained in due course. It suffices here to promise that, in Chapter Three, after a sustained survey of a long and complex chapter, we shall see that the evidence assembled within the taxonomy at hand – Scripture and its uses – defies all reasonable classification, and, therefore, interpretation. That is to say, when, as we shall see, we find everything and its opposite, it is clear that our category of inquiry, to begin with, is flawed. But that result so defies everyone's – including my own, original – reading of matters that it had best be postponed until it can be set forth with all solemn deliberation. It suffices here simply to say: when we ask about "the Torah in the Talmud," we violate the language rules of our writing. And nothing so completely paralyzes thought as the violation of language rules – hence, the destruction of a document's category structure and the paralysis of its media of category formation.

In the next chapter we review the whole of Chapter One of Bavli Qiddushin. In that way we gain a visually compelling picture of the extent to which the Torah plays a role in the Talmud, and the extent to which it does not. At a few points in my exposition I abbreviate the later parts of compositions and composites in which Scripture plays no role at all. In all instances my intent is to analyze and classify the pertinent entries. In Chapter Three, I survey the main points of Chapter Two and underline what I think are the principal results.[2]

---

[2]In Volume Two, in the context of my Yerushalmi Bavli comparison, I proceed systematically to catalogue the types of compositions and composites in which the Torah takes part in the formation of the Talmud. This will give us, for the first time, a differentiated account of how, where, why, and to what purpose the Torah enters into the Talmud. And it is at the point of differentiation within this document and its companion that comparison will take place.

2

Bavli Qiddushin
Chapter One

Folios 2A-41A

Before us is a long and complex chapter of the Talmud of Babylonia. I cannot expect the reader to undertake a detailed exegesis of the text, but I do believe that nearly the whole of at least one chapter should be in the reader's hand, so that the position and proportion of verses of Scripture in the context of the chapter as a whole may be placed on display. In Chapter Three I shall then present some observations on what we find in this chapter. Then, in the second part of this study, we shall undertake the same analysis of the counterpart chapter in the Talmud of the Land of Israel. Examining a complete chapter presents the sole way of affording perspective on the proportions of the whole taken up by the various phenomena I shall identify. I lightly abbreviate those composites that in no way contribute to our inquiry. This involves cutting off the later developments of passages in which Scripture plays no role whatsoever. Where I abbreviate, I place three dots at the end of the passage, to signal omissions. In the concluding chapter I provide charts that summarize the whole of the results of this and the next chapter. To highlight the occurrence of a pericope that utilizes a verse of Scripture, I indent that item; that procedure provides immediate visual evidence on position and proportion of verses of Scripture. Further to highlight the same matter, I represent in boldface type the verse and its context.

1:1

    A. A woman is acquired [as a wife] in three ways, and acquires [freedom for] herself [to be a free agent] in two ways.

    B. She is acquired through money, a writ, or sexual intercourse.

9

    C.   Through money:

    D.   The House of Shammai say, "For a denar or what is worth a denar."

    E.   And the House of Hillel say, "For a perutah or what is worth a perutah."

    F.   And how much is a perutah?

    G.   One eighth of an Italian issar.

    H.   And she acquires herself through a writ of divorce or through the husband's death.

    I.   The deceased childless brother's widow is acquired through an act of sexual relations.

    J.   And acquires [freedom for] herself through a rite of removing the shoe or through the levir's death.

I.1   A.   A woman is acquired [as a wife]:

    B.   *What differentiates the present passage, in which case the Tannaite formula commences,* A woman is acquired [as a wife], *from the passage to come, in which case the Tannaite formula uses the language,* A man effects betrothal [lit.: consecrates] on his own or through his agent [M. 2:1A]? *[Why not say, a woman is betrothed, rather than, is acquired?]*

    C.   *Since the Tannaite framer of the Mishnah passage planned to introduce the matter of acquiring through money [he used language appropriate to a monetary transaction]. For how do we know that a monetary token serves to effect betrothal?* The fact derives from the verbal analogy established by the use of the word "purchase" [or take] with reference to the field of Ephron. Here we have, "if any man take a wife" (Deut. 22:13), and there, "I will give you money for the field, take it from me" (Gen. 23:13). [Freedman: Just as "take" in the latter verse refers to money, so in the former, too, the wife is taken, betrothed, by money.] *And "taking" is referred to as acquisition, in line with the verse,* "The field that Abraham acquired" (Gen. 49:30). *Or, also,* "Men shall acquire fields for money" (Jer. 32:44). Therefore the framer of the Mishnah passage has used the word choice: A woman is acquired [as a wife].

    D.   *Well, then, why not use the same word choice in that other passage [at M. 2:1A], namely,* a man acquires...?

I.2   A.   *And how come the Tannaite framer of the passage uses the feminine form of the word* three, *rather than the masculine form?*

    B.   *The reason is that he will use the word* "way," *which is feminine, too, in the following verse of Scripture:* "And you shall show them the way wherein they must walk" (Ex. 18:20).

    C.   *Well, what about that which is taught on Tannaite authority, where the word* "three" *is used in the masculine form:* In seven ways do they examine the Zab before he is confirmed as to flux [M. Zab. 2:2A]? *Why not use the feminine form?*

    D.   *The reason is that he proposes to speak of* way, *which appears in the masculine form in the following verse:* "They shall come out against you in one way and flee before you in seven ways" (Deut. 28:27).

E.   *Well, then, the two verses prove contradictory, and the Mishnah passages are likewise contradictory!*

F.   *The two verses are not contradictory. Where we find the feminine form, the reference point is the Torah, which is feminine in the verse, "The Torah of the Lord is perfect, restoring the soul" (Ps. 19:8), and hence the feminine form is employed. There, the reference is to warmaking, which men, not women, do, so the masculine form is used. The Mishnah passages are not contradictory: Since the reference here is to a woman, the word is given the feminine form; the reference in the intersecting passage is to a man, for a man is examined, but a woman isn't; a woman contracts that form of uncleanness even though there is no external cause [so no examination is necessary]. Hence the masculine form is used.*

Scripture, along with the Mishnah, provides a fact that requires adjudication. The citation form presents no surprises.

I.3   A.   *Well, then, the Tannaite formulation uses three? It is because the word "ways" is to be used in the feminine? Then let the Tannaite formulation make reference to "things," which is a masculine noun, and use the masculine form of the word for three?*

        B.   *The reason is that the framer of the passage wanted to formulate the Tannaite rule with reference to sexual relations, and sexual relations is called "way," in the verse, "And the way of a man with a maid...such is the way of an adulterous woman" (Prov. 30:19-20).*

I.4   A.   *So there is no problem with respect to betrothal through sexual relations. What is to be said about betrothal through a monetary token or a document of betrothal?*

        B.   *They are formulated as they are in conjunction with the formulation on sexual relations.*

        C.   *And will two items be so formulated because of one?*

        D.   *These, too, are preliminaries to the sex act.*

        E.   *And if you like, I shall say, who is the authority behind the unattributed passage? It is R. Simeon, as has been taught on Tannaite authority:*

        F.   R. Simeon says, "How come the Torah has said, 'If a man take a wife' (Deut. 22:13), and not, 'when a woman is taken by a man'? It is because it is the way of a man to go looking for a woman, but it is not the way of a woman to go looking for a man. The matter may be compared to the case of someone who has lost something: Who looks for whom? The owner of the lost object looks for what he has lost."

Scripture is assumed to formulate its points by making choices in wording, framing matters as it does to make a point beyond its surface allegation, responding to the facts of the world by imposing its word choice on them, or otherwise conducting discourse at more than a single level of thought and communication. Here, too, as we shall now see,

Scripture is simply a source of facts right alongside the Mishnah,
assumed to use language in a manner consistent with the usage of the
Mishnah.

G.   *Well, then, we have learned in the Mishnah:* **In seven ways do they
     examine the Zab before he is confirmed as to flux [M. Zab. 2:2A].**
     Why not use the language, things, *there?*

H.   *In using the language they do there, we are informed that it is the way of
     gluttony to cause a flux, and it is the way of drunkenness to cause a flux.*

I.   *But lo, we have learned in the Mishnah:* **A citron [tree] is like a tree in
     three ways, and like a vegetable in one way [M. Bik. 2:6A].** *Why
     not use the language,* things, *there?*

J.   *It is because he wants to go onward,* **and like a vegetable in one way.**

K.   *Big deal — so use the language,* things, *there, too!*

L.   *[3A] There we are informed that* it is the way of a citron to be like that
     of vegetables. Specifically, just as it is the way of vegetables to
     grow through any sort of water [even artificial irrigation, which
     cannot be done for wheat and vines], and when it is picked it is to
     be tithed, so it is the way of the citron to grow through any sort of
     water [even artificial irrigation, which cannot be done for wheat
     and vines], and when it is picked it is to be tithed.

M.   *And lo, as we have learned in the Mishnah [using the word "way" rather
     than "thing" or "aspect"]:* **A koy [a beast that falls into the taxon of a
     wild beast and also into that of a domesticated beast] — There are
     ways in which it is like a wild animal, and there are ways in
     which it is like a domesticated animal; and there are ways in
     which it is like [both] a domesticated animal and a wild animal;
     and there are ways in which it is like neither a domesticated
     animal nor a wild animal [M. Bik. 2:8].** *Why not use the word
     "thing" here, too? And furthermore we have learned in the Mishnah
     [using the word "way" rather than "thing" or "aspect"]:* **This is one of
     the ways in which writs of divorce for women and writs of
     manumission [M. Git. 1:4C].** *Why not use the word "thing" here, too?
     Rather, in any passage in which there is a point of differentiation, the word
     "ways" is used as the Tannaite formulation, and in any passage in which
     there is no point of differentiation, the word "things" is used. The
     formulation of the Mishnah, closely examined, sustained that view:* R.
     Eliezer says, "It is like a tree in every thing" [M. Bik. 2:6E].

I.5 A.   *What exclusionary purpose — three, no more — is served by specifying the
          number at the opening clause and at the consequent one?*

     B.   *The exclusionary purpose of specifying the number at the opening clause
          serves to eliminate as a means of betrothal the marriage canopy [and its
          rite of consummating the marriage] itself.*

     C.   *Well, then, from the perspective of* R. Huna, *who has said,* "The
          marriage canopy effects acquisition of title to the woman, on the
          strength of an argument a fortiori," *what is eliminated by the
          specification of the number of modes of betrothal?*

     D.   *It serves to exclude the possibility of barter [trading the betrothal of a
          woman in exchange for an object]. It might have entered your mind to say,
          since we have derived the use of the word "take" from the use of the word
          "take" in connection with the field of Ephron, just as the title of a field may*

be acquired through barter, so title to a woman may be acquired through barter. Thus we are informed that that is not the case.

E. *Yeah, so maybe it is the case?*

F. *There is the possibility of an act of barter of something worth less than a penny, but through something worth less than a penny* [3B] *a woman cannot be acquired.*

I.6 A. *The exclusionary purpose of specifying the number at the concluding clause serves to eliminate the rite of removing the shoe. For it might have entered your mind to suppose that the possibility of the rite of removing the shoe should derive by an argument a fortiori from the case of the levirate wife. If a levirate wife, who is not freed by a divorce, is freed by the rite of removing the shoe, then this one [the levirate wife] who is freed by divorce surely should be freed by a rite of removing the shoe. Thus we are informed that that is not the case.*

B. *Yeah, so maybe it is the case?*

C. Scripture is explicit: "Then he shall write her a writ of divorce" (Deut. 24:1) – through a writ he divorces her, but he doesn't divorce her in any other way.

The exegesis of the verse of Scripture yields an important fact for the Talmud's reading of the Mishnah. The principle of reading is simple: the verse is assumed to be exclusive, so when it says, it is done one way, it is assumed to mean, this way, not that way: exclusive and comprehensive.

What follows is the single most important type of Scripture usage in the Talmud; it is long and systematic, and when we identify the traits of thought of the following, we shall have a model by which to classify a vast proportion of the Scripture compositions and composite of the Talmud. Let us examine the way in which the argument unfolds step by step.

II.1 A. She is acquired through money:

B. *What is the scriptural source of this rule?*

C. And furthermore, we have learned in the Mishnah: The father retains control of his daughter [younger than twelve and a half] as to effecting any of the tokens of betrothal: money, document, or sexual intercourse [M. Ket. 4:4A] – *how on the basis of Scripture do we know that fact?*

The premise is that the rule of the Mishnah does not stand on its own but depends upon a statement of the Torah.

D. Said R. Judah said Rab, "Said Scripture, 'Then shall she [the Hebrew slave girl] go out for nothing, without money' (Ex. 21:11). No money is paid to this master, but money is paid to another master, and who would that be? It is the father."

Once more, we read Scripture as both exclusive and comprehensive: this, not that; this, not any other possible that.

E. *But might one say that it goes to her?*

F.   *But how can you suppose so? Since the father has the power to contract her betrothal, as it is written, "I gave my daughter to this man" (Deut. 22:16), can she collect the money? [Obviously she cannot, so the father gets the money.]*

There is another possibility, not considered in our initial proof. Our this, not that, has left an opening, which has now to be closed. It is closed by pointing out that Scripture cannot possibly have entered the alternative possibility, since the facts of the case prevent it.

G.   *But maybe that is the case only for a minor, who has no domain ["hand," with which to effect acquisition], but in the case of a girl, who has a domain for the stated purpose, she may contract the betrothal and also get the money paid for the betrothal?*

H.   Said Scripture, "Being in her youth, in her father's house" (Num. 30:17) – every advantage accruing to her in her youth belongs to her father.

Testing our proposed exclusive reading, we appeal to another scriptural proof to preclude a possibility we have eliminated; and Scripture obliges. But there is another reading of that same matter, and this, too, has to be addressed.

I.   *Then what about what R. Huna said Rab said, "How on the basis of Scripture do we know that the proceeds of a daughter's labor go to the father? 'And if a man sell his daughter to be a maidservant' (Ex. 21:7) – just as the proceeds of the labor of a maidservant go to the master, so the proceeds of the labor of a daughter go to the father"? What need do I have for such a proof, when the same proposition may be deduced from the phrase, "Being in her youth, in her father's house" (Num. 30:17)?*

J.   *Rather, that verse refers to releasing her vows [and not to the matter at hand, as the context at Num. 30:17 makes clear].*

Thus far, we have simply assumed that the correct reading of Scripture on its own solves our problem. But we have now to introduce the issue, is our case appropriately addressed to the verses of Scripture we have chosen? Are there not other verses of Scripture that can have solved our problem? The issue is framed in terms of the corpus of verses that cover a different matter altogether, namely, rules on financial transactions, rather than (as we have assumed to this point) rules on the rights of the father to the property accruing to the daughter.

K.   *And, furthermore, should you say, so let us derive the rule covering money from the rule covering other propositions, in fact, we do not ever derive the rule covering money from the rule covering other propositions!*

L.   *And, furthermore, should you propose, so let us derive the rule
governing the disposition of monetary payments from the rule
governing fines, it is the simple fact that the rule governing
monetary payments is not to be derived from the rule
governing the disposition of fines.*

The argument proposed just now has been dismissed out of hand; the
rules of taxonomy are invoked, and we compare like to like, but not like
to unlike.   A more compelling consideration is now introduced,
particular to the category under discussion, namely, the father's power.
So that category having been defined as governing, we can exclude other
categories, that do not apply.

M.   *Then here is the reason that compensation for humiliation and
damages is assigned to the father:* [add: *if he wanted, he could
hand her over [for marriage] to an ugly man or to a man
afflicted with boils].* [Since he himself could subject her to
indignity and benefit from it, he gets the compensation from
someone who does that to her (Slotki).]

N.   *Rather, it is more reasonable that, when the All-Merciful
excluded another "exodus" [from the household],* [4A] *it was
meant to be like the original.* [Slotki: As in the original, it is
the master, not the slave girl, who would have received the
money for her redemption, but a specific text states to the
contrary, so in the implication it must be the father,
corresponding to the master, who gets the money when she
leaves his control at betrothal.]

O.   *Yes, but the one "exodus" is not really comparable to the other.
For in the case of the master, the slave girl entirely exits from
his control, while in the exodus from the domain of the father,
the exit to the bridal canopy has not yet been completed.*

P.   *Nonetheless, so far as it concerns his power to remit her vows,
she does entirely exit his domain, for we have learned in the
Mishnah:* A betrothed girl – her father and her husband
annul her vows [M. Ned. 10:1A-B].

We have now completed our demonstration and turn to secondary
issues, left open for the purposes of argument. The first concerns our
reading of a key verse, and we now want to know whether that verse
must pertain to our problem; it may be read in a different context
altogether. This consideration has already gained our attention: Are we
sure that the verse is relevant to our problem? If it is, then it solves that
problem; if not, then we are at a loss. So the next initiative tests our use
of evidence from Scripture.

II.2   A.   *But does the verse, "She shall go out for nothing" serve the
present purpose? Surely it is required in line with that which
is taught on Tannaite authority, as follows:*

B. "And she shall go out for nothing" – this refers to the days of
her puberty; "without money" refers to the days just prior to
puberty. [Freedman: Thus the verse merely teaches that
something else, not money, frees her, but implies no other
conclusion.]

The option is now before us: Can the verse not be asked to speak to
another matter altogether? The answer is, it can, but it does not do so,
because the wording of Scripture points toward our problem, and not
that to which another reading wishes to direct the verse.

C. *Said Rabina, "If so, Scripture ought to have said, 'no money.'
Why formulate matters as 'without money'? It is to indicate,
'No money is paid to this master, but money is paid to
another master, and who would that be? It is the father.'"*

The principle of exegesis has now to be articulated and defended. That
principle is, this, not that, and, this, but not any other that. In this case,
when Scripture uses a phrase that can have been omitted without a loss
of meaning, that usage captures our attention and is deemed to be
exclusionary, as I said, this, not that. But we have also to know, this, but
not any other that, thus: How do I know that it is this, not that, when it
can be, this, but not the third thing? In what follows, the model of the
exegesis is shown to pertain to other data, so we are assured that our
reading is not particular to our case.

D. *And on what basis do we perform such an exegesis? It is as
has been taught on Tannaite authority:*
E. "And have no children" (Lev. 22:13) – I know only that that
pertains to her own child; what about her grandchild?
Scripture says, "And have no child," meaning, any child
whatsoever.

As I said, what we know so far is, this, not that. But we do not know,
this but not any other that. That is what now follows.

F. So far I know that that is the case only of a valid offspring;
what about an invalid one?
G. Scripture says, "And have no child," meaning, "hold an
inquiry concerning her."

We have now backtracked and encompassed another that, with no loss to
our argument, so we have, this, not that or anything else. But does not
the verse at hand yield an exclusion, not an extension? That is what now
follows, a problem readily solved by appeal to established facts.

H. *But lo, that clause has yielded the deduction concerning the
grandchild!*

I.   *In point of fact it is not necessary to present a verse of Scripture to prove that grandchildren are in the status of children. Where a verse of Scripture is required is to deal with invalid offspring.*

J.   *And how does the Tannaite authority himself know that such an exegesis is undertaken?*

We do not need a verse of Scripture to make the proposed point, since it is an established fact, beyond the necessity of scriptural demonstration. But how do we know that the exegesis is plausible? The answer lies in a detail of not sense but form. Scripture writes a word one way, rather than in another possible way, and that choice represents a decision of an exegetical character. That is to say, by the writing of a word with (or without) a letter that may be omitted (or included), Scripture accords to us the possibility of drawing a conclusion about the sense of the verse – the conclusion having no relationship to the formal characteristic that has invited us to reexamine the sense of the verse. Here we cross the line from exegesis of sense to exegesis of formal trait and back to the exegesis of sense.

K.   *Say:* **It is written, "Balaam refuses" and "my husband's brother refuses" (Num. 22:14, Deut. 25:7). In these instances, the words are written without the Y that they could have had.** *Now here in the verses treated above, the Y is used, which proves that the Y, which is dispensable, is included for exegetical purposes.*

The proof, as I said, is dialectical, moving from form to sense. The formal character of the spelling tells us that the verse can have a meaning other than that that lies on the surface. But the meaning we choose to impute is not dictated by the formal accident of orthography. The premise, then, is that the verse conducts its discourse on two levels, the one formal, calling attention to a peculiarity implicit in the verse, the other, substantive, dictating what that particular meaning must be. But the form has no bearing on the substance, and that is what I call "dialectical." Our sages perceive a movement that we should never have identified without their guidance; and they moreover impute to that movement – orthography to impllicit sense – a sense that only they, in the context of their thought and inquiry, can have identified. I find this remarkable and subtle, even if I cannot account for all the stages of thought that are represented before us.

It remains to observe that we have asked Scripture to prove two related propositions. Why cannot one proof suffice, with the other proposition derived from the established, scripturally founded one? That is the final, logical question at hand.

II.3   A.   *And it was necessary to provide a verse of Scripture to indicate*
                      that the minor daughter's token of betrothal is assigned to her
                      father, and it also was necessary to find a verse of Scripture to
                      indicate that her wages are assigned to her father. For if the
                      All-Merciful had made reference to the assignment of the token
                      of betrothal to her father, I might have supposed that that was
                      because she has not labored for that item, but as to her wages,
                      for which she has labored, I might have said that they are
                      assigned to her. And if we had been informed of the matter of
                      her wages, in which matter, after all, she is provided for by
                      him, [I might have supposed that since he supports her, she gets
                      her wages], but as to the matter of tokens of betrothal given to
                      her from a third party, I might have supposed that these go to
                      her. So both proofs were required.

The argument is now concluded, a systematic and orderly exposition,
beginning to end; with no loose ends I can discern.

What follows forms an appendix to the foregoing, picking up a detail
of the exegetical composition and expanding on it.

The premise of the question, once more, is that Scripture does not
repeat itself or say what does not have to be said. Here our problem is
that Scripture tells us something that logical inquiry into another point
Scripture makes will have yielded in any event. And the answer is, the
one makes sense of, clarifies, the other. What is important is the interest
in the explanation of Scripture in its own terms, not only in the
framework of an inquiry into the law, on the one side, or the sources of
the Mishnah and their exegesis, on the other. The following, then, is free-
standing in its intellectual dimension, and the form underlines that fact,
for we open with a verse of Scripture, standing at the head of all that will
follow.

II.4   A.   *Reverting to the body of the foregoing:* "And she shall go out
                      for nothing" – this refers to the days of her puberty; "without
                      money" refers to the prepubescent time [days just prior to
                      puberty].
          B.   *But why should the All-Merciful simply make reference to the*
                      prepubescent time [days just prior to puberty], and it would
                      not have been necessary to make reference to the time of her
                      puberty?

Why does Scripture have to tell me something that, on my own, I can
have figured out? There are two possible answers: first, because a fresh
point is at hand, second, because the intersecting passages shed light on
one another; we take the second route.

          C.   Said Rabbah, "The one comes along to impart meaning to the
                      other. *It may be comparable to the case of the words, a*

         sojourner or a hired servant [Lev. 22:10: *toshab, sakir*] *as has been taught on Tannaite authority:*

D.   "'One word refers to a Hebrew slave acquired permanently, the other to one purchased for six years [at Lev. 22:10: "a slave purchased in perpetuity belonging to a priest or a slave purchased for six years shall not eat of the Holy Things"]. If Scripture had referred to the former and not the latter, I would reason, if a slave acquired permanently may not eat Holy Things, how much more so is one acquired only for six years forbidden to do so! And if that were so, I would say, the former word refers to a slave purchased for a limited period, but one acquired in perpetuity may eat. So the word that refers to the slave purchased for a period of six years comes along and illuminates the meaning of the word for the one purchased in perpetuity, by contrast to the one purchased for a period of six years – and neither one may eat.'"

How better to counter that argument than to challenge the comparability of what has been compared? Once we distinguish the two classes, we open the way to a new approach to the solution of the problem, which is to deal with a case that indeed is comparable, but that also exhibits its own distinctive traits; hence the comparable cases require exposition, each in its own terms, since the one will not have yielded the other.

E.   *Said to him Abbayye, "But are the cases truly parallel? In that case, they are two distinct classes of persons, so that, even if Scripture had made explicit reference to a sojourner whose ear had been pierced's not eating, and then made explicit reference to the other, then the hired hand might have been derived by an argument a fortiori. Such matters Scripture does take the trouble to spell out. But here, by contrast, the maidservant is one and the same person. Once she has left the prepubescent period, what business does she have to do with him when she becomes pubescent?"*

F.   *Rather, said Abbayye, "It was necessary to make this point only to deal with the case of a woman who exhibits no signs of puberty even after she has reached the age of twenty years. It might have entered your mind to suppose that when she reaches pubescence, she goes free, but not merely by reaching her majority. So we are informed to the contrary."*

In a sustained, moving exposition, the same challenge raised will be repeated to the one who raised it. We still can have learned the entire matter from one statement and did not require a repetition thereof.

G.   *Objected Mar bar R. Ashi to this proposition:* "But is this not attainable through an argument a fortiori? If the appearance of puberty signs, which do not remove the girl from the domain of the father, do remove the girl from the domain of the master, reaching maturity, which does remove her from

the domain of the father, surely should remove her from the
domain of the master!"

H.   *Rather, said Mar bar R. Ashi, "The proof is required only to*
deal with the matter of the sale of a barren woman [Freedman:
a minor who shows symptoms of constitutional barrenness].
It might have entered your mind to suppose that with one who
will later on produce puberty signs, the sale is valid, but with
one who won't, the sale is null. [4B] *So we are informed by the*
verse, 'and she shall go out for nothing' that that is not the
case."

The process will now be repeated once more, with the same effect. But
then the entire premise of the composition is called into question.
Scripture will indeed state in so many words a proposition that may be
gained through an argument a fortiori.

I.   *But to Mar bar R. Ashi, who has said, "But is this not*
attainable through an argument a fortiori?" haven't we
established the fact that something that can be proved through
an argument a fortiori Scripture will nonetheless trouble to
make explicit?

True, Scripture will do that – but we can concede the possibility only
under duress, and so the exposition draws to a close, perhaps as perfect a
composition as we can imagine for this genre.

J.   *Well, that's true enough where there is no other possible reply,*
but if there is, we give that possible reply [making the verse
pertain to some other matter than the one under discussion
(Freedman)].

Here is another exposition of the meaning of a verse of Scripture, in
which the issue once more is whether or not Scripture repeats itself.

II.5 A.   *[That she is acquired through money] is derived by the*
following Tannaite authority on a different basis, as has been
taught on Tannaite authority:
      B.   "When a man takes a wife and has sexual relations with her,
then it shall be, if she find no favor in his eyes, because he
has found some unseemly thing in her" (Deut. 24:1) – the
sense of "take" refers only to acquisition through a payment
of money, in line with the verse, "I will give the money for
the field; take it from me" (Gen. 23:13).
      C.   But cannot the same be proven by an argument a fortiori: If a
Hebrew slave girl, who cannot be acquired by an act of sexual
relations, can be acquired by money, a wife, who may be
acquired in marriage by an act of sexual relations, surely can
be acquired by money!

What follows is a logical point in no way particular to Scripture exegesis
or argument. It is the simple demonstration that two categories we

thought comparable, with the result that the traits of the one may be imputed to the other, do not yield the result we imputed to the result of that comparison, because there is a third class of persons that is comparable, but that does not produce the same result. This kind of argument on the rules of category formation and comparison appeals to logic, not to the form or sense of Scripture (or of the Mishnah, for that matter); for this Talmud it is an exegetical initiative common to the reading of both documents.

D.   A levirate wife proves the contrary, since she may be acquired by sexual relations but not by a money payment.

E.   But what distinguishes the levirate wife is that she cannot be acquired by a deed, and can you say the same of an ordinary wife, who can be acquired by a deed? So it is necessary for Scripture to teach, "When a man takes a wife and has sexual relations with her, then it shall be, if she find no favor in his eyes, because he has found some unseemly thing in her" (Deut. 24:1) – the sense of "take" refers only to acquisition through a payment of money, in line with the verse, "I will give the money for the field; take it from me" (Gen. 23:13) [Sifré Deut. CCLXVIII.I.1].

F.   But what need do I have for a verse of Scripture, *since it has been yielded by the argument a fortiori [the case of the levirate wife having been refuted]?*

G.   *Said R. Ashi, "It is because one may raise the following disqualifying argument to begin with: Whence have you derived proof for the matter? From the case of the Hebrew slave girl?* But what distinguishes the Hebrew slave girl is that she goes out from bondage with a money payment. Will you say the same in this case, in which she does not go forth through a money payment? So it is necessary for Scripture to teach, 'When a man takes a wife and has sexual relations with her, then it shall be, if she find no favor in his eyes, because he has found some unseemly thing in her' (Deut. 24:1) – the sense of 'take' refers only to acquisition through a payment of money, in line with the verse, 'I will give the money for the field; take it from me' (Gen. 23:13)."*

H.   *And it was necessary for Scripture to deal with the case, "and she shall go out for nothing" and also "when a man takes." For had Scripture made reference to "when a man takes," I might have thought, the token of betrothal that the husband gives to her is her own; therefore Scripture states, "and she shall go out for nothing." And if Scripture had said only, "and she shall go out for nothing," I might have supposed, if the wife gives him the money and betroths him, it is a valid act of betrothal. Therefore Scripture stated, "when a man takes," but not, "when a woman takes."*

The polemic that follows forms an integral part of a sustained argument that correct category formation proceeds only from Scripture;

the traits of things, by themselves, do not provide reliable classification of things. The argument is as follows: Scripture teaches a rule about a given classification of persons, in this case, a woman and how she is acquired as a wife. Scripture alone is pertinent in the demonstration of that rule. Reason, uncorrected by revelation, will have yielded a different, and wrong conclusion. We now show how reason will have erred. This demonstration follows self-evident formal rules; it is not particular to the Talmud, but it is the foundation of Sifra, as I have shown in *Uniting the Dual Torah: Sifra and the Problem of the Mishnah* (Cambridge and New York, 1989: Cambridge University Press).

II.6 A.   "...And possesses her [has sexual relations with her]":
B.   This teaches that a woman is acquired through an act of sexual relations.
C.   One might have reasoned as follows:
D.   If a deceased childless brother's widow, who may not be acquired through a money payment, may be acquired through an act of sexual relations, a woman, who may be acquired through a money payment, logically should be available for acquisition through an act of sexual relations.

Reason ungoverned by Scripture errs, because we can find a further, comparable classification, which does not yield the same characteristic:

E.   But a Hebrew slave girl will prove the contrary, for she may be acquired through a money payment, but she is not acquired through an act of sexual relations. [On that account, you should not find it surprising for an ordinary woman, who, even though she may be acquired through a money payment, may not be acquired through an act of sexual relations] [Sifré Deut. CCLXVIII.I.2].
F.   What characterizes the Hebrew slave girl is that she is not acquired for a wife. But will you say the same in this case, in which the woman is acquired for a wife?
G.   So Scripture states, "...and possesses her [has sexual relations with her]."
H.   But then why do I need a verse of Scripture [in light of F]? *Lo, the matter has been proven without it!*
I.   *Said R. Ashi, "Because there is the possibility of stating that at the foundations of the logical argument there is a flaw, namely, from whence do you derive the case? From the deceased childless brother's widow. But what characterizes the levirate widow is that she is already subject to a relationship to the levir, but can you say the same in this instance, where the woman hardly is subject to any relationship whatever to this unrelated man? So it is necessary to state: '...And possesses her [has sexual relations with her]' – This teaches that a woman is acquired through an act of sexual relations."*

The next composition goes over the same program as the foregoing, an interest in the necessity of appealing to the Torah for a proper basis of comparing classes of things.

III.1   A.   [5A] And how on the basis of Scripture do we know that a woman may be acquired by a deed?

B.   It is a matter of logic.

C.   If a payment of money, which does not serve to remove a woman from a man's domain [as does a writ of divorce], lo, it has the power of effecting acquisition.

D.   A deed [namely, a writ of marriage or a marriage contract], which does [in the form of a writ of divorce] have the power to remove a woman from the domain of a man, surely should have the power of effecting acquisition.

E.   No, if you have made that statement concerning the payment of money, which does have the power of effecting acquisition of things that have been designated as Holy and of produce in the status of second tithe [there being an exchange of money for such objects, by which the objects become secular and the money becomes consecrated], will you make the same statement concerning a writ, which does not have the power of effecting acquisitions of Holy Things and produce in the status of second tithe, for it is written, "And if he who sanctifies the field will in any manner redeem it, then he shall add the fifth part of the money of your estimation, and it shall be assigned to him" (Lev. 27:19)?

F.   Scripture says, "and he writes her a bill of divorcement, hands it to her, and sends her away from his house; she leaves his household and becomes the wife of another man."

G.   Her relationship to the latter is comparable to her leaving the former. Just as her leaving the former is effected through a writ, so her becoming wife to the latter may be effected through a writ [Sifré Deut. CCLXVIII.I.3].

H.   *Well, why not draw the comparison in the opposite direction, namely, the going forth from the marriage to the establishment of the marriage: Just as the establishment of the marriage is through money, so the going forth from the marriage is through money?*

I.   Said Abbayye, "People will say, money brings the woman into the marriage and money takes her out of it? Then will the defense attorney turn into the prosecutor?"

J.   *If we accept that argument, then the deed of betrothal likewise will be subject to the saying, a writ removes her from the marriage, and a writ brings her into it? So will the prosecutor turn into the defense attorney?*

K.   *Yes, but the substance of this document is distinct from the substance of that document.*

L.   *Yeah, well, then, the purpose of this money payment is different from the purpose of that money payment!*

M.   *Nonetheless, all coins have the same mint mark! [So who knows the difference? But the documents contain different wordings.]*

III.2   A.   Raba said, "Said Scripture, 'And he shall write for her' (Deut. 24:1) – through what is in writing a woman is divorced, and she is not divorced through a money payment."

       B.   *Why not say:* Through writing a woman is divorced, but she is not betrothed through what is in writing?

       C.   Lo, it is written, "And when she goes forth, then she may marry," so comparing divorce to marriage.

       D.   Why choose that reading rather than the contrary one [excluding money for divorce and but accept a deed for marriage? Why not reverse it?]

       E.   *It stands to reason that when we deal with divorce, we exclude a conceivable means for effecting divorce; when dealing with divorce should we exclude what is a means of effecting a betrothal?*

       F.   *Now how, for his part, does R. Yosé the Galilean attain that same principle, [since he interprets the language of the verse at hand for another purpose], how does he know that a woman is not divorced through a money payment?*

       G.   *He derives that lesson from the language, "a writ of divorce," meaning, "A writ is what cuts the relationship," and no other consideration cuts the relationship.*

       H.   *And rabbis – how do they deal with the language, "a writ of divorce"?*

       I.   *That formulation is required to indicate that the relationship is broken off through something that effectively severs the tie between him and her. For it has been taught on Tannaite authority:* [If the husband said], "Lo, here is your writ of divorce, on the condition that you not drink wine, that you not go to your father's house forever," this is not an act of totally severing the relationship. [If he said,] "...for thirty days...," lo, this is an act of severing the relationship. [The husband cannot impose a permanent condition, for if he could do so, then the relationship will not have been completely and finally severed.]

       J.   And R. Yosé?

       K.   *He derives the same lesson from the use of the language, "total cutting off" as against merely "cutting off."*

       L.   And rabbis?

       M.   *The rabbis do not derive any lesson from the variation in the language at hand.*

The issue that follows is secondary to the foregoing. What is interesting is the evidence of a sustained inquiry, in which Scripture's reading is at issue throughout: Why does Scripture not give us two items, and let us infer the third – a continuing of the prior demonstration, in precisely the same terms. Not only does Scripture effect monothetic taxonomy, but Scripture, and that alone, makes possible even polythetic taxonomy! It is hardly surprising that Scripture also forms the arena of analysis, and here we see how the Torah, as much as the Mishnah, defines sustained discourse.

III.3   A.   *While it is not possible to derive the rule governing one mode of acquisition from another [the various arguments having failed], maybe it's possible to infer one from two others [so that if we can show that it is possible to effect acquisition through two modes that work elsewhere and also that work in respect to a betrothal, then a third, that works elsewhere, can work in this case, too]?*

        B.   *Which two?*
        C.   *Perhaps the All-Merciful should not make reference in Scripture to a deed, and that might be derived from the other two modes of acquisition [sexual relations, money payment]? But then one might argue that what characterizes these other two modes of acquisition is that a good deal of benefit derives from them, which is not the case for a mere piece of paper.*

        D.   *Then perhaps Scripture should not make written reference to the mode of sexual relations, and that might be derived from the other two? But then one might argue that what is characteristic of the other two is that they serve to effect acquisition in a wide variety of matters, while that is not so in the instance of sexual relations!*

        E.   *Then let Scripture not make reference to the matter of money, and let that derive from the other two? But what characterizes the other two is that they take effect even contrary to the woman's will, which is not the case of money [she must be willing to accept it]. And should you say that money, too, may take effect willy-nilly in the case of a Hebrew slave girl, nonetheless, in the matter of effecting a marriage, we find no such instance.*

III.4   A.   Said R. Huna, "The marriage canopy effects acquisition of title to the woman, on the strength of an argument a fortiori: If a money payment, which on its own does not confer the right to eat priestly rations, effects transfer of title to the husband over the woman, the marriage canopy, which does confer the right to eat priestly rations, surely should effect the transfer of title."

        B.   But doesn't acquisition through a money payment confer the right to eat priestly rations? And hasn't Ulla said, "By the law of the Torah, a girl of Israelite caste who was betrothed to a priest is permitted to eat priestly rations: 'But if a priest buy any soul, the purchase of his money...' (Lev. 22:11) – *and this one also falls into the class of* 'purchased of his money.' And what is the reason that they have said that she may not eat priestly rations? Lest a cup of wine in the status of priestly rations be mixed for her in her father's house and she share it with her brother or sister [who are not in the priestly caste]"?

        C.   *Then raise the following question:* What characterizes a money payment is that it does not effect the completion of the acquisition of the wife but nonetheless effects transfer of title, [5B] the marriage canopy, which does effect the completion of the acquisition of the wife, surely should effect transfer of title and hence betrothal!

D.   The particular trait of a money payment is that with it things that have been consecrated and second tithe may be redeemed.

E.   But sexual relations prove to the contrary [having no bearing on that matter].

F.   The distinguishing trait of sexual relations is that that is a means for acquiring a levirate widow as a wife.

G.   A money payment, inoperative there, proves the disqualifying exception.

H.   So we find ourselves going around in circles. The distinctive trait that pertains to the one is not the same as the distinctive trait that applies to the other, and the generative quality of the other is not the same as the generative quality of the one. But then, the generative trait that pertains to them all is that they effect transfer of title in general and they also effect transfer of title here. So I shall introduce the matter of the marriage canopy, which effects transfer of title in general and should also effect transfer of title here.

I.   But the generative quality that is characteristic of the set is that they produce a considerable benefit.

J.   A writ, a mere piece of paper, proves the disqualifying exception.

K.   The distinctive quality of the deed is that it can remove an Israelite woman from a marriage.

L.   A money payment and sexual relations provide the disqualifying exceptions.

M.   So we find ourselves going around in circles. The distinctive trait that pertains to the one is not the same as the distinctive trait that applies to the other, and the generative quality of the other is not the same as the generative quality of the one. But then, the generative trait that pertains to them all is that they effect transfer of title in general and they also effect transfer of title here. So I shall introduce the matter of the marriage canopy, which effects transfer of title in general and should also effect transfer of title here.

N.   But the generative quality that is characteristic of the set is that they serve under compulsion.

O.   And R. Huna?

P.   *In any event, we don't find any aspect of compulsion when it comes to the money payment.*

III.5 A.   [As to R. Huna's statement,] said Rabbah, "There are two refutations of what he has said: *First, we learn in the Mishnah the language, three, not four; and furthermore, isn't it the simple fact that the marriage canopy completes the relationship only in consequence of an act of betrothal? But can the marriage canopy complete the relationship not in the aftermath of an act of betrothal, so that we may deduce that,*

B.

> *when it is not in consequence of an act of betrothal, there is the same result as the marriage canopy following such an act?"*
>
> *He said to Abbayye, "As to what you have said, namely, first, we learn in the Mishnah the language, three, not four, the Tannaite authority makes explicit reference only to what is explicitly stated in Scripture, but not what is not explicitly stated [and we have shown that the media of money and deed derive from exegesis, if not from an explicit statement of Scripture, but the validity of the marriage canopy is only derived by an argument a fortiori]. And as to your statement, isn't it the simple fact that the marriage canopy completes the relationship only in consequence of an act of betrothal? As a matter of fact, that is R. Huna's argument: If a money payment, which does not complete the relationship after a prior payment of a money payment, the marriage canopy, which does complete the relationship after a money payment, surely should effect transfer of title just as well!"*

We have now concluded our sustained inquiry into the role of Scripture in the determination of the classification of persons and shown that comparison and contrast based on the inherent traits of things prove null. All things have to be made explicit – and that is solely through the Torah.

What follows expounds the data of the Mishnah law; a different type of composition is at hand. Scripture now proves contingent and unimportant. I abbreviate secondary developments of the compositions that follow, so far as I can, preserving the indications of the main lines of structure of the composites. This is indicated by the insertion of three dots, to show that a passage continues.

III.6   A.   *Our rabbis have taught on Tannaite authority:*
        B.   With money, how so?
        C.   If he gave her money or what is worth money and said to her, "Lo, you are consecrated to me," "Lo, you are betrothed to me," "Lo, you are for me as a wife," lo, this one is consecrated. But if she gave it to him and said to him, "Lo, I am consecrated to you," "Lo, I am betrothed to you," "Lo, I am yours as a wife," she is not consecrated [T. Qid. 1:1B-D].

III.7   A.   *Objected R. Pappa, "So is the operative consideration only that he gave the money and he made the statement? Then if he gave the money and she made the statement, she is not betrothed? Then note what follows: But if she gave it to him and said to him, "Lo, I am consecrated to you," "Lo, I am betrothed to you," "Lo, I am yours as a wife," she is not consecrated! So the operative consideration is that she gave the money and she made the statement. Lo, if he gave the money and she made the statement, there would be a valid betrothal!"*
        B.   The opening clause describes precisely the details of the transaction, and the concluding one states them in more general terms....

III.8   A.   Said Samuel, "In the matter of a betrothal, if he gave her money or
what is worth money and said to her, 'Lo, you are sanctified,' 'Lo
you are betrothed,' 'Lo, you are a wife to me,' lo, this woman is
consecrated. 'Lo, I am your man,' 'Lo, I am your husband,' 'Lo, I
am your betrothed,' there is no basis for taking account of the
possibility that a betrothal has taken place. And so as to a writ of
divorce: If he gave her the document and said to her, 'Lo, you are
sent forth,' 'Lo, you are divorced,' 'Lo, you are permitted to any
man,' lo, this woman is divorced. 'I am not your man,' 'I am not
your husband,' 'I am not your betrothed,' there is no basis for
taking account of the possibility that a divorce has taken place."

         B.   *Said R. Pappa to Abbayye, "Does this bear the implication that Samuel
takes the view,* 'Inexplicit abbreviations [such as the language that is
used and then spelled out, for example, "I am forbidden by a vow
from you" *means, "I am not going to speak to you."* "I am separated
from you by a vow" *means, "I am not going to do any business with
you."* "I am removed from you" *means, "I am not going to stand
within four cubits of you"*] are null [and take effect only if they are
made explicit]'? *And have we not learned in the Mishnah:* **He who
says, 'I will be [such]' – lo, this one is a Nazir [M. Naz. 1:1B]?** *And
in reflecting on it, we stated: 'But maybe the sense of,* I will b e [such], *is
I will fast?' And said Samuel, 'But that rule that the Mishnah states
pertains to a case in which a Nazirite was walking by at just that
moment.' So the operative consideration is that* a Nazirite was walking
by at just that moment. Lo, if that were not the case, it would not be
the rule! [So Samuel maintains that inexplicit abbreviations are
valid only if made explicit.]"...

III.9   A.   *Our rabbis have taught on Tannaite authority:*
         B.   "Lo, you are my wife," "Lo, you are my betrothed," "Lo, you are
acquired by me," she is consecrated.
         C.   "Lo, you are mine," "Lo, you are in my domain," "Lo, you are
subject to me," she is betrothed.

III.10   A.   *So why not form them all into a single Tannaite statement?*
         B.   *The Tannaite had heard them in groups of three and that is how he
memorized them.*

III.11   A.   *The question was raised:* "If he used the language, 'Singled out for
me,' '...designated for me,' '...my helpmate,' 'you are suitable for
me,' 'you are gathered in to me,' 'you are my rib,' 'you are closed in
to me,' 'you are my replacement, ' 'you are seized to me,' 'you are
taken by me,' [what is the consequence]?"
         B.   *In any event you can solve one of these problems on the basis of that which
has been taught on Tannaite authority:* If he said, "You are taken by
me," she is betrothed, in line with the language, "when a man takes
a wife."

   In the composition that follows, Scripture supplies evidence on the
meaning or use of words; it plays no role in the amplification of the
proposition at hand.

III.12   A.   *The question was raised,* "If he said, 'You are my [betrothed]
bondmaid,' what is the law?"

B. *Come and take note of what has been taught on Tannaite authority:*

C. If he said, "You are my [betrothed] bondmaid," she is consecrated, for in Judea a betrothed woman is called a betrothed bondmaid.

D. *So is Judea the majority of the world at large?*

E. *This is the sense of the statement:* If he said, "You are my [betrothed] bondmaid," she is consecrated, for it is said, "that a betrothed bondman belonging to a man" (Lev. 19:20). Moreover, in Judea a betrothed woman is called a betrothed bondmaid.

F. *So do I need to know a custom in Judea in order to sustain what Scripture says?*

G. *This is the sense of the statement:* If in the territory of Judea he said, "You are my [betrothed] bondmaid," she is consecrated, for it is said, "that a betrothed bondmaid belonging to a man" (Lev. 19:20), for in Judea a betrothed woman is called a betrothed bondmaid.

The verse is adduced in evidence because it contains a fact that is required for the analysis at hand.

III.13 A. *With what situation do we deal [in the interpretation of the language just now cited as effective]? Should I say that it is a situation in which he is not talking with her about business having to do with her writ of divorce or her betrothal? Then how in the world should she know what he is talking about with her?! But rather, it is a case in which he is talking with her about business having to do with her writ of divorce or her betrothal. Then, even if he said nothing at all, but merely gave her money, she is still betrothed, for we have learned in the Mishnah:* [If] he was speaking to his wife about matters relevant to her divorce contract or her bride price and did not make it explicit – R. Yosé says, "It is sufficient for him [simply to give her the contract or bride price without a declaration." R. Judah says, "He must make it explicit" [M. M.S. 4:7]. And said R. Huna said Samuel, "The decided law accords with R. Yosé."

B. *Say:* In point of fact, *it is a case in which* he is talking with her about business having to do with her writ of divorce or her betrothal. *If he had given her money and then shut up, that would indeed be the rule [she would be divorced or betrothed], but here with what situation do we deal? It is one in which he gave her the item and stated to her the language that has just now been set forth, and this is what is at issue here: When he used this language, was it for purposes of betrothal? Or was it for purposes of work? And that question stands over.*

III.14 A. *Reverting to the body of the foregoing:*

B. [If] he was speaking to his wife about matters relevant to her divorce contract or her bride price and did not make it explicit –

C. R. Yosé says, "It is sufficient for him [simply to give her the contract or bride price without a declaration.]"

D. R. Judah says, "He must make it explicit" [M. M.S. 4:7].

E.   Said R. Judah said Samuel, "And that is the case in which they were engaged in discussing that very same matter."

F.   And so said R. Eleazar said R. Oshayya, "And that is the case in which they were engaged in discussing that very same matter."

G.   *There is a Tannaite dispute on the same matter:*

H.   Rabbi says, "And that is the case in which they were engaged in discussing that very same matter."

I.   R. Eleazar b. R. Judah says, "Even though they were not engaged in discussing that very same matter" [cf. T. Qid. 2:8]].

III.15 A.   *Well, if they were not engaged in discussing that very same matter, then how in the world should she know what he is talking about with her?*

B.   Said Abbayye, "It is a case in which they moved from one topic to another in the same context."

III.16 A.   Said R. Huna said Samuel, "The decided law accords with R. Yosé."

B.   *Said R. Yemar to R. Ashi, "But what about what R. Judah said Samuel said, 'Whoever is not expert in the character of writs of divorce and betrothals should not get involved in dealing with them' – is that the case even if he has heard nothing of this ruling of R. Huna in Samuel's name?"*

C.   He said to him, "Yes indeed."

III.17 A.   And so as to a writ of divorce: If he gave her the document and said to her, "Lo, you are sent forth," "Lo, you are divorced," "Lo, you are permitted to any man," lo, this woman is divorced.

B.   *It is obvious that* if he gave her her writ of divorce and said to his wife, "Lo, you are a free woman," [6B] he has not said anything effective. If he said to his female slave, "Lo, you are permitted to any man," he has not said anything effective. If he said to his wife, "Lo, you are your own property," what is the law? *Do we say that he made that statement with respect to work? Or perhaps, he meant it to cover the entirety of the relationship?*

C.   *Said Rabina to R. Ashi, "Come and take note of what we have learned in the Mishnah: The text of the writ of divorce [is as follows]: "Lo, you are permitted to any man." R. Judah says, "[In Aramaic]: Let this be from me your writ of divorce, letter of dismissal, and deed of liberation, that you may marry anyone you want." The text of a writ of emancipation [is as follows]: "Lo, you are free, lo, you are your own [possession]" [cf. Deut. 21:14] [M. Git. 9:3]. Now if, in the case of a Canaanite slave, whose body belongs to the master, when the master says to him, lo, you are your own [possession], he makes that statement covering the entirety of the relationship, when he makes such a statement to his wife, whose person he does not acquire as his possession, all the more so should it yield the same meaning!"*

III.18 A.   Said Rabina to R. Ashi, "If he said to his slave, 'I have no business in you,' *what is the upshot? Do we say that the sense is,* I have no business in you in any way whatsoever? *Or perhaps he made that statement with respect to work?"*

B.   *Said R. Nahman to R. Ashi, and others say, R. Hanin of Khuzistan to R. Ashi, "Come and take note:* He who sells his slave to gentiles – the slave has come forth to freedom, but he requires a writ of emancipation from his first master. Said Rabban Simeon b. Gamaliel, 'Under what circumstances? If he did not write out a deed of sale for him. But if he wrote out a deed of sale for him, this constitutes his act of emancipation' [T. A.Z. 3:16A-C]."

C. *What is a deed of sale?*

D. *Said R. Sheshet, "He wrote for him the following language: 'When you escape from him, I have no claim on you.'"*

III.19   A. Said Abbayye, "If someone effects a betrothal with a loan, the woman is not betrothed. If it is with the benefit of a debt, she is betrothed, but this is not to be done, because it constitutes usury accomplished through subterfuge."

B. *What is the definition of the benefit of a debt? Should I say that he treated the interest as a loan, saying, "I am lending you four zuz for five"? But that is actual usury. And it is in fact a debt.*

C. *The rule pertains to a case in which he gave her extra time to pay the debt.*

III.20   A. Said Raba, "If someone said, 'Take this maneh on the stipulation that you return it to me,' in regard to a purchase, he does not acquire title [for example, real estate would not be acquired if the money has to be returned]; in the case of a woman, she is not betrothed; in the case of redeeming the firstborn, the firstborn is not redeemed; in the case of priestly rations, he has carried out the duty of handing it over, but it is not permitted to do it that way, since it appears to be the case of a priest who assists in the threshing floor [in order to get the priestly rations, and that is not permitted because of the indignity]."

B. *What is Raba's operative theory? If he maintains that a gift that is made on the stipulation that it will be returned is classified as a gift, then even the others, too, should be valid; and if he maintains that it is not a valid gift, then even in the case of priestly rations, it should not be valid. Not only so, lo, Raba is the one who said, "A gift that is given on the stipulation that it is returned is classified as a gift," for said Raba, "'Here is this citron [as a gift to you] on condition that you return it to me' – if one has taken it and carried out his obligation and returned it to the other, he has carried out his obligation, but if he did not return it, he did not carry out his obligation." [So a conditional gift is entirely valid.]*

C. *Rather, said R. Ashi, "In all cases the gift that rests on a stipulation is valid, except the case of a woman, because a woman is not acquired through barter."*

D. *Said R. Huna Mar b. R. Nehemiah to R. Ashi, "This is what we say in Raba's name, precisely as you have said it."*

III.21   A. Said Raba, "If a woman said, 'Give a maneh to Mr. So-and-so [7A] and I shall be betrothed to you,' she is betrothed under the law of surety, *namely: Even though a surety does not derive benefit from the loan, he obligates himself to repay it; so this woman, too, though she derives no benefit from the money, still obligates and cedes herself as betrothed.*

B. "If someone said, 'Here is a maneh, and be betrothed to Mr. So-and-so' – she is betrothed under the law governing a Canaanite slave, *namely: In the case of a Canaanite slave, even though he himself loses nothing when someone else gives his master money to free him, he nonetheless acquires ownership to himself, so even though this man personally loses nothing, he acquires the woman....*

III.22   A.   *Raba raised this question:* "'Here is a maneh and I'll become betrothed to you' [Freedman: and the man accepted it saying, 'Be betrothed to me with it'], [what is the law?]"

          B.   Said Mar Zutra in the name of R. Pappa, "She is betrothed."

          C.   *Said R. Ashi to Mar Zutra,* "*If so, you have a case in which* property that is secured [real estate] is acquired along with property that is not secured [movables], *while in the Mishnah we have learned the opposite, namely:* Property for which there is no security is acquired along with property for which there is security through money, writ, and usucaption. And property for which there is no security imposes the need for an oath on property for which there is security [M. 1:5C-D]." [Freedman: A creditor could collect his debt out of the debtor's real estate, even if sold after the debt was contracted, but not out of movables, if sold; hence the former is termed property that ranks as security, the latter, not. Human beings are on a par with the former, and Ashi assumes that the woman is acquired in conjunction with the maneh.]...

III.23   A.   Said Raba, "If a man said, 'Be betrothed to half of me,' she is betrothed; 'half of you be betrothed to me,' she is not betrothed."

          B.   *Objected Abbayye to Raba,* "*What's the difference between the language,* 'Be betrothed to half of me,' *and the language,* 'half of you be betrothed to me,' *so that in the latter case she is not betrothed? Is it because Scripture has said,* 'when a man take a wife' *(Deut. 24:1) but not half a wife? Then Scripture also says,* 'a man,' *but not half a man!*"

          C.   *He said to him,* "*How are the cases parallel! In that case a woman cannot be assigned to two men, but can't a man be assigned to two or more women? So this is what he meant to say to her:* 'If I want to marry another woman, I'll do just that.'"...

III.24   A.   *Raba raised the question,* "If one said, 'Half of you is betrothed with half of this penny, and half of you is betrothed with the other half,' what is the law? *Once he said to her,* 'a half penny,' *he has divided the money [and there is no valid betrothal], or maybe what he was doing was just counting out the matter [betrothing her for the penny, half for half]? If, then, you should maintain that he was just counting the matter out, what if he said,* 'half of you for a penny, and half of you for a penny,' *what is the law? Since he has said,* 'for a penny,' *and* 'for a penny,' *he has divided his statement [and it is null], or maybe, if the procedure was on a single day, what he was doing was counting out the matter? And if you say that, if it was on the same day, he was counting out the matter, then what if he said,* 'half of you for a penny today, and the other half of you for a penny tomorrow'? *Since he said,* 'tomorrow,' *he has divided it up and the transaction is null, or perhaps this is what he meant: The betrothal starts right away but won't be finished until tomorrow? And if he said,* 'both halves of you for a penny,' *here he certainly has made the entire proposition all together, or maybe a woman can't be betrothed by halves?*"

          B.   *The questions stand.*

III.25   A.   *Raba raised the question,* "What if a man said, 'Your two daughters are betrothed to my two sons for a penny'? *Do we invoke as the operative criterion the one who gives and the one who receives, so there is a* valid monetary transaction [one person gives and one person receives the penny, there is no transaction under that sum]? Or perhaps we invoke the criterion of the one who betroths and the one who is betrothed, so there is no monetary transaction here?"

B.   *The question stands.*

III.26   A.   *R. Pappa raised the question,* "What if a man said, 'Your daughter and your cow are mine for a penny'? *Do we interpret the language to mean,* 'your daughter for a half-penny and your cow for a half-penny,' *or perhaps* 'your daughter for a penny,' and ownership of title to your cow by the act of drawing it?"

B.   *The question stands.*

III.27   A.   *R. Ashi raised the question,* "What if a man said, 'Your daughter and your real estate are mine for a penny'? *Do we interpret the language to mean,* 'your daughter for a half-penny and your property for a half-penny,' *or perhaps* 'your daughter for a penny, and ownership of title to your property through usucaption'?"

B.   *The question stands.*

III.28   A.   *There was a man who betrothed a woman with a token of silk. Said Rabbah, "It is not necessary to perform an act of valuation in advance [to inform the woman of its value]."*

B.   *R. Joseph said, "It is necessary to perform an act of valuation in advance [to inform the woman of its value]."*

C.   If he said to her, "Be betrothed for what is worth any piddling sum," all parties concur that it is not necessary to make an up-front valuation of the silk. If he said to her, "For fifty zuz," and this silk is not worth that much, then it isn't worth that [and the transaction is null]. Where there is a point of difference, it is a case in which he said, "Fifty...," and the silk is worth fifty.

D.   *Rabbah said, "It is not necessary to perform an act of valuation in advance, since, after all, it is worthy fifty."*

E.   *R. Joseph said, "It is necessary to perform an act of valuation in advance, since a woman is not necessarily an expert in the value of the silk, she will not depend on that, without an expert evaluation."*

F.   *There are those who say, even in a case in which the transaction was for any piddling value there is a dispute.*

G.   R. Joseph said, "The equivalent of cash must be treated like cash itself: Just as a cash transaction must involve an articulated sum, [8A] so cash equivalent must involve an articulated sum."

In the following, the form of the composition appeals to a verse of Scripture for its foundation. We then introduce a proposition that that verse is supposed to yield, and then the purpose for which the verse and accompanying proposition are introduced is addressed, C. So the Scripture component is a complete exegesis: verse, statement of its sense. This is then followed by the utilization of that fact for the issue at hand. On that basis I treat B as free-standing.

III.29   A.   *Said R. Joseph, "How do I know it? Because it has been taught on Tannaite authority:*

B.   "'If there be yet many years, according to them he shall give back the price of his redemption out of the money with which he was acquired' (Lev. 25:51) – he may be acquired by money, not by produce or utensils.

C.   [*Joseph continues,*] "*Now what is the meaning of 'produce or utensils'? Should I say that there is no possibility of acquiring title through a transaction symbolized by these in any way at all? But Scripture has said, 'he shall return the price of his redemption' (Lev. 25:51), which serves to encompass a cash equivalent as much as actual cash. And if these are of insufficient value to add up to a penny, then why make reference in particular to produce or utensils, when the same is the rule governing ready cash? So does it not mean that they are worth a penny, but, since they do not add up to an articulated sum, they do not serve that purpose.*"

D.   *And the other party?*

E.   *This is the sense of the matter:* He is acquired under the torah governing cash, but he is not acquired under the torah governing produce and utensils. *And what might that involve? Barter.* [Freedman: Whatever is given for a slave, whether money or cash equivalents, must be given in money; produce and utensils can be given in that way, but not as barter, in exchange for the slave, for barter can acquire only movables, but human beings rank as real estate].

F.   *Well, then, from the perspective of R. Nahman, who has said, "Produce cannot effect a barter" [though a utensil can], what is to be said?*

G.   *Rather, in point of fact, these objects [produce, utensils] are worth at least a penny, and as to your question – Then why make reference in particular to produce or utensils, when the same is the rule governing ready cash? – the intent of the Tannaite framer is to make the point in the form of a statement, it goes without saying, thus: It is not necessary to make that point in respect to cash, for if it is worth a penny, the transaction is valid, and if not, it is not valid, but even with regard to produce and utensils, where I might argue, since the benefit from these is close at hand, the slave permits himself to be acquired – so we are informed that that is not the case.*

H.   *Said R. Joseph, "How do I know it? Because it has been taught on Tannaite authority:*

I.   "[If someone said,] 'This calf is for the redemption of my firstborn son,' 'this cloak is for the redemption of my firstborn son,' he has said nothing whatsoever. '...This calf, worth five selas, is for the redemption of my son,' 'this cloak, worth five selas, is for the redemption of my son' – his son is redeemed [T. Bekh. 6:13].

J.   [*Joseph continues,*] "*Now what is the meaning of redemption? Should I say that the calf or cloak is not worth five selas? Then does he have the power to make such a decision [when that is what is owing]? So isn't it a case in which that is so even though they are worth the stated sum, but since there is no fixed value assigned to them that is made articulate, they are not acceptable?*"

K. *Not at all. In point of fact it is a case in which they do not have the requisite value, but it is, for example, a case in which the priest accepted the object as full value for the redemption, as in the case of R. Kahana, who took a scarf in exchange for the redemption of the firstborn, saying to the father, "To me it's worth five selas."*

L. *Said R. Ashi, "Well, we make that rule only with someone such as R. Kahana, who is an eminent authority and needs a scarf for his head, but not with everybody in general."*

M. *That is like Mar bar R. Ashi, who bought a scarf from the mother of Rabbah of Kubi worth ten zuz for thirteen.*

III.30 A. Said R. Eleazar, "[If the man said,] 'Be betrothed to me for a maneh,' but he gave her a denar, lo, this woman is betrothed, and he has to make up the full amount that he has promised. *Why is that the rule? Since he referred to a maneh but gave her only a denar, it is as though he had said to her, '...on the stipulation...,'* and said R. Huna said Rab, 'Whoever uses the language, "on the stipulation that...," is as though he says, "...as of now."'" [Freedman: Thus it is as though he said, "Be betrothed to me immediately for a denar, on condition that I gave you a maneh later."]

B. *An objection was raised:* [If the man said,] "Be betrothed to me for a maneh," and he was continuing to count out the money, and one of the parties wanted to retract, even up to the final denar, he or she has every right to do so.

C. *Here with what situation do we deal? It is one in which he said, "...for this particular maneh...."*...

III.31 A. *As to a denar of copper, with what sort of a case do we deal? If she knew about its character, well, then she was informed and accepted it!*

B. *Not at all, the specific reference is required to deal with a case in which he gave it to her at night, or she found it among other coins.*

III.32 A. *As to a debased denar, with what sort of a case do we deal? If it is not in circulation, then isn't it in the same class as a copper denar?*

B. *Said R. Pappa, "It would be one that circulates but only with difficulty."*

III.33 A. Said R. Nahman, "If he said to her, 'Be betrothed to me with a maneh,' and he gave her a pledge for it, she is not betrothed. [8B] There is no maneh here, there is no pledge here." [Freedman: She neither received the maneh nor did he actually give her a pledge, since that has to be returned.]

B. *Raba objected to R. Nahman,* "If he betrothed her with a pledge, she is betrothed."

What follows once more appeals to Scripture as the source for a known fact:

C. *That refers to a pledge belonging to a third party, in accord with what R. Isaac said, for said R. Isaac, "How on the basis of Scripture do we know that the creditor acquires title to the pledge [while it is in his possession and so is responsible for any accident that occurs]? Scripture states, 'In any case you shall deliver the pledge again when the sun goes down...and it shall be righteousness for you' (Deut. 24:13). Now if he doesn't have title to the object, whence the righteousness?*

This proves that the creditor takes the title to the pledge."
[Freedman: It is legally his while in his possession, therefore
he may validly offer it for a token of betrothal.]

III.34   A.   *The sons of R. Huna bar Abin bought a female slave for copper coins. They*
didn't have the coins in hand, so they gave as a pledge a silver ingot. The
slave's value increased. They came before R. Ammi. He said to them,
"There are here neither coins nor an ingot" [and the transaction can be
cancelled].

III.35   A.   *Our rabbis have taught on Tannaite authority:*

         B.   "Be betrothed to me with a maneh," and she took it and threw it
into the sea or fire or anywhere where it is lost – she is not
betrothed [T. Qid. 2:8A-C].

III.36   A.   *So if she threw it down before him, is it a valid betrothal? Lo, in so doing,*
she says to him, "You take it, I don't want it."

         B.   *The formulation means to say, it is not necessary to say..., thus: It is not*
necessary to say that if she throw it back before him, this is not a valid
betrothal, but if she threw it into the sea or into the fire, I might have
supposed that, since she now is liable for the money, she has most certainly
allowed herself to be betrothed, and the reason that she did what she did is
that she was thinking, "I'll test him to see whether he is temperamental or
not." So we are informed that that is not the case.

III.37   A.   *Our rabbis have taught on Tannaite authority:*

         B.   "Be betrothed to me with this maneh" –

         C.   "Give it to my father or your father" –

         D.   she is not betrothed.

         E.   "...On condition that they accept it for me" –

         F.   she is betrothed [T. Qid. 2:8D-E].

III.38   A.   *The Tannaite formulation has made reference to "father" to show you the*
full extent of the application of the rule of the first clause [even then she is
not betrothed], and the usage of "your father" shows how far we go in the
second clause [that she is then betrothed].

III.39   A.   "Be betrothed to me with a maneh" –

         B.   "Give them to Mr. So-and-so."

         C.   She is not betrothed .

         D.   "...On condition that Mr. So-and-so accept the money for me," she
is betrothed [T. Qid. D-G].

III.40   A.   *And it was necessary to specify both cases. For if we had been informed of*
the cases of her referring to her father or his father, it would be in such a
case in which if she said, "on condition that they receive them for me," she
would have accomplished a valid betrothal, for she would have relied on
them, assuming that they would carry out her commission. But that
would not be the case when she merely made reference to Mr. So-and-so.
And had we been informed of her referring to Mr. So-and-so, it would be
in this case in particular that the rule would apply, for if she said, "Give
them to Mr. So-and-so," she would not be betrothed, for she would not
have known the man well enough to give him the money as a gift. But as
for her referring to her father or his father, with whom she is closely
related, one might have supposed that her intent was to make a gift of the
money to them. So both cases are required.

III.41   A.   *Our rabbis have taught on Tannaite authority:*

         B.   "Be betrothed to me for this maneh" –

	C.	"Put it on a rock" –
	D.	she is not betrothed.
	E.	But if the rock belonged to her, she is betrothed.

III.42
- A. *R. Bibi raised this question:* "If the rock belonged to the two of them, what is the law?"
- B. *That question stands.*

III.43
- A. "Be betrothed for this loaf of bread" –
- B. "Give it to a dog" –
- C. she is not betrothed.
- D. But if the dog belonged to her, she is betrothed.

III.44
- A. *R. Mari raised this question:* "If the dog was running after her, what is the law? In exchange for the benefit that she gets in being saved from the dog, she has determined to assign to him title over herself? Or perhaps she has the power to say, 'By the law of the Torah, you were obligated to save us?'"
- B. *That question stands.*

III.45
- A. "Be betrothed to me for this loaf of bread" –
- B. "Give it to that poor man" –
- C. she is not betrothed, even if it was a poor man who depended on her.

III.46
- A. *How come?*
- B. *She can say to the man, "Just as I have an obligation to him, so you have an obligation to him."*

III.47
- A. *There was someone who was selling* [9A] *glass beads. A woman came to him. She said to him, "Give me one string."*
- B. *He said to her, "If I give it to you, will you become betrothed to me?"*
- C. *She said to him, "Give it to me, do."*
- D. *Said R. Hama, "Any case in which someone said, 'Give it to me, do,' means absolutely nothing."*

III.48
- A. There was someone who was drinking wine in a wine shop. A woman came. She said to me, "Give me a cup."
- B. *He said to her, "If I give it to you, will you be betrothed to me?"*
- C. *She said to him, "Oh, let me have a drink."*
- D. *Said R. Hama, "Any case in which someone said, 'Oh let me have a drink,' means absolutely nothing."*

III.49
- A. *There was someone who was throwing down dates from a date palm. A woman came along and said to him, "Throw me down two."*
- B. *He said to her, "If I throw them down to you, will you become betrothed to me?"*
- C. *She said to him, "Oh, throw them down to me."*
- D. *Said R. Zebid, "Every usage such as, 'Oh, throw them down to me,' is null."*

III.50
- A. *The question was raised:* "What if she said, 'give me,' 'let me drink,' or 'throw them down'?"
- B. Said Rabina, "She is betrothed."
- C. R. Sama bar Raqata said, "By the king's crown, she's not betrothed."
- D. *And the decided law is, she's not betrothed.*
- E. *And the decided law is, silk doesn't have to be evaluated.*
- F. *And the decided law is in accord with R. Eleazar.*
- G. *And the decided law is in accord with Raba as stated by R. Nahman.*

IV.1
- A. [A writ:] *Our rabbis have taught on Tannaite authority:*

    B.   A writ: How so?

    C.   If one wrote on a parchment or on a potsherd, even though they themselves were of no intrinsic value, "Lo, your daughter is betrothed to me," "Your daughter is engaged to me," "Your daughter is a wife for me" – lo, this woman is betrothed.

    D.   *Objected R. Zira bar Mammel, "Lo, this writ is not comparable to a writ of purchase, for there, the seller writes, 'My field is sold to me,' while here, it is* the prospective husband who writes, 'Your daughter is consecrated to me.'"

In the following, Scripture supplies a fact on the usage of the language:

    E.   *Said Raba, "There the formulation derives from the expression of Scripture, and here the formulation derives from the expression of Scripture. In reference to that other matter it is written, 'and he sell some of his possessions' (Lev. 25:25), so it is on the seller that the All-Merciful has made the matter depend. Here it is written, 'when a man takes a woman' (Deut. 24:1), so it is on the husband that Scripture had made the matter depend."*

    F.   *But in that other context, it is also written, "Men shall buy fields for money" (Jer. 32:44).*

    G.   *Read the letters as though they bore vowels to yield, "Men shall transmit" [that is, sell].*

    H.   *Well, then, if you read the word to yield "transmit," because it is written "and he sell," then here, too, read "if a man be taken," since it is written, "I gave my daughter to this man for a wife" (Deut. 22:16)!*

    I.   *Rather said Raba, "What we have is a law by decree, and our rabbis have then found support for the law in verses of Scripture. Or, if you prefer, I shall say, there, too, it is also written, 'So I took the deed of the purchase' (Jer. 32:11)."* [Freedman: This shows that Jeremiah, the purchaser, received the deed, which must have been drawn up by the vendor.]

What is interesting here is the distinction between a decree for which scriptural support is to be identified and a solid proof on the strength of Scripture. What leads to the conclusion that all we have is the former is the contrary evidence; it is not a solid proof, so serves as a mere indication of the state of matters.

IV.2   A.   Said Raba said R. Nahman, "If one wrote on a piece of paper or a sherd, even though these were not worth a penny, 'Your daughter is consecrated to me,' 'Your daughter is betrothed to me,' 'Your daughter is mine as a wife,' whether this is effected through her father or through herself, she is betrothed by the father's consent. That is the case if she had not reached maturity. If one wrote for her on a piece of paper or a sherd, even though these were not worth a penny, 'You are consecrated to me,' 'You are betrothed to

me,' 'You are mine as a wife,' whether this is effected through her
father or through herself, she is betrothed by her own consent."

IV.3   A.   R. Simeon b. Laqish raised the question, "As to a deed of betrothal
that was not written for the purpose of betrothing this particular
woman, what is the law? *Do we treat as comparable the formation of a
marriage and its dissolution, so that, [9B] just as in the case of its
dissolution, we require that the writ of divorce be written for the particular
purpose of divorcing this woman, so in the case of the formation of the
marriage, we require the writ of betrothal to be written for the particular
purpose of betrothing this woman? Or do we treat as comparable the
several modes for effecting a betrothal: Just as the betrothal by a monetary
token need not be accomplished by a token prepared for her sake in
particular, so betrothal by a deed does not have to be through a deed
prepared for this particular woman?"*

    B.   *After he raised the question, he went and solved it: "We do
indeed treat as comparable the formation of a marriage and its
dissolution. For said Scripture, 'and when she has gone
forth...she may be another man's wife' (Deut. 24:1)."*

What is of special interest in the following is the range and variety of
appeals to Scripture. First, we ask Scripture to serve as the source of
Mishnah rules, and this application is made explicit in the common
formula. Since there are two potential sources for the same proposition,
we ask why one is unsatisfactory, or, why both are required. That
inquiry into the need for multiple statements of a point is familiar in
Mishnah exegesis as well. V.1.E reads Scripture precisely as, elsewhere,
the Talmud reads the Mishnah. We further show, M, that all parties to
the dispute take up each detail of Scripture and read it in a manner
coherent with the proposition at hand; the correct disposition of all
details from all viewpoints is integral, for example, at P-Q, among several
points. Does Scripture here form the substrate of discourse and impose
organization on it? Not at all. It is critical, but not definitive.

IV.4   A.   *It has been stated:*
    B.   *If someone wrote a deed of betrothal in her name but without
her knowledge and consent –*
    C.   *Rabbah and Rabina say, "She is betrothed."*
    D.   *R. Pappa and R. Sherabayya say, "She is not betrothed."*
    E.   *Said R. Pappa, "I shall state their scriptural foundations and I
shall state mine. I shall state their reason: It is written, 'and
when she has gone forth...she may be another man's wife'
(Deut. 24:1). Scripture treats as comparable the betrothal and
the divorce: Just as the writ of divorce must be written for the
purpose of divorcing this particular woman yet without her
knowledge and consent, so the writ of betrothal must be
written for her own sake, and without her consent. And I shall
state the scriptural foundation of my position: 'And when she
has gone forth...she may be another man's wife' (Deut. 24:1).
This treats betrothal as comparable to divorce: Just as in the*

divorce, the knowledge of the giver is required [the husband has obviously to concur], so in betrothal the giver's knowledge is essential [and it is the woman who gives herself]."

F. *An objection was raised:* They write the documents of betrothal and marriage only with the knowledge and consent of both parties [M. B.B. 10:4A]. *Doesn't this mean literally, documents of betrothal and marriage?*

G. *No, it means deeds of apportionment [designating how much the families are giving to the son and daughter], in accord with what R. Giddal said R. Rab said, for said R. Giddal said Rab, "How much are you going to give to your son?' 'Thus and so.' 'How much are you going to give to your daughter?' 'Thus and so.' If they then arose and declared the formula of sanctification, they have effected transfer of the right of ownership. These statements represent matters in which the right of ownership is transferred verbally."*

V.1   A. Or sexual intercourse:

B. *What is the scriptural source of this rule?*

C. *Said R. Abbahu said R. Yohanan, "Said Scripture, 'If a man be found lying with a woman who had intercourse with a husband' (Deut. 22:22) – this teaches that he became her husband through an act of sexual relations."*

D. Said R. Zira to R. Abbahu, and some say, R. Simeon b. Laqish to R. Yohanan, "Is then what Rabbi taught unsatisfactory, namely, '"and has intercourse with her" (Deut. 24:1) – this teaches that he became her husband through an act of sexual relations'?"

E. *If I had to derive proof from that verse, I might have supposed that he first has to betroth her [with a monetary token] and only then have sexual relations with her. So we are informed that that is not the case.*

F. *Objected R. Abba bar Mammel, "If so, then in the case of the betrothed maiden, where Scripture decrees stoning as the death penalty should she commit adultery, how can we find a concrete case in which that would be the upshot? If he first betrothed her and then had sexual relations, she is in the classification of a woman who has had sexual relations [and stoning is the death penalty for a virgin alone]; if he betrothed her but did not have sexual relations with her, then it is on this hypothesis null anyhow!"*

G. *Rabbis stated the solution to this conundrum before Abbayye: "You would find such a case if the prospective groom had sexual relations with her through the anus."*

H. *Said to them Abbayye, "But in point of fact, even Rabbi and rabbis conduct their dispute only with regard to an outsider; but as to the husband, all concur that if the prospective groom had sexual relations with her through the anus, she is classified as one who has had sexual relations."*

I. *What is the pertinent passage? As has been taught on Tannaite authority:*

J.   It ten men had intercourse with her and she remained yet a virgin, all of them are put to death by stoning.

K.   Rabbi says, "The first is put to death by stoning, and the others by strangulation" [T. San. 10:9C-D].

L.   *Said R. Nahman bar Isaac, "You would find such a case, for instance, if he betrothed her with a writ.* Since a writ is wholly sufficient to sever the marital bond, it also is sufficient fully to effect it." [Freedman: Yet it might be that money betrothal must be followed by sexual relations.]

M.   And as to the clause, "and has intercourse with her" (Deut. 24:1), *how does R. Yohanan make use of that item?*

N.   *He requires it to show the following:* A wife is acquired by sexual relations, but a Hebrew slave girl is not acquired by sexual relations. *For it might have entered your mind to maintain that the contrary may be inferred by an argument a fortiori from the case of the levirate wife:* If a levirate wife, who is not acquired by a money payment is acquired through an act of sexual relations, this woman, who is acquired by a money payment, surely should be acquired by an act of sexual relations!

O.   [But the verse is not required for that purpose, for one may well respond:] what characterizes the levirate wife is that she is already subject to the bond to the husband [which obviously does not pertain to the slave girl].

P.   *Well, it might have entered your mind to maintain:* Since it is written, "If he take another wife" (Ex. 21:10) [in addition to the slave girl] – just as the other is acquired by intercourse, so a Hebrew slave girl would be acquired through an act of sexual relations. *So by this verse we are informed to the contrary.*

Q.   *And how does Rabbi deal with this theoretical proposition?*

R.   *If it is so [that verse yields only the proposition that sexual relations is a medium of betrothal], Scripture should have written, "and he have sexual relations." Why say, "and he have sexual relations with her"? That yields both points.*

S.   *And from the perspective of Raba, who said, "Bar Ahina explained to me, '"When a man takes a woman and has sexual relations with her" (Deut. 24:1) – a betrothal that can be followed by sexual relations is valid, but a betrothal that cannot be followed by sexual relations is not valid,"' what is to be said?*

T.   *If that were the sole point, Scripture could have written, "or has sexual relations with her." Why, "and has sexual relations with her"? This yields all the pertinent points.*

U.   *And how does Rabbi deal with the phrase, "who had intercourse with a husband"?*

V.   *He uses it to teach the following proposition:* A husband's act of anal intercourse renders her a woman who is no longer a virgin, but a third party's action does not.

W.   *Well, now, is that Rabbi's position? Hasn't it been taught on Tannaite authority:*

X.   It ten men had intercourse with her and she remained yet a virgin, all of them are put to death by stoning.

Y.   Rabbi says, "The first is put to death by stoning, and the others by strangulation" [T. San. 10:9C-D].

Z.   [10A] Said R. Zira, "Rabbi concedes that, in regard to the extrajudicial sanction, all have to pay the fine. *And how come this is different from the death penalty [in which case Rabbi classifies her as a virgin]? That is differentiated by Scripture itself:* 'Then the man alone that lay with her shall die' (Deut. 22:25)."

AA.   *And rabbis – how do they deal with the word "alone"?*

BB.   *They require it in line with that which has been taught on Tannaite authority:*

CC.   "'Then they shall both of them die' (Deut. 22:22) means that a penalty is imposed only when the two of them are equal," the words of R. Josiah.

DD.   R. Jonathan says, "'Then the man only that lay with her shall die' (Deut. 22:25)."

EE.   *And whence does R. Yohanan derive this thesis?*

FF.   *If it were so, Scripture should have said,* "who has had intercourse with a man." *Why say,* "Who had had intercourse with a husband"? *That is to yield both matters.*

V.2   A.   *The question was raised:* Is it the beginning of the act of intercourse that effects the acquisition of the woman, or the end of the act of sexual relations that does? *The practical difference would derive from a case in which* he performed the initial stage of sexual relations, then she put out her hand and accepted a token of betrothal from someone else; *or the case of whether a high priest may acquire a virgin through an act of sexual relations. What is the rule?*

        B.   Said Amemar in the name of Raba, "Whoever has sexual relations is thinking about the completion of the act of sexual relations [not only the commencement of the act]."

V.3   A.   *The question was raised:* Do sexual relations effect a consummated marriage or merely a betrothal? *The practical difference would pertain to the question of* whether he inherits her estate, contracts uncleanness to bury her [if he is a priest], and abrogates her vows. *If you maintain that* sexual relations effect a consummated marriage, then he inherits her estate, contracts uncleanness to bury her [if he is a priest], and abrogates her vows. *If you maintain that* sexual relations effect only betrothal, then he does not inherit her estate, contract uncleanness to bury her [if he is a priest], and abrogate her vows. *What is the rule?*

        B.   Said Abbayye, "The father retains control of his daughter [younger than twelve and a half] as to effecting any of the tokens of betrothal: Money, document, or sexual intercourse. And he retains control of what she finds, of the fruit of her labor, and of abrogating her vows. And he receives her writ of divorce [from a betrothal]. But he does not dispose of the return [on property received by the girl from her mother] during her lifetime. When she is married, the husband exceeds the father, for he disposes of the return [on property received by the girl from her mother] during her lifetime. But he is liable to maintain her, and to ransom her, and to bury her [M. Ket. 4:4]. *Now there is a clear reference to sexual relations, and yet the Tannaite formulation also qualifies the matter,* When she is married."

C. *But the clause,* When she is married, *may refer to other matters.*

D. *Said Raba,* "Come and take note: A girl three years and one day old is betrothed by intercourse. And if a levir has had intercourse with her, he has acquired her. And they are liable on her account because of the law [prohibiting intercourse with] a married woman. And she imparts uncleanness to him who has intercourse with her [when she is menstruating] [10B] to convey uncleanness to the lower as to the upper layer. [If] she was married to a priest, she eats heave-offering. [If] one of those who are unfit [for marriage] has intercourse with her, he has rendered her unfit to marry into the priesthood. [If one of all those who are forbidden in the Torah to have intercourse with her did so, they are put to death on her account. But she is free of responsibility. If she is younger than that age, intercourse with her is like putting a finger in the eye] [M. Nid. 5:4]. *Now there is a clear reference to sexual relations, and yet the Tannaite formulation also qualifies the matter,* When she is married."

E. *This is the sense of the passage: If this intercourse mentioned at the outset is with a priest, then she may eat priestly rations.*

F. *Come and take note:* It is the fact that Yohanan b. Bag Bag sent word to R. Judah b. Beterah in Nisibis, "I heard in your regard that you maintain, an Israelite woman who is betrothed to a priest may eat priestly rations." He replied, "And don't you concur? I have it on good authority in your regard that you are an expert in the innermost chambers of the Torah, knowing how to compose an argument a fortiori. So don't you know the following: 'If a Canaanite slave girl, upon whom an act of sexual relations does not confer the right to eat priestly rations, may eat priestly rations by reason of a money purchase of ownership to her, this one, upon whom an act of sexual relations does confer the right to eat priestly rations, surely should be permitted to eat priestly rations by means of the transfer of a token of betrothal!' But what can I do? For lo, sages have ruled: An Israelite girl betrothed to a priest may not eat priestly rations until she enters the marriage canopy." *Now how are we to understand the case here? If it is sexual relations after the marriage canopy and a betrothal through a monetary token followed by a marriage canopy, in both cases there is obviously no doubt that she may eat priestly rations. If it is intercourse with the marriage canopy or money without, then here there are two operative analogies, there, only one [and how can the rule governing money without a marriage canopy be deduced from the rules governing intercourse with]? So the passage surely must speak to both intercourse and money payment without a marriage canopy. If you maintain that intercourse brings about the consummated marriage, well and good; it is self-evident that sexual relations have a greater effect than money; but if you maintain that it effects only the betrothal, then what makes him certain in the one case and doubtful in the other?*

G. *Said R. Nahman bar Isaac, "In point of fact, I shall explain the matter to you to refer to sexual relations accompanied by the marriage canopy or monetary token without. And as to your objection, here there are two operative analogies, there, only one [and how can the rule governing money without a marriage canopy be deduced from the rules governing intercourse with]? Still there is an argument a fortiori that remains entirely valid. And this is what he sent to him by way of reply:* If a Canaanite slave girl, upon whom an act of sexual relations does not confer the right to eat priestly rations, even via the marriage canopy, may eat priestly rations by reason of a money purchase of ownership to her – without the intrusion of the rite of the marriage canopy, this one, upon whom an act of sexual relations does confer the right to eat priestly rations by means of the marriage canopy, surely should be permitted to eat priestly rations by means of the transfer of a token of betrothal – without the intrusion of the rite of the marriage canopy! But what can I do? For lo, sages have ruled: An Israelite girl betrothed to a priest may not eat priestly rations until she enters the marriage canopy.

A piece of evidence now is drawn from a reading of a clause of Scripture:

> That is on account of what Ulla said ['By the law of the Torah, a girl of Israelite caste who was betrothed to a priest is permitted to eat priestly rations: "But if a priest buy any soul, the purchase of his money..." (Lev. 22:11) – *and this one also falls into the class of* "purchased of his money." And what is the reason that they have said that she may not eat priestly rations? Lest a cup of wine in the status of priestly rations be mixed for her in her father's house and she share it with her brother or sister who are not in the priestly caste']."

H. *And Ben Bag Bag [doesn't he accept the argument a fortiori]?*

I. *In the acquisition of the gentile slave girl, the man has left out nothing in acquiring her [once he pays the money, she is his], but as to her, he has left out part of the process of acquiring her [for only after the marriage canopy does he inherit her and so forth].*

J. *Rabina said, "On the basis of the law of the Torah, [Ben Bag Bag] was quite certain that she may eat priestly rations, but it was only with respect to the position of rabbinical law that he sent word to him claiming that she is forbidden to do so, and this is the character of his inquiry:* 'I have heard in your regard that you maintain, an Israelite woman betrothed to a priest may eat priestly rations, thus disregarding the possibility of nullification' [for example, through discovery of an invalidating cause to nullify the betrothal; this then has no bearing on the question of status conferred by intercourse, since all concur that a betrothed girl may eat priestly rations so far as the law of the Torah is concerned (Freedman)]. And he sent word back, 'And don't you take the same position? I have it on good authority in your regard that you are an expert in the innermost chambers of the Torah, knowing how to compose an argument a fortiori. So don't you know the following: If a Canaanite slave girl, upon whom an act of sexual relations does not confer the right to eat priestly rations, may eat priestly rations by reason of a money purchase of ownership to her, *and we don't take account of the possibility of nullification of the betrothal* – this one, upon whom an act of sexual relations does confer the right to eat priestly rations, surely should be permitted to eat priestly rations by means of the transfer of a token of betrothal – *and we shouldn't take account of the possibility of nullification of the betrothal.* But what can I do?

For lo, sages have ruled: **An Israelite girl betrothed to a priest may not eat priestly rations [11A] until she enters the marriage canopy, on account of what Ulla said ["By the law of the Torah, a girl of Israelite caste who was betrothed to a priest is permitted to eat priestly rations: 'But if a priest buy any soul, the purchase of his money...' (Lev. 22:11) –** *and this one also falls into the class of* **'purchased of his money.'** **And what is the reason that they have said that she may not eat priestly rations? Lest a cup of wine in the status of priestly rations be mixed for her in her father's house and she share it with her brother or sister who are not in the priestly caste"].'"**

K. And Ben Bag Bag?
L. *He does not concede that a possibility of invalidating the transaction can take place in the sale of slaves. For if these were defects that were visible, then he has seen them and accepted them; if it was on account of defects that were concealed, what difference does it make to him? He wants the slave for work, and it wouldn't matter to him. If the slave turns out to be a thief or a rogue, he still belongs to the purchaser [since most slaves are that way anyhow]. So what can you say, that he turned out to be an thug or an outlaw? These would be known defects.*
M. *Now since both parties concur that a betrothed woman may not eat priestly rations, what's at issue?*
N. At issue is a case in which the husband accepted the body defects; or the father handed her over to the husband's messengers to be taken to her husband's house; or if the father's messengers were en route with the husband's. [In the first case, Ben Bag Bag lets her eat priestly rations; in Judah b. Batera's view, she cannot do so, by reason of Ulla's explanation; in the second, Ulla's consideration no longer pertains, there being no family around, but there can be nullification; and the third is governed by the same rule (Freedman).]

VI.1　A. **Through money: The House of Shammai say, "For a denar or what is worth a denar":**
B. *What is the operative consideration in the mind of the House of Shammai?*
C. Said R. Zira, "For a woman is particular about herself and is not going to allow herself to become betrothed for less than a denar."
D. *Said to him Abbayye, "Well, then what about the daughters of R. Yannai, who were so particular about themselves that they would not become betrothed for less than a tubful of denarii! If she should put out her hand and accept a coin from a stranger as a token of betrothal, is she then betrothed?!"*
E. *He said to him, "Well, if she put out her hand and accepted the token, I don't take that position. I speak of a case in which he conducts the*

betrothal at night [so doesn't know what she got] or if she appointed an agent."

F.   *R. Joseph said, "The operative consideration in the mind of the House of Shammai accords with what R. Judah said R. Assi said, for* said R. Judah said R. Assi, 'Whenever "money" is mentioned in the Torah, what is meant is Tyrian coinage; when rabbis speak of money, they refer to the coinage that circulates in the provinces.' [The betrothal token is Scriptural, so it must be a valuable coin, not a copper coin, hence a denar.]"

VI.2   A.   *Reverting to the body of the foregoing:* Said R. Judah said R. Assi, "Whenever 'money' is mentioned in the Torah, what is meant is Tyrian coinage; when rabbis speak of money, they refer to the coinage that circulates in the provinces."

In the next item a verse of Scripture provides a minor detail.

B.   *Is this a ubiquitous principle?* Lo, there is the case of a claim, concerning which Scripture states, "If a man shall deliver to his neighbor money or utensils to keep" (Ex. 22:6), *and yet we have learned in the Mishnah:* The oath imposed by judges [is required if] the claim is [at least] two pieces of silver, and the concession [on the part of the defendant is that he owes] at least a penny's [perutah's] worth [M. Shebu. 6:1A].

C.   *There the governing analogy is utensils:* Just as utensils are two, so the coins must be two; just as money speaks of what has intrinsic worth, so utensils speaks of something that is of worth.

D.   Lo, there is the case of a second tithe, concerning which Scripture states, "And you shall turn it into money and bind up the money in your hand," *and yet we have learned in the Mishnah:* One who exchanges a [silver] sela [sanctified as] second tithe [for other coins] in Jerusalem – The House of Shammai say, "The whole sela [he receives must consist] of [copper] coins." And the House of Hillel say, "[The sela he receives may consist] of one sheqel of silver [coins] and one sheqel of [copper] coins." The disputants before the sages say, "[The sela may consist] of three silver denars and [one] denar of [copper] coins." R. Aqiba says, "[The sela may consist] of three silver denars and a quarter [of the fourth denar must consist of] [copper] coins." R. Tarfon says, "[The fourth denar may consist of] four aspers of silver [equal to four-fifths of the denar's value and the remaining asper must be of copper]." Shammai says, "Let him deposit it in a shop and consume its value [in produce]" [M. M.S. 2:9]....

The next item gives a scriptural basis for a rule of the Mishnah:

VI.3   A.   R. Simeon b. Laqish says, *"The operative consideration behind the ruling of the House of Shammai is in accord with Hezekiah, for* said Hezekiah, 'Said Scripture, "then shall he let her be redeemed" (Ex. 21:8) – this teaches that she deducts from her redemption money and goes out free.' *Now if you maintain that the master gives her a denar [when he buys her, which*

		would be the counterpart to the token of betrothal], then there is no problem; but if you say it was a mere penny, then what deduction can be made from a penny?"
	B.	But maybe this is the sense of what the All-Merciful has meant to say: In a case in which he gave her a denar, there is a deduction made until a penny is left; but if he gave her a penny, there is no deduction made at all?
	C.	*[12A] Don't let it enter your mind. For it is comparable to the act of designating a Hebrew handmaid [for betrothal, once the Hebrew slave girl has been purchased; there is no further token of betrothal required]: Just as, in the case of such a designation, even though the master can designate her or refrain from doing so, as he prefers, where he doesn't designate her for marriage, the sale is invalid, so here, too, where we cannot make such a deduction, the sale is invalid. And the House of Shammai derive the rule governing the betrothal of a woman from the rule governing the Hebrew slave girl. Just as a Hebrew slave girl cannot be acquired for a penny, so a woman cannot be betrothed for a penny.*
	D.	*Well why not say half a denar or two pennies?*
	E.	*Once the penny was excluded as a measure, the matter was set at a denar.*

VI.4   A.   *Raba said, "This is the operative consideration for the position of the House of Shammai:* So that Israelite women won't be treated as ownerless property."

VII.1   A.   And the House of Hillel say, "For a perutah or what is worth a perutah":

       B.   *R. Joseph considered ruling, "A penny, of any sort [however debased]."*

       C.   *Said to him Abbayye, "But lo, there is a Tannaite clarification of this matter in so many words:* And how much is a perutah? One eighth of an Italian issar. *And should you say, that ruling addresses the time of Moses, while at the present time, it is as generally valued, lo, when R. Dimi came,* he said, 'R. Simai estimated the value in his time to determine how much a penny is, and determined, an eighth of an Italian issar,' *and when Rabin came,* he said, 'R. Dosetai, R. Yannai, and R. Oshayya estimated how much a penny is worth, and determined, a sixth of an Italian issar.'"...

VII.2   A.   *Reverting to the body of the foregoing: When R. Dimi came,* he said, "R. Simai estimated the value in his time to determine how much a penny is, and determined, an eighth of an Italian issar," *and when Rabin came,* he said, "R. Dosetai, R. Yannai, and R. Oshayya estimated how much a penny is worth, and determined, a sixth of an Italian issar."...

VII.3   A.   Said Samuel, "If one betrothed a woman with a date, even if a kor of dates were at a denar, she is deemed betrothed, *for we take account of the possibility that in Media it may be worth a penny."*

       B.   *But lo, we have learned in the Mishnah:* And the House of Hillel say, "For a perutah or what is worth a perutah"!

       C.   *No problem, the one speaks of a betrothal that is beyond all doubt, the other, a betrothal that is subject to doubt.*

VII.4   A.   *There was someone who betrothed a woman with a bundle of tow cotton [Freedman]. In session before Rab, R. Shimi bar Hiyya examined the question: "If it contains the value of a penny, she would be betrothed, if not, not."*

          B.   *... If not, not? But didn't Samuel say, "for we take account of the possibility that in Media it may be worth a penny"?*

          C.   *No problem, the one speaks of a betrothal that is beyond all doubt, the other, a betrothal that is subject to doubt.*

VII.5   A.   *There was someone who betrothed a woman with a black marble stone. In session, R. Hisda estimated its value: "If it contains the value of a penny, she would be betrothed, if not, not."*

          B.   *... If not, not? But didn't Samuel say, "for we take account of the possibility that in Media it may be worth a penny"?*

          C.   *R. Hisda does not view matters as does Samuel....*

VII.6   A.   *There was someone who in the marketplace betrothed a woman with a myrtle branch. R. Aha bar Huna sent word to R. Joseph, "In such a case, what is the ruling?"*

          B.   *He sent back, "Flog him in accord with the position of Rab, but require him to issue a writ of divorce in accord with the position of Samuel."...*

VII.7   A.   *There was someone who in the marketplace betrothed a woman with a mat made of myrtle twigs. They said to him, "But it's not worth a penny!"*

          B.   *He said to them, "Let her be betrothed for the four zuz that it contains [wrapped up in the mat]."*

          C.   *She took the mat and shut up.*

          D.   *Said Raba,* "You have then a case of silence following receipt of funds, and that kind of silence is null."

          E.   *Said Raba, "How do I know it? Because it has been taught on Tannaite authority:*

          F.   "'Take this sela as a bailment,' and then he said to her, 'Be betrothed to me with it' – if this was at the moment that he handed over the money, she is betrothed; if it was afterward, if she wanted, she is betrothed, but if she didn't want, she is not betrothed [T. Qid. 2:7A-D].

          G.   *"Now what is the meaning of if she wanted, and what is the meaning of if she didn't want? Shall we say that the meaning of, if she wanted, is, she said yes, and the meaning of if she didn't want is, she said no? Then it would follow that the first clause bears the meaning,* [13A] *even if she said no, it is a valid act of betrothal. But why should that be the case? Lo, she has said no! Rather, is not the meaning of, if she wanted, she said yes, and would not the language, if she didn't want, mean, she remained silent? Then it would follow,* silence following receipt of funds is null."...

VII.8   A.   *There was a woman who was selling silk skeins [Freedman]. Someone came along and grabbed a piece of silk from her. She said to him, "Give it back to me."*

          B.   *He said to her, "If I give it back to you, will you be betrothed to me?"*

          C.   *She took it from him and shut up.*

          D.   *And said R. Nahman, "She has every right to claim, 'Yes, I took it, but I took what was mine!'"...*

VII.9   A.   *When R. Assi died, rabbis assembled to collect his traditions. Said one of the rabbis, R. Jacob by name, "This is what R. Assi said R. Mani said,*

'Just as a woman may not be acquired with less than a penny, so real estate cannot be acquired for less than a penny.'"

B. *They said to him, "But hasn't it been taught on Tannaite authority:* Even though a woman may not be acquired with less than a penny, real estate can be acquired for less than a penny?"

C. *He said to them, "When that Tannaite ruling was set forth, it had to do with barter, for it has been taught on Tannaite authority:* Transfer of title may take place with a utensil even though the utensil is not worth a penny."

Scripture is alleged to serve as a source for good counsel given by a sage, and then, of special interest, we ask how in particular the verse proves the point that is imputed to it:

VII.10 A. *Further, in session they said, "Lo, in regard to what* R. Judah said Samuel said, 'Whoever doesn't know the essentials of writs of divorce and betrothals should not get involved in them,' said R. Assi said R. Yohanan, 'And such folk are more of a problem to the world than the generation of the flood, for it has been stated, "By swearing, lying, killing, stealing, and committing adultery, they spread forth and blood touches blood"' (Hos. 4:2)."

B. *How does that verse bear the alleged implication?*

C. *It is in line with the way in which R. Joseph interpreted the verse in his translation, "They beget children by their neighbors' wives, piling evil upon evil."*

D. *[Reverting to A:] "And it is written, 'Therefore shall the land mourn and everyone who dwells therein shall languish, with the beasts of the field and the fowl of heaven, yes the fish of the sea also shall be taken away' (Hos. 4:3). By contrast, with respect to the generation of the flood, there was no decree against the fish of the sea: 'Of all that was in the dry land died' (Gen. 7:22) – but not the fish in the sea; here even the fish in the sea are covered."*

E. *But might one say that that penalty was inflicted only when all of the sins listed were committed [not only adultery]?*

F. *Don't imagine it! For it is written, "For because of swearing the land mourns" (Jer. 23:10) [a single crime suffices (Freedman)].*

G. *Well, maybe swearing stands on its own terms, and the others combined on theirs?*

H. *[13B] Is it written, "and they spread forth"? What is written is, "they spread forth."*

One important way in which Scripture serves is to provide grounds for the distinction between a ruling or law deriving from the Torah and one deriving from scribes or rabbis. Here, a specific verse of Scripture may or may not be invoked; but the Torah always is invoked. So here the Torah serves as a source of taxonomic differentiaton. In the following we have an example of differentiating between the rule of the

Torah and the rule driving from Scribes, without an explicit introduction
of a verse of Scripture.

VII.11   A.   *Further, in session they said, "Lo, in regard to what we have*
                learned in the Mishnah, the woman who brought her sin-
                offering, and died – let the heirs bring her burnt-offering. [If
                she brought] her burnt-offering and died, the heirs do not
                bring her sin-offering [M. Qin. 2:5O-Q], and, in which regard,
                said R. Judah said Samuel, 'That rule applies to a case in
                which she had designated the offering while she was yet
                alive, but not otherwise,' *therefore taking the view that the*
                obligation incurred by a debt is not based on the law of the
                Torah [Freedman: if a man borrows money, we do not say
                that his property is automatically mortgaged for its
                repayment, so that in the event of his death, his heirs are
                liable on the law of the Torah, since they inherit mortgaged
                property unless the debtor explicitly mortgages his goods in a
                bond; here, too, the woman is under an obligation to God to
                bring a sacrifice, yet, since she did not designate an animal
                for it, no obligation lies on the heirs] – said R. Assi said R.
                Yohanan, 'That rule applies even though she had not
                designated the offering while she was yet alive, but not
                otherwise,' *therefore taking the view that the obligation*
                incurred by a debt is based on the law of the Torah – in that
                context, lo, the dispute was set forth in another connection
                [and hardly required repetition].
         B.   *"For Rab and Samuel both say, 'A debt attested only orally*
                cannot be collected from the heirs or the purchasers of the
                indentured property,' and both R. Yohanan and R. Simeon b.
                Laqish say, 'A debt attested only orally can be collected from
                the heirs or the purchasers of the indentured property.'"
         C.   *Well, as a matter of fact, both versions of the dispute had to be*
                set forth. For if it had been stated in the latter case only, I
                should have supposed that it is only in that case that Samuel
                took the position that he did, because it is not a debt the type
                of which is set forth in the Torah, but in the other case, I might
                have said that he concurs with R. Yohanan and R. Simeon b.
                Laqish. And if it had been stated in the former case only, I
                should have supposed that it is only in that case that R.
                Yohanan took the position that he did, because a class of debt
                that is known in Scripture is equivalent to one that is written
                out in a bond, but in the latter case, I might have supposed that
                he concurs with Samuel. So both versions of the dispute had to
                be set forth.
         D.   Said R. Pappa, "The decided law is, 'A loan that is only
                verbal is collected from an estate but may not be collected
                from purchasers [of the property from the now-deceased
                testator].'
         E.   "It is collected from an estate, *since the indenture derives from*
                the Torah, but it may not be collected from purchasers [of the

property from the now-deceased testator], *since it will not be widely known [so the purchasers cannot protect themselves]."*

What is striking in the foregoing is that a verse of Scripture does not come into play, so here we find the presence of the Torah without an explicit exegetical initiative.

VIII.1 A.   And she acquires herself through a writ of divorce or through the husband's death:

B.   *Well, there is no problem identifying the source for the rule concerning divorce, since it is written, "And he shall write for her a writ of divorce" (Deut. 24:1). But as to the husband's death, how do we know it?*

C.   *It is a matter of reasoning:* He binds her [to himself, forbidding her to all other men] so he can free her.

D.   *Well, what about the case of consanguineous relations, from whom he forbids her, but for whom he cannot release her [even after he dies]?*

E.   *Rather, since the All-Merciful has said,* a levirate widow without children is forbidden, it must follow that, lo, if she has children [after the husband's death] she is permitted [to remarry].

F.   *Well, maybe, if she has no children, she is forbidden to everybody but forbidden to the levir, and if she has children, she is forbidden to everybody without exception?*

G.   *Rather, since Scripture has said that a widow is forbidden to marry a high priest, lo, she is permitted to marry an ordinary priest [and any other man].*

H.   *Well, maybe, she is forbidden by a negative commandment to a high priest but to everyone else by a positive commandment?*

I.   *So what's this alleged positive commandment doing here? If her husband's death matters, she should be wholly free to remarry, but if not, let her stay as she was.* [Freedman: As a married woman, she is forbidden to others by a negative commandment; there are no grounds for supposing that her husband's death leaves the prohibition but changes its nature.]

J.   *Well, how come not? The husband's death can remove her from liability to the death penalty and place her under the prohibition involved in an affirmative commandment. It would then be comparable to the case of animals that have been consecrated but then rendered unfit for sacrifice. Before they were unfit, they would be subject to sacrilege and not sheared or worked with; when redeemed, they are no longer subject to the laws of sacrilege, but they still are not to be sheared or worked with.*

K.   Rather, Scripture said, "What man is there...his house, lest he die in battle and another man take her" (Deut. 20:7).

L.   *Objected R. Shisha b. R. Idi, "But might I then say, who is 'another man'? It is the levir."*

M.   Said R. Ashi, "There are two replies in this matter. *The first is, the levir is not classified as 'another.' Furthermore, it is written, 'and if the latter husband hate her and write her a writ of divorce...or if the latter husband die...' (Deut. 24:3) – so death is treated as wholly comparable to a writ of divorce; just as the writ of divorce leaves her completely free, so death leaves her completely free."*

IX.1   A.   The deceased childless brother's widow is acquired through an act of sexual relations:

B.   *How do we know that she is acquired by an act of sexual relations?*

C.   Said Scripture, [14A] "Her husband's brother shall go in to her and take her to him as a wife" (Deut. 25:5).

D.   *Might I say that she is his wife in every regard [so that she can be acquired by money or a deed]?*

E.   *Don't let it enter your mind, for it has been taught on Tannaite authority:* Might one suppose that a money payment or a writ serve to complete the bond to her, as much as sexual relations does? Scripture says, "Her husband's brother shall go in to her and take her to him as a wife" (Deut. 25:5) – sexual relations complete the relationship to her, but a money payment or a writ do not do so.

F.   *Might I say, what is the meaning of* take her to him as a wife? *Even against her will he enters into levirate marriage with her?*

G.   *If so, Scripture should have said, "and take her...." Why say, "and take her to wife"? It bears both meanings just now under discussion.*

X.1   A.   And acquires [freedom for] herself through a rite of removing the shoe:

B.   *How do we know it?*

C.   Said Scripture, "And his name shall be called in Israel, the house of him who has had his shoe removed" (Deut. 25:12) – once his shoe has been removed by her, she is permitted for all Israel.

D.   *Is this the purpose of the word "Israel" in this context? Isn't it required in line with that which R. Samuel bar Judah taught as a Tannaite statement: "'In Israel' (Deut. 25:7) means that the rite of removing the shoe must be done in front of a court of Israelites by birth, not a court of proselytes"?*

E.   *There are two references in context to "in Israel."*

F.   *Nonetheless, it is required in line with that which has been taught on Tannaite authority:* Said R. Judah, "Once we were in session before R. Tarfon, and a levirate woman came to perform the rite of removing the shoe, and he said to us, 'All of you respond: "The man who has had his shoe removed"' (Deut. 25:10)."

G.   *That is derived from the formulation, "and his name shall be called" [with "in Israel" free for its own purpose].*

In what follows, the same procedure as dominated in the foregoing continues without revision; we simply ask for the source of hard facts, and we are satisfied to find the source in either Scripture or reasoning on other facts from the known to the unknown. At **XI.1** we read the Mishnah rule just as we did before; but instead of finding a verse of Sdripture to guide us, we turn to reason: an argument a fortiori based on a known case. Reason and Scripture serve equally well, and I see no material point of differentiation in the outcome. An analytical problem may be brought to Scripture or to a work of hierarchical classification from the known to the unknown (a fortiori), and the form will not vary beyond what is necessitated by citation language.

XI.1   A.   **And through the levir's death:**
       B.   *How do we know it?*
       C.   It derives from an argument a fortiori: If a married woman, who, if she commits adultery, is put to death through strangulation, is released by the death of the husband, a levirate widow, who is forbidden merely by a negative commandment [from marrying someone else] all the more so should be freed by the death of the levir!
       D.   But what distinguishes a married woman is that she goes forth with a writ of divorce. Will you say the same of this woman, who does not go forth with a writ of divorce?
       E.   But she, too, goes forth with the rite of removing the shoe [which is comparable to a writ of divorce].
       F.   Rather: What is special about the married woman is that the one who forbids her to other men also frees her [which is not the case with the levirate widow, since she is forbidden to others because of her childless deceased husband, but that the death of the levir frees her has yet to be proved].
       G.   *Said R. Ashi, "Lo, here, too, he who forbids her also frees her: The levir forbids her, the levir frees her"* [since if there were no levir, her husband's death alone would have freed her, so he really is responsible (Freedman)].

XI.2   A.   **A married woman also should be freed through the rite of removing the shoe, by reason of an argument a fortiori based on the levirate widow, namely: If a levirate wife, who is not freed by a divorce, is freed by the rite of removing the shoe, then this one [the levirate wife] who is freed by divorce surely should be freed by a rite of removing the shoe. Thus we are informed that that is not the case. Said Scripture, "Then he shall writ her a writ of divorce" (Deut. 24:1) – through a writ he divorces her, but he doesn't divorce her in any other way.**
       B.   **Then a levirate widow should go forth through a writ of divorce, by reason of an argument a fortiori, namely: If a married woman, who does not go forth through the rite of removing the shoe, goes forth through a writ of divorce, this one, who does go forth through the rite of removing the shoe, surely should go forth with a writ of divorce. So Scripture says to the contrary, "Thus it shall be done" (Deut. 25:9) –** *this*

*is the only possible way, and in any circumstance in which
there is a clear indication of what is indispensable, an
argument a fortiori is not composed.*

C.   Then what about the case of the Day of Atonement, in
connection with which there is clear scriptural reference to
"lot" and "statute" (Lev. 16:9) [and "statute" is a sign of an
indispensable detail], *and it has been taught on Tannaite
authority:* "And Aaron shall present the goat upon which the
lot fell for the Lord and make it a sin-offering" (Lev. 16:9) –
the lot is what designates the goat as a sin-offering, and mere
designation of the classification of the goat is not what turns
it into a sin-offering, nor does the priest designate it as a sin-
offering. For one might have argued to the contrary: Is it not
a matter of logic? If in a case in which the lot does not
consecrate an offering for a particular purpose, the
designation does consecrate the offering for a particular
purpose, in a case in which the lot does consecrate the
offering for a particular purpose, is it not a matter of logic
that the designation for a given purpose serves also to
designate what is offered for a given purpose? For that
reason Scripture states, "And Aaron shall present the goat
upon which the lot fell for the Lord and make it a sin-
offering" (Lev. 16:9) – the lot is what designates the goat as a
sin-offering, and mere designation of the classification of the
goat is not what turns it into a sin-offering. *So the operative
consideration is that Scripture is what excludes that
possibility. Then if it were not for that, we should have
composed an argument a fortiori, even though the word
"statute" is written in that connection!*

D.   [There is another reason altogether, namely,] said Scripture,
"Then he shall write her a writ of divorce" (Deut. 24:1), for
her, not for a levirate widow.

E.   *But might one say, "for her," meaning, for her in particular?*

F.   *There are two Scripture references to "for her."*

G.   *Nonetheless, they are needed for another purpose, one reference
to, "for her," means, for her sake in particular, and the other
reference to "her" meaning, but not for her and another
woman.*

H.   Rather, said Scripture, "The house of him that has had a shoe
removed" – *a shoe alone permits her to remarry, nothing else.*

I.   *Well, is that the purpose served by the reference to shoe? Isn't
it necessary in line with that which has been taught on
Tannaite authority:*

J.   "...Pull the sandal off his foot":

K.   I know only that the rule speaks of a sandal belonging to
him. How on the basis of Scripture do I know that it is all
right if the sandal belongs to someone else?

L.   Scripture says, "pull the sandal" – under any circumstances.

M.   If so, why does Scripture say, "his sandal"?

N.   It excludes the case of a large shoe, in which one cannot
actually walk, or a small one, which does not cover the larger

part of his foot, [14B] or a slipper lacking a heel. [In such instances the act of removing the shoe is null] [Sifré Deut. CCXCI:II.2].

O. *If so, Scripture should have said merely "shoe." Why "the shoe"? To yield both propositions.*

Let me briefly describe the complex composite we have now completed. I.1 presents an exegetical question for clarifying the formulation of the commencement of the Mishnah tractate. Nos. 2-4, 5-6 follow suit. II.1+2-3, 4-5 work on the problem of the scriptural origins of the Mishnah's rule. III.1-2, 3, 4-5 go through the same exercise. No. 6, with its talmud at Nos. 7-8, and No. 9, with its talmud at Nos. 10-12, then move on to a Tannaite complement to the Mishnah paragraph. Nos. 13+14-17 then extend the discussion of the foregoing set of entries in more general terms. Nos. 18-19 proceed to a variety of important theoretical questions, well within the framework of the foregoing. Nos. 20-25 present a sequence of systematic theoretical problems in the name of a single individual. There follow further theoretical questions along the same lines, Nos. 26-27. Then comes a case, No. 28, which yields a further theoretical problem, extending beyond the range of our particular topic. No. 29 extends the foregoing. No. 30, with a talmud at Nos. 31-32, resumes the analysis of theoretical questions pertinent to the protracted thematic appendix at hand. No. 33 proceeds with another, related theoretical problem. No. 34 illustrates the foregoing. No. 35, with a talmud at No. 36, then No. 37, with its talmud at No. 38, No. 39, with a talmud at No. 40, No. 41, analyzed by No. 42, No. 43, analyzed by No. 44, No. 45, analyzed at No. 46, in a coherent pattern and following a cogent program, all provide Tannaite complements to the same general theme as has been under discussion. Then come a set of cases, Nos. 47-50. IV.1 starts back at the starting point, with the exposition of the Mishnah's rule. No. 2 then expands on the same theme. Nos. 3-4 raise secondary questions of refinement of the now-established facts. V.1 finds the scriptural basis for the Mishnah's rule. Nos. 2, 3 proceed to theoretical questions, clarifying the fact given by the Mishnah rule. VI.1, with a footnote at No. 2, supplies an explanation of the Mishnah statement. Nos. 3, 4 continue the inquiry of No. 1. VII.1, with a footnote at No. 2, continues the exposition of the rule of the Mishnah. Nos. 3+4-8, 9+10-11 then move on to the elaboration and extension of the Mishnah's rule. VIII.1, IX.1, X.1, XI.1+2 ask about the sources of the rule of the Mishnah, whether scriptural, whether logical. The former is preferred.

1:2

A. A Hebrew slave is acquired through money and a writ.

B.   And he acquires himself through the passage of years, by the Jubilee Year, and by deduction from the purchase price [redeeming himself at this outstanding value (Lev. 25:50-51)].

C.   The Hebrew slave girl has an advantage over him.

D.   For she acquires herself [in addition] through the appearance of tokens [of puberty].

E.   The slave whose ear is pierced is acquired through an act of piercing the ear (Ex. 21:5).

F.   And he acquires himself by the Jubilee and by the death of the master.

A typical starting point in Mishnah exegesis is simply, "How [on the basis of Scripture] do we know this? Said Scripture...."

I.1   A.   A Hebrew slave is acquired through money and a writ:

B.   *How do we know this?*

C.   Said Scripture, "He shall give back the price of his redemption out of the money that he was bought for" (Lev. 25:51).

D.   So we have found the source of the rule governing a Hebrew slave sold to a gentile, since the only way of acquiring him is by money. How do we know that the same rule applies to one sold to an Israelite?

E.   Said Scripture, "Then he shall let her be redeemed" (Ex. 21:8) – this teaches that she deducts part of her redemption money and goes free.

F.   So we have found the rule governing the Hebrew slave girl; since she is betrothed with a money payment, she is acquired with a money payment. How do we know of it a Hebrew slave boy?

G.   Said Scripture, "If your brother, a Hebrew man or a Hebrew woman, is sold to you and serves you six years" (Deut. 15:12) – Scripture treats as comparable the Hebrew slave boy and the Hebrew slave girl.

H.   So we have found the rule governing those sold by a court, since they are sold willy-nilly. If they have sold themselves, how do we know that that is the case?

I.   We derive the parallel between the one and the other because of the use of the word "hired hand" [Lev. 25:39: One who sells himself; one sold by a court, Deut. 15:12ff.; the same word appears in both cases, so the same method of purchase applies to both (Freedman)].

J.   *Well, that poses no problems to him who accepts the consequences drawn from the verbal analogy established by the use of the word "hired hand," but for him who denies that analogy and its consequences, what is to be said?*

K.   Said Scripture, "And if a stranger or sojourner with you gets rich" (Lev. 25:47) – thus adding to the discussion that is just prior, teaching rules governing what is prior on the basis of rules that govern in what is to follow. [The "and" links Lev. 25:47-55, one who sells himself to a non-Jew, to Lev. 25:39-46, one who sells himself to a Jew; just as the purchase in the one case is carried out by money, so is that of the other (Freedman)].

I.2 A. *And who is the Tannaite authority who declines to establish a verbal analogy based on the recurrent usage of the word "hired hand" in the several passages?*

B. *It is the Tannaite authority behind the following, which has been taught on Tannaite authority:*

C. He who sells himself may be sold for six years or more than six years; if it is by a court, he may be sold for six years only.

D. He who sells himself may not have his ear bored as a mark of perpetual slavery; if sold by the court, he may have his ear bored.

E. He who sells himself has no severance pay coming to him; if he is sold by a court, he has severance pay coming to him.

F. To him who sells himself, the master cannot assign a Canaanite slave girl; if sold by a court, the master can give him a Canaanite slave girl.

G. R. Eleazar says, "Neither one nor the other may be sold for more than six years; both may have the ear bored; to both severance pay is given; to both the master may assign a Canaanite slave girl."

H. *Isn't this what is at stake: The initial Tannaite authority does not establish a verbal analogy based on the appearance of "hired hand" in both passages, while R. Eleazar does establish a verbal analogy based on the occurrence of "hired hand" in both passages?*

I. *Said R. Tabyumi in the name of Abbayye, "All parties concur that we do establish a verbal analogy based on the appearance in both passages of 'hired hand.' And here, this is what is the operative consideration behind the position of the initial Tannaite authority, who has said, He who sells himself may be sold for six years or more than six years? Scripture has stated a limitation in the context of one sold by a court:* 'And he shall serve you six years' (Deut. 15:12), *meaning, he but not one who sells himself."*

J. *And the other party?*

K. *"And he shall serve you" – not your heir.*

L. *And the other party?*

M. *There is another "serve you" in context [at Deut. 15:18].*

N. *And the other party?*

O. *That is written to tell you that* the master must be prepared to give severance pay.

I.3 A. *And what is the scriptural foundation for the position of the initial Tannaite authority, who has said, He who sells himself may not have his ear bored as a mark of perpetual slavery; if sold by the court, he may have his ear bored?*

B. *Because the All-Merciful has already imposed a limitation in the context of one sold by a court, namely:* "And his master shall bore his ear through with an awl" (Ex. 21:6) – his ear, but not the ear of the one who has sold himself.

	C.	[15A] *And the other party?*
	D.	*That comes for the purpose of establishing a verbal analogy, for it has been taught on Tannaite authority:*
	E.	R. Eliezer says, "How on the basis of Scripture do we know that the boring of the ear of the Hebrew slave (Ex. 21:5) must be the right ear? Here we find a reference to 'ear,' and elsewhere, the same word is used [at Lev. 14:14]. Just as in the latter case, the right ear is meant, so here, too, the right ear is meant."
	F.	*And the other party?*
	G.	*If so, Scripture should have said merely,* "ear." *Why* "his ear"?
	H.	*And the other party?*
	I.	*That is required to make the point,* "his ear" *not* "her ear."
	J.	*And the other party?*
	K.	*That point derives from the statement,* "But if the slave shall plainly say..." (Ex. 21:5) – *the slave boy, not the slave girl.*
	L.	*And the other party?*
	M.	*That verse is required to make the point,* he must make the statement while he is still a slave.
	N.	*And the other party?*
	O.	*That fact derives from the use of the language* "the slave," rather than simply, "slave."
	P.	*And the other party?*
	Q.	*He draws no such conclusion from the use of the language* "the slave," rather than simply, "slave."
I.4	A.	*And what is the scriptural basis for the position of the initial Tannaite authority, who has said,* He who sells himself has no severance pay coming to him; if he is sold by a court, he has severance pay coming to him?
	B.	*The All-Merciful expressed an exclusionary clause in regard to one sold by a court, namely,* "You shall furnish him liberally": (Deut. 15:14) – *him, but not one who sells himself.*
	C.	*And the other party?*
	D.	*That verse is required to make the point,* "You shall furnish him liberally": (Deut. 15:14) – *him, but not his heir.*
	E.	*But why not provide for his heirs? For Scripture has classified him as a hired hand:* Just as the wages of a hired hand belong to his heirs, so here, too, his wages belong to his heirs!
	F.	*Rather: Him – and not his creditor. [And it is necessary to make that point, for] since we concur in general with R. Nathan, as it has been taught on Tannaite authority:* R. Nathan says, "How on the basis of Scripture do we know that if someone claims a maneh from someone else, and the other party claims the same amount of money from a third party, the money is collected from the third party and paid out directly to the original claimant? 'And give it to him against whom he has trespassed' (Num. 5:7)," *the word* "him" *in the present case serves to exclude that rule here.*
	G.	*And the other party?*
	H.	*Otherwise, too, we do in point of fact differ from R. Nathan.*

I.5   A.   *And what is the scriptural basis for the position of the initial Tannaite authority, who has said,* To him who sells himself, the master cannot assign a Canaanite slave girl; if sold by a court, the master can give him a Canaanite slave girl?

B.   *The All-Merciful expressed an exclusionary clause in regard to one sold by a court, namely,* "If his master give him a wife" (Ex. 21:4) – *him, but not one who sells himself.*

C.   *And the other party?*

D.   "Him" – *even against his will.*

E.   *And the other party?*

F.   *He derives that rule from the phrase,* "for to the double of the hire of a hired servant has he served you" (Deut. 15:18), *for it has been taught on Tannaite authority:* "For to the double of the hire of a hired servant has he served you" (Deut. 15:18) – a hired hand works only by day, but a Hebrew slave works by day and night.

G.   Well, now can you really imagine that a Hebrew slave works day and night? But has not Scripture stated, "Because he is well off with you" (Deut. 15:16), meaning, he has to be right there with you in eat and drink [eating what you eat and living like you], and said R. Isaac, "On this basis it is the rule that his master gives him a Canaanite slave girl."

H.   *And the other party?*

I.   *If I had to derive the rule from that passage, I might have supposed that that is the case only with his full knowledge and consent, but if it is against his will, I might have thought that that is not so. So we are informed that that is not the case.*

I.6   A.   *And who is the Tannaite authority who declines to establish a verbal analogy based on the recurrent usage of the word "hired hand" in the several passages?*

B.   *It is the Tannaite authority behind the following, which has been taught on Tannaite authority:*

C.   "And go back to his own family, and return to the possession of his fathers":

D.   Said R. Eliezer b. R. Jacob, "Concerning what classification of slave does Scripture speak?

E.   "If it concerns a slave who has had his ear pierced to the doorjamb with an awl, lo, that classification has already been covered.

F.   "If it concerns the one who has sold himself, lo, that one has already been covered.

G.   "Lo, Scripture speaks only of one who has sold himself for one or two years prior to the Jubilee.

H.   "The Jubilee in his case frees him" [Sifra CCLVI:I.12 Parashat Behar Pereq 7].

I.   *Now if it should enter your mind that R. Eliezer b. Jacob accepts the verbal analogy based on the recurrent usage of the word "hired hand" in the several passages, what need do I have for this verse and its exegesis? Let him derive the point from the verbal analogy.*

J.   Said R. Nahman bar Isaac, "In point of fact he does accept the verbal analogy involving the hired hand. But nonetheless, the proof we required is given here. For it might have entered your mind to suppose that it is one who sells himself alone who is subject to the law, for he has done no prohibited deed, but if the court has sold the man, in which case it is because he has done a prohibited deed, I might have supposed that we impose an extrajudicial penalty on him and deny him the present advantage. So we are informed that that is not so."

I.7   A.   The master has said: "If it concerns a slave who has had his ear pierced to the doorjamb with an awl, lo, that classification has already been covered": *Where?*

B.   *It is as has been taught on Tannaite authority:*

C.   "When each of you shall return to his property and each of you shall return to his family":

D.   Said R. Eliezer b. Jacob, "Concerning what classification of slave does Scripture speak here?

E.   "If it concerns a [Hebrew slave] sold for six years, that of course has already been dealt with. And if it concerns a person sold for a year or two, that of course has already been dealt with.

F.   "The passage therefore addresses only the case of the slave who before the Jubilee has had his ear pierced to the doorjamb so as to serve in perpetuity.

G.   "The Jubilee serves to release him" [Sifra CCXLVIII:I.1 Parashat Behar Pereq 2].

H.   *How so?*

I.   Said Raba bar Shila, "Said Scripture, 'And you shall return, every man' (Lev. 25:10) – now what is the rule that applies to a man but not to a woman? You have to say, it is the boring of the ear."

J.   *Now it was necessary for Scripture to deal with the case of the court's selling him, and it was necessary for Scripture to deal with the one whose ear has been bored. For had we been informed of the case of the one whom the court has sold, that might have been because his term had not yet expired, but as for him whose ear was bored, since his term had expired, I might have said that we impose an extrajudicial penalty on him. And if we had been informed of the case of the one whose ear was pierced, that might have been because he had already worked for six years, but as to the one who was sold by the court, who has not yet served for six years, I might have maintained that he is not set free. So it was necessary for Scripture to make both points explicit.*

K.   *And it was further necessary for Scripture to state both "and you shall return" and also "and he shall serve forever." For if the All-Merciful had said only "and he shall serve forever," I might have supposed that that is meant literally. So the All-Merciful found it necessary to state also "and you shall return." And if the All-Merciful had said only "and you shall return," I might have supposed that that is the case when he has not served for six years, but in a case in which he has served for six years, then his latter phase of service should not be subject to a more stringent rule than his former:* Just as the first phase of service, when he was sold, was for six years, so his last phase of service should be for only six years; so "forever" *informs us,* forever to the end of the Jubilee.

I.8   A.   *And who is the Tannaite authority who declines to establish a verbal analogy based on the recurrent usage of the word "hired hand" in the several passages?*

       B.   *It is Rabbi, for it has been taught on Tannaite authority:*

       C.   [15B] "And if he be not redeemed by these" (Lev. 25:54) –

       D.   Rabbi says, "Through these he is redeemed, but not by the passage of six years. For is not the contrary not plausible, namely, if he who cannot be redeemed by these [a Hebrew slave sold to a Jew, who cannot be redeemed by relatives], can be redeemed through the passage of six years, then this one, who can be redeemed by these, surely should be redeemed through working for six years! So it was necessary to say, 'And if he be not redeemed by these' – through these he is redeemed, but not by the passage of six years."

       E.   *Now if it should enter your mind that Rabbi agrees to establish a verbal analogy based on the recurrent usage of the word "hired hand" in the several passages, then why does he say,* if he who cannot be redeemed by these? *Why not deduce the comparable law from the verbal analogy established by the repeated use of "hired hand"?*

       F.   *Said R. Nahman bar Isaac, "In point of fact, he does agree to establish a verbal analogy based on the recurrent usage of the word 'hired hand' in the several passages. But the case at hand is exceptional, since Scripture has said, 'one of his brothers shall redeem him' (Lev. 25:48) – but not another"* [a slave sold to a Jew (Freedman)].

I.9   A.   *And who is the Tannaite authority who differs from Rabbi?*

       B.   *It is R. Yosé the Galilean and R. Aqiba, for it has been taught on Tannaite authority:*

       C.   "And if he be not redeemed by these" (Lev. 25:54) –

       D.   R. Yosé the Galilean says, "'By these' persons for emancipation, but by anybody else for further subjugation [until the Jubilee]. [If anyone other than the listed relatives redeems him, it is for continued slavery.]"

       E.   R. Aqiba says, "'By these persons' for further subjugation [until the Jubilee], but by anybody else for emancipation" [Sifra CCLXIX:I.1 Parashat Behar Pereq 9].

       F.   *What is the scriptural basis for the position of R. Yosé the Galilean?*

       G.   Said Scripture, "And if he be not redeemed by these" – but by a stranger – "then he shall go out in the year of Jubilee."

       H.   And R. Aqiba?

       I.   "And if he be not redeemed by these" – by any but these – "then he shall go out in the year of Jubilee."

       J.   And R. Yosé the Galilean?

K.   *Is the language, "by any but these"?*

L.   *Rather, they differ on the following verse:* "Or his uncle, or his uncle's son, may redeem him" (Lev. 25:59) – this speaks of redemption by a relative. "Or if he gets rich" (Lev. 25:39) – this speaks of redeeming oneself. "And he shall be redeemed" (Lev. 25:49) – this speaks of redemption by strangers.

M.   *R. Yosé the Galilean takes the view that the verse is read in the context of what precedes, which join redemption by relatives with redemption of oneself:* Just as when one redeems oneself, it is for freedom, so if relatives do so, it has the same result.

N.   *And R. Aqiba maintains that a verse of Scripture is read in the context of what follows, which joins the act of redemption by others to the redemption of oneself:* Just as redemption of himself leads to liberation, so redemption by outsiders yields freedom.

O.   *Well, then, why say "by these"?*

P.   *If the phrase, "by these," were not set forth, I might have supposed,* a verse of Scripture is read in the context of either what precedes or what follows, with the result that redemption of any kind yields freedom.

Q.   *If so, our problem comes home again. Rather, it must be that at issue between them is a matter of logic. R. Yosé the Galilean takes the view that it is logic that redemption carried out by others should yield slavery, for if you say it would yield liberation, people would refrain and not redeem him. But R. Aqiba finds more reasonable the view that redemption by relatives yields slavery. For if you say it yields freedom, then every day the man is going to go out and sell himself.*

I.10   A.   Said R. Hiyya bar Abba said R. Yohanan, "Well, then, that represents the view of R. Yosé the Galilean and R. Aqiba. But sages say, 'Redemption by any party at all yields liberation.'"

B.   *Who are "sages"?*

C.   *It is Rabbi, who utilizes "by these" for a different interpretation,* while the verse indeed is read in the context of either what precedes or what follows, with the result that redemption of any kind yields freedom.]

D.   *Then how does Rabbi read the verse,* "Then he shall go out in the year of Jubilee"?

E.   *He requires it in line with that which has been taught on Tannaite authority:*

F.   "Then he shall go forth in the Jubilee Year": [16A] Scripture speaks of a gentile who is subject to your authority.

G.   Well, maybe it speaks of a gentile who is not subject to your authority?

H.   How can you say so, for, if so, what can be done to him [Freedman: how can he be forced to provide facilities for redemption]?

I.   You must say, therefore, Scripture speaks of a gentile who is subject to your authority.

II.1　A.　[A Hebrew slave is acquired through money] or a writ:

　　　B.　*How on the basis of Scripture do we know that fact?*

　　　C.　Said Ulla, "Said Scripture, 'If he take him another wife' (Ex. 21:10) [in addition to the Hebrew slave girl] – Scripture thus treats the Hebrew slave girl as another wife: Just as another wife would be acquired by a writ, so a Hebrew slave girl is acquired through a writ."

　　　D.　*Well, that proof would clearly pose no problem to him who says,* "The writ of a Hebrew slave girl – the master writes it," *but from the perspective of him who says,* "The father writes it," *what is to be said? For it has been stated:*

　　　E.　The writ of a Hebrew slave girl – who writes it?

　　　F.　R. Huna said, "The master writes it."

　　　G.　R. Hisda said, "The father writes it."

　　　H.　*So the proposed derivation from Scripture poses no problems, but from the perspective of R. Hisda, what is to be said?*

　　　I.　Said R. Aha bar Jacob, "Said Scripture, 'She shall not go forth as slave boys do' (Ex. 21:7) [if the master blinds them or knocks out their teeth] – but she may be purchased in the manner in which slave boys are purchased. *And what might that way be? A writ.*"

　　　J.　*Well, why not say:* But she may be purchased in the manner in which slave boys are purchased. *And what might that way be? Usucaption?*

　　　K.　Said Scripture, "And you shall make [gentile slaves] an inheritance for your children after you" (Lev. 25:46) – they are acquired by usucaption, and slaves of no other classification are acquired by usucaption.

　　　L.　*Well, why not say:* They are acquired by a writ, and slaves of no other classification are acquired by a writ?

　　　M.　But isn't it written, "She shall not go forth as slave boys do" (Ex. 21:7)?

　　　N.　Well, then, how come you prefer the one reading rather than the other?

　　　O.　*It stands to reason that a writ is encompassed as a medium of acquiring title,* since a writ serves to divorce an Israelite woman [Freedman: just as it is effective in one instance, so in another].

　　　P.　*To the contrary, usucaption should have been encompassed as a medium of acquiring title,* since it serves to effect acquisition of the property of an heirless proselyte.

　　　Q.　*But we don't find such a medium of acquisition relevant when it comes to matters of marital relationship. Or, if you prefer, I shall say that the language,* "if he takes another" *serves to make that very point.* [Freedman: "She shall not go out" teaches that she may be acquired by deed, as is implied by the analogy of "another".]

　　　R.　*Now how does R. Huna deal with the clause,* "She shall not go forth as slave boys do" (Ex. 21:7) [if the master blinds them or knocks out their teeth]?

S.   *He requires that verse to indicate that she does not go forth at the loss of the major limbs, as does a slave boy.*

T.   And R. Hisda?

U.   *If so, Scripture should have said, "She shall not go forth like slave boys." Why say, "She shall not go forth as slave boys do"* (Ex. 21:7) [if the master blinds them or knocks out their teeth]? *That yields two points.*

III.1   A.   And he acquires himself through the passage of years:

        B.   *For it is written,* "Six years he shall serve, and in the seventh he shall go free for nothing" (Ex. 21:2).

IV.1   A.   By the Jubilee Year:

        B.   *For it is written,* "He shall serve with you into the year of Jubilee" (Lev. 25:40).

V.1   A.   And by deduction from the purchase price [redeeming himself at this outstanding value]:

        B.   Said Hezekiah, "For said Scripture, 'Then shall he let her be redeemed' (Ex. 21:8) – this teaches that she makes a deduction from her redemption money and goes out free."

V.2   A.   *A Tannaite statement:* And he acquires title to himself through money or a cash equivalent or through a writ.

        B.   *Now with respect to money, there is no difficulty, for it is written in so many words,* "He shall give back the price of his redemption out of the money he was bought for" (Lev. 25:51). *And as to a cash equivalent, too:* "He shall give back the price of his redemption," the All-Merciful has said, extended the law covering cash to a cash equivalent. *But as to this writ, how is it to be imagined? Should we say that the slave writes a bond for the redemption money? Then it is tantamount to money. But if it is a writ of manumission, then why a deed? Let the master say to the slave in the presence of two witnesses of a court: "Go"?*

        C.   Said Raba, "That is to say, a Hebrew slave is owned by his master as to his very body, so a master who remitted the deduction – the deduction is not remitted."

VI.1   A.   The Hebrew slave girl has an advantage over him. For she acquires herself [in addition] through the appearance of tokens [of puberty].

        B.   Said R. Simeon b. Laqish, "A Hebrew slave girl has acquired from the domain of her master possession of herself [as a free woman] upon the death of her father. That is the result of an argument a fortiori: If the appearance of puberty signs, which do not free her from her father's authority, free her from the authority of her master, then death, which does free her from her father's authority [the father's heirs have no claim on her], surely should free her from her master's authority [whose heirs should not inherit her]!"

        C.   *Objected R. Oshayya,* "The Hebrew slave girl has an advantage over him. For she acquires herself [in addition] through the appearance of tokens [of puberty]. *But if what he has said were so, then the list should include reference to her father's death as well!*"

        D.   *The Tannaite authority has listed some items and left out others.*

        E.   *Well, then, what else has he left out, if he has left out this item?*

F. *He leaves out reference to her master's death.*

G. *Well, if that is all he has left out, then he has left out nothing; since that would pertain also to a male slave as well, it is omitted anyhow.*

H. *But why not include it?*

I. *The Tannaite framer of the passage has encompassed what is subject to a fixed limit [the six years, the proportionate repayment of the purchase price, the Jubilee], but what is not subject to a fixed limit he does not include in his Tannaite rule.*

J. *But lo, there is the matter of puberty signs, which are not subject to a fixed limit, but the Tannaite framer of the passage has covered them, too.*

K. Said R. Safra, "They have no fixed limit above, but they are subject to a fixed limit [16B] below. *For it has been taught on Tannaite authority:* A boy aged nine who produced two puberty hairs – these are classified as a mere mole; from the age of nine years to twelve years and one day, they are classified as a mere mole. R. Yosé b. R. Judah says, 'They are classified as a mark of puberty.' From thirteen years and one day onward, all parties concur that they are classified as a mark of puberty."

L. *Objected R. Sheshet,* "R. Simeon says, 'Four are given severance pay, three in the case of males, three in the case of females. And you cannot say there are four in the case of the male, because puberty signs are not effective in the case of a male, and you cannot say there is boring of the ear in the case of the female.' *Now if what R. Simeon b. Laqish has said were valid* ['A Hebrew slave girl has acquired from the domain of her master possession of herself as a free woman upon the death of her father'], *then the death of the father also should be included here. And should you say, the Tannaite authority has listed some items and left out others, lo, he has said matters explicitly in terms of four items! And if you should say, the Tannaite framer of the passage has encompassed what is subject to a fixed limit [the six years, the proportionate repayment of the purchase price, the Jubilee], but he has left off what is not subject to a fixed limit, lo, there is the matter of puberty signs, which are not subject to a fixed limit, and he has encompassed them in the Tannaite statement. And should you say, here as a matter of fact he, too, accords with R. Safra, well, then, there is the matter of the death of the master, which is not subject to a fixed definition as to time, and yet the Tannaite framer has included it. So what are the four items to which reference is made?"*

M. [1] Years, [2] Jubilee, [3] Jubilee for the one whose ear was bored, and [4] the Hebrew slave girl freed by puberty signs. *And that stands to reason, since the concluding clause goes on to say,* and you cannot say there are four in the case of the male, because puberty signs are not effective in the case of a male, and you cannot say there is boring of the ear in the case of the female. *But if it were the case [that the master's death is covered], then you would have four items for the woman. So that's decisive proof.*

N. *Objected R. Amram,* "And these are the ones that get severance pay: Slaves freed by the passage of six years of service, the Jubilee, the master's death, and the Hebrew slave girl freed by the advent of puberty signs. *And if the stated proposition were valid, the father's death also should be on the list. And should you say, the Tannaite authority has*

listed some items and left out others, lo, he has said, and these are the
ones [which is exclusionary, these – no others]. *And if you should
say, the Tannaite framer of the passage has encompassed what is subject to
a fixed limit [the six years, the proportionate repayment of the purchase
price, the Jubilee], but he has left off what is not subject to a fixed limit, lo,
there is the matter of puberty signs, which are not subject to a fixed limit,
and he has encompassed them in the Tannaite statement. And should you
say, here as a matter of fact he, too, accords with R. Safra, well, then, there
is the matter of the death of the master. So isn't this a refutation of R.
Simeon b. Laqish's position?"*

O.   *Sure is.*

P.   *But lo, R. Simeon b. Laqish has set forth an argument a fortiori!*

Q.   *It's a flawed argument a fortiori, along these lines:* The distinguishing
trait of puberty signs is that they mark a change in the body of the
girl, but will you say the same of the death of the father, by which
the body of the girl is left unaffected?

VI.2   A.   *One Tannaite version states,* The severance pay [the gifts given at the
end of six years] of a Hebrew slave boy belongs to himself and that
of a Hebrew slave girl belongs to herself. *Another Tannaite version
states,* The severance pay [the gifts given at the end of six years] of a
Hebrew slave girl and things that she finds belong to her father, and
her master has a claim only to a fee for loss of time [taken up by
finding the lost object]. *Is it not the case that the one speaks of a girl
who goes forth by reason of the advent of puberty signs [in which case the
severance pay goes to the father], the other liberated at the death of the
father?*

B.   *Not at all, both speak of freedom by reason of puberty signs, but there is
still no conflict, in the one case, the father is alive, in the other, not.*

C.   *There is no problem with the statement,* The severance pay
[the gifts given at the end of six years] of a Hebrew slave girl
belongs to herself, *for it serves to exclude any assignment to
her brothers, as has been taught on Tannaite authority:* "And
you make them an inheritance for your children after you"
(Lev. 25:46, speaking of Canaanite slaves] – them you leave to
your sons, and your daughters you do not leave to your sons.
This states that a man does not leave title to his daughter as
an inheritance to his son. *But as to the statement,* The
severance pay [the gifts given at the end of six years] of a
Hebrew slave boy belongs to himself, *surely that is obvious!
Who else should get it?*

D.   *Said R. Joseph, "I see here a molehill made into a mountain.
[This is all redundant.]"*

E.   Abbayye said, "This is what R. Sheshet said: 'Who is the
authority behind this unattributed statement? It is Totai. For
it has been taught on Tannaite authority: Totai says, "'You
shall furnish him' (Deut. 15:14) – him, not his creditor"' [and
that is the point of the statement at hand]."

VI.3   A.   *Reverting to the body of the foregoing:* And these are the ones that get
severance pay: Slaves freed by the passage of six years of service,
the Jubilee, the master's death, and the Hebrew slave girl freed by

the advent of puberty signs. But one who runs away or who is
freed by deduction from the purchase price don't get severance pay.

B.   R. Meir says, "A runaway doesn't get severance pay, but he who is
freed by deduction from the purchase price does get severance
pay."

C.   R. Simeon says, "Four are given severance pay, three in the case of
males, three in the case of females. And you cannot say there are
four in the case of the male, because puberty signs are not effective
in the case of a male, and you cannot say there is boring of the ear in
the case of the female."

D.   *What is the source of these rulings?*

E.   *It is in line with that which our rabbis have taught on Tannaite authority:*

F.   Is it possible to suppose that a gift is provided only to those
who go forth after six years of work? How on the basis of
Scripture do we know that one who goes forth on the
occasion of the Jubilee, or on the death of the owner, or a
female slave who goes forth on the appearance of puberty
signs [also gets a liberal gift]?

G.   Scripture says, "When you set him free," "When you do set
him free."

H.   Is it possible to suppose that a runaway and one who goes
out through a deduction get it? Scripture states, "When you
do set him free," meaning, to him whom you set free you give
a gift, and you do not give a gift to him who is set free on his
own account [Sifré Deut. CXIX:I.1].

I.   R. Meir says, "A runaway doesn't get severance pay, since his
liberation is not on your account, but he who is freed by
deduction from the purchase price does get severance pay, for
his liberation is on your account."

VI.4 A.   *A runaway?! But he has to serve out his term of service. For it
has been taught on Tannaite authority:* How on the basis of
Scripture do we know that a runaway has to complete his
term of service? Scripture states, "Six years he shall serve"
(Ex. 21:2).

B.   [17A] Might one suppose that that is so even if he got sick?

C.   Scripture says, "And in the Seventh Year he shall go out
free."

D.   *Said R. Sheshet, "Here with what situation do we deal? With a slave that
ran away and the Jubilee Year came into force for him. What might you
have thought? Since the Jubilee Year is what has sent him forth, we
classify the case as one in which you are the one who has sent him forth,
and we do not impose a judicial penalty on him but rather we give him
severance pay? So we are informed that that is not the case."*

VI.5 A.   A master has said: "Might one suppose that that is so even if he got
sick? Scripture says, 'And in the Seventh Year he shall go out free –
even if he were sick all six years'":

B.   *But has it not been taught on Tannaite authority:* If he was sick for three
years and worked for three years, he doesn't have to make up the
lost time. If he was sick all six years, he is obligated to make up the
time?

C.   Said R. Sheshet, "It is a case in which he could still do needlework."

D.   *Lo, there is an internal contradiction. You have said,* If he was sick for three years and worked for three years, he doesn't have to make up the lost time. Lo, if it were four, he would have to make up the time. *Then note the concluding clause:* If he was sick all six years, he is obligated to make up the time. Lo, if it were four, he would not have to make up the time!

E.   *This is the sense of the matter:* If he was sick for four years, he is treated as though he were sick all six, and he does have to make up the time.

VI.6   A.   *Our rabbis have taught on Tannaite authority:*

B.   How much do they give in severance pay?

C.   "Five selas worth of each kind mentioned in Scripture [Deut. 15:14: 'Out of your flock and out of your threshing floor and out of your wine press'], that is, fifteen in all," the words of R. Meir.

D.   R. Judah says, "Thirty, as in the thirty paid for a gentile slave" (Ex. 21:32).

E.   R. Simeon says, "Fifty, as in the fifty for valuations" (Lev. 27:3).

VI.7   A.   The master has said, "'Five selas worth of each kind mentioned in Scripture [Deut. 15:14: "Out of your flock and out of your threshing floor and out of your wine press"], that is, fifteen in all,' the words of R. Meir."

B.   [With reference to "that is, fifteen in all," we ask:] *Well, then, is it R. Meir's intention to inform us how to count?*

C.   *What he proposes to tell us is that he may not diminish the total, but if he gives less of one classification and more of another, we have no objection.*

D.   *What is the scriptural basis for R. Meir's conclusion?*

E.   *He forms a verbal analogy on the basis of the occurrence of the word "empty-handed" here and with reference to the firstborn* [Deut. 15:13: "You shall not let him go empty-handed"; Ex. 34:20: "All the firstborn of your sons you shall redeem, none shall appear before me empty-handed"]. *Just as in that case, five selas is the fixed sum, so here, too, five selas is the fixed sum.*

F.   *Might one say then, there must be five selas worth of each item?*

G.   *If the word "empty-handed" had been written at the end of the verse, it might be as you say; but since the word "empty-handed" is written at the outset, the word "empty-handed" pertains to "flock," "threshing floor," and "wine press," item by item.*

H.   *Why not derive the meaning of the word "empty-handed" from the verbal analogy deriving from the burnt-offering brought at one's appearance on the pilgrim festival [and much less than five selas is required there]?*

I.   Said Scripture, "As the Lord your God has blessed you you shall give to him" (Deut. 15:14).

VI.8   A.   R. Judah says, "Thirty, as in the thirty paid for a gentile slave" (Ex. 21:32):

	B.	*What is the scriptural basis for the position of R. Judah?*
	C.	*He establishes a verbal authority on the basis of the occurrence of the word "giving" here and in the case of the slave. Just as in that case, thirty selas is involved, so here, too, thirty selas is involved.*
	D.	*Why not establish the verbal analogy with the common use of the word "giving" with reference to severance pay and valuations, with the result: Just as in that case, fifty selas is involved, so here, too, fifty selas is involved.*
	E.	*First of all, if you hold onto a great deal, you hold nothing, but if you hold onto a little, you will hold onto it, and, furthermore, you should establish the verbal analogy on the basis of passages that speak in particular of slaves.*
VI.9	A.	R. Simeon says, "Fifty, as in the fifty for valuations" (Lev. 27:3).
	B.	*What is the scriptural basis for the position of R. Simeon?*
	C.	*He establishes a verbal authority on the basis of the occurrence of the word "giving" here and in the case of valuations. Just as in that case, fifty selas is involved, so here, too, fifty selas is involved.*
	D.	*Might one say it may be the least sum that will serve for a valuation [which is five sheqels, Lev. 27:6]?*
	E.	"...As the Lord your God has blessed you" (Deut. 15:14).
	F.	*And why not establish a verbal authority on the basis of the occurrence of the word "giving" here and in the case of the slave. Just as in that case, thirty selas is involved, so here, too, thirty selas is involved, for, after all, first, if you hold onto a great deal, you hold nothing, but if you hold onto a little, you will hold onto it, and, furthermore, you should establish the verbal analogy on the basis of passages that speak in particular of slaves?*
	G.	*R. Simeon draws his verbal analogy on the basis of the recurrent word "poverty" [Lev. 25:39 for the slave, Lev. 27:8 for the valuation].*
VI.10	A.	*Well, now, from R. Meir's perspective, we can understand why Scripture states, "out of your flock and out of your threshing floor and out of your wine press" (Deut. 15:14). But from R. Judah's and R. Simeon's viewpoint, why are these items – flock and threshing floor and wine press – required?*
	B.	*These are required in line with that which has been taught on Tannaite authority:*
	C.	"...Of the flock, threshing floor, and vat":
	D.	Might one suppose that one furnishes a gift solely from the flock, threshing floor, and vat in particular? How on the basis of Scripture do I know to encompass every sort of thing?
	E.	Scripture says, "Furnish him...with whatever the Lord your God has blessed you, you shall give to him," which serves to encompass every sort of thing.
	F.	If so, why is it said, "...of the flock, threshing floor, and vat"?

G.   "Just as the flock, threshing floor, and vat are characterized by being worthy of blessing, so is excluded a payment of cash, which is not the occasion for a blessing": The words of R. Simeon.

H.   R. Eliezer b. Jacob says, "What is excluded are mules, which do not produce offspring" [Sifré Deut. CXIX:II.3].

VI.11 A.   And R. Simeon?

B.   *Mules themselves can increase in value.*

C.   And R. Eliezer b. Jacob?

D.   *One can do business with ready cash.*

VI.12 A.   *And it was necessary for all of these items to be made articulate. For if the All-Merciful had made reference to the flock, I might have thought that the law applies to animate creatures but not to what grows from the soil. So the All-Merciful has written, "threshing floor." And if the Scripture had made reference only to threshing floor, I might have thought that the gift may be what grows from the soil but not animate creatures. So Scripture wrote, "flock."*

B.   *What need do I have for a reference to the vat?*

C.   [17B] *In the view of one master, it serves to exclude ready cash, of the other, mules.*

VI.13 A.   *Our rabbis have taught on Tannaite authority:*

B.   "Furnishing him, you shall furnish him liberally" (Deut.15:14):

C.   I know only that if the household of the master has been blessed on account of the slave, that one must give a present. How do I know that even if the household of the master was not blessed on account of the slave, a gift must be given?

D.   Scripture says, "Furnishing him, you shall furnish him liberally" (Deut.15:14) – under all circumstances.

E.   R. Eleazar b. Azariah says, "If the household has been blessed for the sake of the slave, a present must be given, but if not, then the present need not be made" [Sifré Deut. CXIX:III.1].

F.   *Then what is the sense of* "Furnishing him"?

G.   In this case Scripture used language in an ordinary way.

VI.14 A.   *Our rabbis have taught on Tannaite authority:*

B.   The Hebrew slave boy serves the son but doesn't serve the daughter. The Hebrew slave girl serves neither the son nor the daughter. The slave whose ear has been bored and the slave that is sold to a gentile serves neither the son nor the daughter.

VI.15 A.   The master has said, "The Hebrew slave boy serves the son but doesn't serve the daughter":

B.   *What is the source for that ruling?*

C.   *It is in line with that which has been taught on Tannaite authority:*

D.   "[If a fellow Hebrew, man or woman, is sold to you,] he shall serve you six years":

E.   ["You,"] and also your son. [The Hebrew slave remains the possession of the son, if the father dies within the six-year spell.]

F. Might one think that the same rule applies to the heir [other than the son]?

G. Scripture says, "Six years he shall serve you."

H. What is it that moved you to include the son but to exclude any other heir?

I. I include the son because the son takes the father's place in [Hammer:] designating [the Hebrew bondwoman as his wife], and in recovering for his family an ancestral field that has been alienated.

J. But I exclude any other heir, because any other heir does not take the father's place in [Hammer:] designating [the Hebrew bondwoman as his wife], and in recovering for his family an ancestral field that has been alienated [CXVIII:IV.1] [given in Sifré Deut.'s wording].

K. But to the contrary: I should encompass the brother, who takes the place of the deceased childless brother for a levirate marriage! Is there a levirate marriage except where there is no offspring? If there is an offspring, there is no levirate marriage.

L. *Then the operative consideration is that there is this refutation, but otherwise, would the brother be preferable?*

M. *Why not infer the opposite: Here where there is a son, there are two points in his favor, there, only one?*

N. *The consideration of the son in regard to the field of inheritance is also inferred from this same refutation, namely: Is there a levirate marriage except where there is no son?*

VI.16 A. The Hebrew slave girl serves neither the son nor the daughter.

B. *What is the source for that ruling?*

C. Said R. Peda, "Said Scripture, 'And if he say to you, I will not go out from you...then you shall take an awl and thrust it through his ear...and also to your slave girl you shall do likewise' (Deut. 15:16-17). In this way Scripture has treated her as comparable to him whose ear is bored: Just as the latter serves neither the son nor the daughter, so the former serves neither the son nor the daughter."

D. *Well, is that the purpose that is served by this verse? It surely is required in line with that which have been taught on Tannaite authority:*

E. "Do the same with your female slave":

F. That refers to providing a generous gift when she leaves.

G. What about piercing her ear to the door?

H. Scripture says, "But should he say to you...," the slave, not the slave girl [Sifré Deut. CXXI.V.3].

I. How then do I deal with the clause, "and also to your female slave do the same"?

J. It is in regard to the severance pay.

K. *If so, Scripture should have said, "and also to your slave girl likewise," why add, "you shall do"? It makes both points.*

VI.17 A. The slave whose ear has been bored and the slave that is sold to a gentile serves neither the son nor the daughter.

B.   The slave whose ear has been bored: "And his master shall bore his ear through with an awl, and he shall serve him forever" (Ex. 21:6) – him but not his son or daughter.

C.   And the slave that is sold to a gentile serves neither the son nor the daughter: *What is the source for that ruling?*

D.   Said Hezekiah, "Said Scripture, 'And he shall reckon with his purchaser' (Lev. 25:50) – but not with his purchaser's heirs."

VI.18 A.   Said Raba, "By the law of the Torah, a gentile may inherit his father's estate, as it is said, 'And he shall reckon with his purchaser,' but not with his purchaser's heirs, *which proves that he has heirs.* A proselyte's inheriting from a gentile is not based on the law of the Torah but only on the rulings of scribes. *For we have learned in the Mishnah:* A proselyte and a gentile who inherited [the property of] their father, [who was] a gentile – he [the proselyte brother] may say to him [the gentile brother], "You take the idols and I [will take] the coins; you [take] the libation wine and I [will take] the produce." And if [he said this] after it [the property] came into his possession, this [arrangement] is forbidden [M. Dem. 6:9A-E]. *Now if it should enter your mind that it is by the law of the Torah that the proselyte inherits his gentile father's estate, then even if the goods have not yet come into his possession, when he takes the money or produce, he is taking something in exchange for an idol* [which would be forbidden, since the inheritance is automatically of a half-share of everything, whether he has taken possession or not (Freedman)]. *So it follows that it is by rabbinical law, a preventive measure enacted by rabbis to take account of the threat that he may return to his wickedness."*

B.   *So, too, it has been taught on Tannaite authority:* Under what circumstances? In a case of inheritance. But in a case of mere partnership, such an arrangement is forbidden [and the proselyte may not derive benefit from an idol or libation wine].

C.   [Raba continues,] "A gentile inherits the estate of a proselyte, or a proselyte inherits the estate of a proselyte, neither by the law of the Torah nor by the law of the scribes. *For it has been taught on Tannaite authority:* A man who borrows money from a proselyte whose children converted with him must not return the money to the children [who are not his heirs], and if he does, sages are not pleased with him."

D.   *But it also has been taught on Tannaite authority,* and if he does, sages are pleased with him!

E.   *No problem,* the former refers to a case in which his conception and birth were not in a circumstance of sanctification, [18A] the latter, a case in which his conception was not in conditions of sanctification, but his birth was in conditions of sanctification.

F.   R. Hiyya bar Abin said R. Yohanan said, "A gentile inherits his father's estate by the law of the Torah, as it is written, 'Because I have given Mount Seir to Esau for an inheritance' (Deut. 2:5)."

G.   *But perhaps the case of an Israelite apostate is exceptional?*

H.   *Rather, proof derives from the following:* "Because I have given to the children of Lot Ar as an inheritance" (Deut. 2:9).

       I.   *And how come R. Hiyya bar Abin does not rule as does Raba?*

       J.   *Is it written,* "and he shall reckon with his purchaser but not his purchaser's heirs"?

       K.   *And how come Raba does not rule as does R. Hiyya bar Abin?*

       L.   *Because the honor owing to Abraham makes the situation exceptional.*

VI.19   A.   *Our rabbis have taught on Tannaite authority:*

       B.   "...A fellow Hebrew, man or woman":

       C.   Rules pertain to the Hebrew male that do not pertain to the Hebrew female,

       D.   and rules pertain to the Hebrew female that do not pertain to the Hebrew male:

       E.   Rules pertain to the Hebrew male: For a Hebrew male goes forth through the passage of years and at the Jubilee and through the deduction of the years yet to be served by the payment of money and through the death of the master, none of which applies to the Hebrew female slave.

       F.   A Hebrew female slave goes forth when she produces puberty signs, she may not be sold to third parties, she may be redeemed even against her wishes, none of which applies to the Hebrew male slave.

       G.   Lo, since it is the fact, therefore, that rules pertain to the Hebrew male that do not pertain to the Hebrew female, and rules pertain to the Hebrew female that do not pertain to the Hebrew male, it is necessary to make explicit both the Hebrew man and the Hebrew woman [Sifré Deut. CXVIII:III.2].

VI.20   A.   The master has said: "Rules pertain to the Hebrew male that do not pertain to the Hebrew female":

       B.   *By way of contradiction:* The Hebrew slave girl has an advantage over him. For she acquires herself [in addition] through the appearance of tokens [of puberty]!

       C.   Said R. Sheshet, "For instance, if he designated her as his wife" [in which case these signs would not apply].

       D.   *If he designated her as his wife? Obviously! She would require a writ of divorce in that case!*

       E.   *What might you imagine? In her instance the rules pertaining to a Hebrew slave girl are not suspended? So we are informed that that is not the case.*

       F.   *If so, then how come she goes forth through the advent of the tokens of puberty?*

       G.   *This is the sense of the matter:* If he did not designate her for marriage, then she would go forth by the advent of the tokens of puberty as well.

VI.21   A.   She may not be sold to third parties: *So does that imply that a slave boy may be sold to third parties? But has it not been taught on Tannaite authority:*

       B.   "If he have nothing, then he shall be sold for his theft" (Ex. 22:2) – but not for paying the double indemnity [that is owing by a thief, Ex. 22:3].

C. "If he have nothing, then he shall be sold for his theft" (Ex. 22:2) – but not for paying the indemnity brought on him by testimony of his that has been shown part of a conspiracy of perjury.

D. "If he have nothing, then he shall be sold for his theft" (Ex. 22:2) – once he has been sold one time, you are not again permitted to sell him. [There can be no sale to third parties.]

E. *Said Raba, "No problem, the one speaks of a single act of theft, the other of multiple acts of theft."*

F. *Said to him Abbayye, "'...for his theft...' bears the sense of any number of thefts."*

G. *Rather, said Abbayye, "No problem, the one speaks of a single individual, the other of two or more."*

VI.22 A. *Our rabbis have taught on Tannaite authority:*

B. If the theft was worth a thousand zuz and the thief is worth only five hundred, he is sold and resold. If his theft was worth five hundred zuz and he was worth a thousand, he is not sold at all.

C. R. Eliezer says, "If his theft was worth his sale price, he is sold, and if not, he is not sold."

VI.23 A. *Said Raba, "In this matter R. Eliezer got the better of rabbis, for what difference does it make whether what he stole is worth five hundred and he is worth a thousand, in which case he is not sold? It is because Scripture says, 'then he shall be sold,' meaning, all of him, not half. Well, here, too, Scripture says, 'he shall be sold for his theft,' but not for half of his theft."*

VI.24 A. **She may be redeemed even against her wishes, none of which applies to the Hebrew male slave:**

B. *Raba considered interpreting, "...against the wishes of the master."*

C. *Said to him Abbayye, "What would be the case? That a bond is written for the master covering her value? But then why does he have to accept the bond? The guy's holding a pearl in his hand, shall we give him a sherd?"*

D. *Rather, said Abbayye, "The meaning can only be, against the father's will, because of the embarrassment of the family."*

E. *If so, then the same should apply to the Hebrew slave – let the members of his family be forced to redeem him because of the embarrassment of his family.*

F. *But he may just go and sell himself again, and here, too, the father will just go and sell her again!*

G. *But hasn't it been taught as part of the Tannaite statement at hand:* **She may not be sold to third parties?** *[So that can't happen]. And who is the authority? It is R. Simeon, for it has been taught on Tannaite authority:* A man may sell his daughter into marriage, then do the same for bondage, then do the same for marriage after bondage, but he may not sell her into bondage after she has been married. R. Simeon says, "Just as he may not sell his daughter into bondage after marriage, so a man may not sell his daughter into bondage after he has sold her into bondage."

H. *This involves the dispute of the following Tannaite statements, as has been taught on Tannaite authority:*

I. "To sell her unto a strange people he shall have no power, since he has dealt deceitfully with her" (Ex. 21:8):

J. [18B] "Since he spread his cloth over her [reading the letters that yield 'dealt deceitfully' as though they bore the vowels to yield 'his cloth'], he may not again sell her," the words of R. Aqiba.

K. R. Eliezer says, "'...since he has dealt deceitfully with her' (Ex. 21:8) – he may not again sell her."

L. What is at issue here? R. Eliezer rejects the view that the reading supplied by the vowels dictates the sense of Scripture, R. Aqiba affirms the view that the reading supplied by the vowels dictates the sense of Scripture, R. Simeon both maintains and denies the view that the reading supplied by the vowels dictates the sense of Scripture.

Here, the principle we adopt will govern how we read the verse at hand and the facts that we shall derive from it. The same considerations govern in what follows.

VI.25 A. *Rabbah bar Abbuha raised this question:* "Does designating the slave girl for marriage effect the status of a fully consummated marriage or does it bring about the status of betrothal? *The upshot is the familiar issue of* whether or not he inherits her estate, contracts uncleanness to bury her if he is a priest and she dies, and abrogates her vows. *What is the law?*"

B. *Come and take note:* "Since he spread his cloth over her [reading the letters that yield 'dealt deceitfully' as though they bore the vowels to yield 'his cloth'], he may not again sell her" – *so what he can't do is sell her, but lo, he may designate her for marriage. Now, if you maintain that the designation effects a consummated marriage, then, once she has married, her father has no more power over here. So must it not follow that the designation effects only a betrothal?"*

C. *Said R. Nahman bar Isaac,* "Here the issue concerns a betrothal in general [not only the slave girl's being designated by her master for marriage to himself or his son], and this is the sense of the statement: Since the father has handed her over to one who accepts liability to provide for 'her food, clothing, and conjugal rights' (Ex. 21:10) [and so betrothed her], he may not sell her again."

D. *Come and take note:* The father may not sell her to relatives [who because of consanguinity cannot designate her as a wife]. In the name of R. Eliezer, they have said, "He may sell her to relatives." But both sides concur that, if she is a widow, he may nonetheless sell her to a high priest, and, if she is a divorcée or a woman who has executed the rite of removing the shoe, he may sell her to an ordinary priest." *Now as to the widow, what sort of a situation confronts us? Shall we say that she accepted a betrothal in her own behalf? Then can she be classified as a widow?* [Freedman: Not at all, her actions are null, as would be the case of any other minor.] *So it must mean that her father has betrothed her. But can he*

*have sold his daughter for bondage after she was married?
And lo, a man may not sell his daughter into bondage after
she has been married, and in that connection said R. Amram
said R. Isaac, "Here we deal with a case of designation, within
the theory of R. Yosé b. R. Judah, who has said, 'The original
money for her was not given for betrothal.'"* [The money
paid for the slave girl is not for betrothal; when the girl is
designated for marriage, it is via the work she owes him, not
the money he has given; therefore the father can resell her
after the master's death, and it is not regarded as bondage
after betrothal, since he didn't accept the original money as
betrothal money (Freedman).] *Now, if you take the position
that the designation has effected a consummated marriage,
then, once she is married, her father has no longer got any
authority over her?*

E.   *Yes, but, what's the sense of "it effects a betrothal" or of "and
both agree"? For lo, a man may not sell his daughter into
bondage after she has been married! Rather, what do you
have to say? An act of betrothal done by her is different from
one done by her father?* [Freedman: When her father receives
a token of betrothal on her behalf, he loses his authority to
sell her later on; but when she gets it, for example, through
her labor, meaning, renunciation of the work she owes, her
father still has the right to sell her.] *But then, even if you
maintain that designation effects a fully consummated
marriage, her own arrangement of the fully consummated
marriage still will differ in effect from her father's.*

F.   *But how are the matters parallel? True enough, the act of
betrothal that she undertakes will produce a different result
from the act of betrothal that her father undertakes, but will
there be any difference between an act of consummated
marriage done by her and one done by her father?*

G.   *[19A] And from the perspective of R. Nahman bar Isaac, who said even
from the viewpoint of R. Yosé b. R. Judah, "The original money for her
was not given for betrothal," how are you going to explain the matter?*

H.   *It will be in accord with R. Eliezer, who has said, "It is for a condition of
subjugation after another condition of subjugation that he cannot sell her,
but he can sell her for subjugation after marriage."*

VI.26 A.   *R. Simeon b. Laqish raised this question:* "What is the law on
designating the slave girl for his minor son? 'His son' (Ex.
21:9) *is what Scripture has said, meaning, his son of any
classification? Or perhaps, 'his son' comparable to him,
meaning,* just as he is an adult, so his son must be an adult?"

B.   *Said R. Zira, "Come and take note:* ['And the man who
commits adultery with another man's wife, even he who
commits adultery with his neighbor's wife, the adulterer and
the adulteress shall surely be put to death' (Lev. 20:10)]. 'A
man' – excluding a minor. '...Who commits adultery with
another man's wife' – excluding the wife of a minor. Now if
you say that he can designate [her for a minor], then you find
the possibility of a matrimonial bond in the case of a minor."

C. *So what's the upshot? That he can't designate her for a minor son? Then why should Scripture exclude that possibility? Rather, on this basis, solve the problem to indicate that he can designate her for a minor [since that's the only way a minor male can be legally married]!*

D. *Said R. Ashi, "In this case we deal with a levir who is nine years and a day old who has sexual relations with his levirate bride, in which case, on the basis of the law of the Torah, she is a suitable wife for him. Now what might you have said? Since on the strength of the law of the Torah, she is a suitable wife for him, and his act of sexual relations is valid, then he who has sexual relations with her is liable on the count of doing so with a married woman? So we are informed to the contrary."*

E. *So what's the upshot of the matter?*

F. *Come and take note:* Said R. Yannai, "The designation of the slave girl for a wife can take place only with an adult male; the designation of a slave girl for a wife may take place only with full knowledge and consent of the man," [which solves Simeon b. Laqish's problem].

G. *Two items?*

H. *The sense of the matter is what is set forth, that is, how come the designation of the slave girl for a wife can take place only with an adult male? It is because* the designation of a slave girl for a wife may take place only with full knowledge and consent of the man.

I. *But why not say, what is the meaning of* full knowledge and consent? *It must be full knowledge and consent of the woman!*

J. *For Abbayye b. R. Abbahu repeated as a Tannaite statement:* "'If she does not please her master, who has not espoused her' – this teaches that he has to inform her that he plans to designate her." He is the one who repeated it, and he is the one who explained it: "It refers to the betrothal effected by designation, *and accords with the position of R. Yosé b. R. Judah,* who said, 'The original money for her was not given for betrothal.'"

K. *R. Nahman bar Isaac said, "You may even maintain that the money was given for betrothal, but this case is exceptional, for the All-Merciful has said, 'designate' [meaning, designate with full knowledge and consent]."*

VI.27 A. *What is the source for the position of R. Yosé b. R. Judah?*

B. *It is in line with that which has been taught on Tannaite authority:*

C. "If she does not please her master, who has espoused her to himself, then he shall let her be redeemed" – there must be enough time in the day to allow redeeming her. [Freedman: If her master wishes to designate her on the very last day of her servitude, her labor still owing must be worth at least a penny, so that she could be redeemed from the work; otherwise he cannot designate her.] On the strength of that fact, said R. Yosé b. R. Judah, "If there is enough time left on that last day for her to work for him to the value of a penny, she is betrothed, and if not, she is not betrothed." *Therefore he takes the position that* the original money for her was not given for betrothal.

D.   *R. Nahman bar Isaac said, "You may even maintain that the original money for her was given for betrothal, but this case is different, for said the All-Merciful, 'then he shall let her be redeemed.'"*

VI.28   A.   Said Raba said R. Nahman, "A man may say to his minor daughter, 'Go, accept your own token of betrothal.' *This is on the basis of what R. Yosé b. R. Judah has said. For didn't he say that* the original money for her was not given for betrothal? *But when the master leaves her only a penny's worth of her labor, that serves for a token of betrothal, so here, too, it is no different."*

VI.29   A.   And said Raba said R. Nahman, "He who betroths a woman through transfer of a debt on which there is a pledge – she is betrothed. *This is on the basis of what R. Yosé b. R. Judah has said. For didn't he say that* the original money for her was not given for betrothal? [19B] *But this work represents a loan, for which she herself is pledge, when the master leaves her only a penny's worth of her labor, that serves for a token of betrothal, so here, too, it is no different."*

VI.30   A.   *Our rabbis have taught on Tannaite authority:*
        B.   How is the religious duty of designating the slave girl carried out?
        C.   The master says to her in the presence of two valid witnesses, "Lo, you are consecrated to me," "Lo, you are betrothed to me,"
        D.   – even at the end of six years, even near sunset at the end of that time.
        E.   And he then deals with her in the custom of a matrimonial bond and he does not deal with her in the custom of servitude.
        F.   R. Yosé b. R. Judah says, "If there is enough time left on that last day for her to work for him to the value of a penny, she is betrothed, and if not, she is not betrothed."
        G.   This matter may be compared to one who says to a woman, "Be betrothed to me as from now, after thirty days have gone by," and someone else comes along and betroths her within the thirty days. So far as the law of designation is concerned, she is betrothed to the first party.

VI.31   A.   *Now whose position is served by this parable? Should we say the parable pertains to the position of R. Yosé b. R. Judah? Lo,* if there is enough time left on that last day for her to work for him to the value of a penny, she is betrothed, and if not, she is not betrothed! [Freedman: This proves that the betrothal commences not at the beginning of her servitude but only at the last moment; here, too, the betrothal commences at the end of thirty days, and therefore if another man betroths her in the meantime, she is betrothed to the second.]
        B.   *Said R. Aha b. Raba, "The parable serves to illustrate the position of rabbis."*
        C.   *Yeah, so what else is new?*
        D.   *What might you otherwise have supposed? The master didn't say, "As from now"?* [Freedman: Therefore in the analogous case, even if he says, "You are betrothed after...," and another does so within the

thirty days, she is betrothed to the first.] *So we are informed that that consideration does not come into play.*

VI.32 A. *It has further been taught on Tannaite authority:*

B. "He who sells his daughter and went and accepted betrothal for her with a second party has treated the master shabbily, and she is betrothed to the second party," the words of R. Yosé b. R. Judah.

C. But sages say, "If he wants to designate her as a wife for himself or for a son, he may do so."

D. This matter may be compared to one who says to a woman, "Be betrothed to me after thirty days have gone by," and someone else comes along and betroths her within the thirty days. So far as the law of designation is concerned, she is betrothed to the second party.

VI.33 A. *Now whose position is served by this parable? Should we say the parable serves the position of rabbis? Lo, rabbis maintain, "If he wants to designate her as a wife for himself or for a son, he may do so." Said R. Aha b. Raba, "The parable serves to illustrate the position of rabbis."*

B. *Yeah, so what else is new?*

C. *What might you otherwise have supposed? Lo, he did not say to her, "After thirty days"? So we are informed that that is not the operative consideration.* [Freedman: Her master did not say he would designate her after a certain period, therefore the second man's betrothal is valid; but if he said, "Be betrothed after..," I might have thought she is betrothed to him, and the second man's betrothal is null. Now, since Scripture empowered him to designate her through purchase, it is as though he had said he would subsequently designate her; the cases are analogous.]

VI.34 A. *It has further been taught on Tannaite authority:*

B. "He who sells his daughter and agreed that it was on condition that her master not designate her as a wife for himself or his son, the stipulation is valid," the words of R. Meir.

C. And sages say, "If he wanted to designate her as a wife for himself or his son, he may do so, since he has made a stipulation contrary to what is written in the Torah, and any stipulation in violation of what is written in the Torah is null."

VI.35 A. *Well, then, from R. Meir's perspective, is his stipulation valid? And hasn't it been taught on Tannaite authority:*

B. "He who says to a woman, 'Lo, you are betrothed to me on the stipulation that you have no claim upon me for provision of food, clothing, and sex' – lo, she is betrothed, and his stipulation is null," the words of R. Meir.

C. And R. Judah says, "With respect to property matters [food, clothing], his stipulation is valid."

D. *Said Hezekiah, "This case is exceptional, for* Scripture has said, '...and if a man sell his daughter to be a slave girl' (Ex. 21:7) – there are occasions on which he may sell her only to be a slave girl alone."

E. *And as to rabbis, how do they deal with this statement, "and if a man sell his daughter to be a slave girl" (Ex. 21:7)?*

F. *They require it in line with that which has been taught on Tannaite authority:*

G.   "And if a man sell his daughter to be a slave girl" (Ex. 21:7) –
      this teaches that he may sell her to those who are invalid to
      marry her [for example, a mamzer].

H.   But does that fact not follow merely from a logical argument,
      namely, if he can betroth her to unfit persons, can't he sell
      her to unfit persons?

I.   But what makes it possible for him to betroth her to unfit
      persons is that a man may betroth his daughter when she is
      in the status of pubescent, but can he sell her to unfit
      persons, since he cannot sell his daughter when she is
      pubescent? Therefore it is required to prove that point from
      Scripture's explicit statement, "he may sell her to those who
      are invalid to marry her [for example, a mamzer]," which
      teaches that he may sell her to those who are invalid to marry
      her [for example, a mamzer].

J.   R. Eliezer says, "If the purpose is to indicate that he may sell
      her to those who are invalid to marry her [for example, a
      mamzer], lo, that is already indicated by the verse, 'if she
      displease her master so that he has not espoused her,'
      meaning, she was displeasing in regard to an entirely valid
      matrimonial bond. So what is the point of the verse, 'and if a
      man sell his daughter to be a slave girl' (Ex. 21:7)? This
      teaches that he may sell her [20A] to relatives."

K.   But does that fact not follow merely from a logical argument,
      namely, if he can betroth her to unfit persons, can't he sell
      her to relatives?

L.   What makes it possible for him to sell her to unfit persons is
      that, if he wanted to designate her as a wife, he may do so,
      but can he sell her to relatives, who, if one of them wished to
      designate her as a wife, may not do so? So it was necessary
      for Scripture to say, "he may sell her to those who are invalid
      to marry her [for example, a mamzer]," which teaches that he
      may sell her to relatives.

M.   And R. Meir?

N.   *That he may sell her to unfit persons is a proposition he*
      derives from the same verse used by R. Eliezer for that
      proposition, and as to selling her to relatives, he concurs with
      rabbis, who take the position that he may not sell her to
      relatives.

VI.36   A.   *One Tannaite statement holds:* He may not sell her to relatives, *and*
             another Tannaite statement, he may sell her to his father, but he may
             not sell her to his son, and yet another Tannaite statement, he may not
             sell her either to his father or to his son.

        B.   *Now there is no problem understanding the position,* he may not sell her
             either to his father or to his son, *since this would accord with rabbis.*
             But in accord with what authority is the position, he may sell her to his
             father, but he may not sell her to his son? *This is neither in accord*
             with rabbis nor with R. Eliezer?

        C.   *In point of fact it is in accord with rabbis, for rabbis concede in a case in*
             which there is a possibility of designating her as a wife [the father for the

son, who may be her uncle; but the son cannot betroth her for himself nor designate her for his son (Freedman)].

VI.37   A.   *Our rabbis have taught on Tannaite authority:*

         B.   "If he came in by himself, he shall go out by himself" (Ex. 21:3) – he comes in with his body whole and undamaged, and he goes out in the same condition.

         C.   R. Eliezer b. Jacob says, "He comes in single, he goes out single."

VI.38   A.   *What is the meaning of the phrase,* he comes in with his body whole and undamaged, and he goes out in the same condition?

         B.   Said Raba, "This is to say that he is not freed through loss of his major limbs, as a gentile slave is."

         C.   *Said to him Abbayye, "That proposition derives from the language, 'She shall not go out as slave boys do' (Ex. 21:7)."*

         D.   *"If I had to rely on that verse, I should have thought that he has to pay him, at least, the value of his eye, at which point he also frees him. So we are informed that that is not the case."*

VI.39   A.   *What is the meaning of the phrase,* he comes in single, he goes out single?

         B.   *Said R. Nahman bar Isaac, "This is the sense of the statement:* If a Hebrew slave does not have a wife and children, his master cannot give him a Canaanite slave girl. If he does have a wife and children, his master may give him a Canaanite slave girl."

VI.40   A.   *Our rabbis have taught on Tannaite authority:*

         B.   If a person was sold as a slave for a maneh and increased in value so that he was then worth two hundred zuz, how do we know that they reckon with his value only at the rate of a maneh?

         C.   As it is said, "He shall give back the price of his redemption out of the money that he was bought for" (Lev. 25:51).

         D.   If he was sold for two hundred zuz and lost value and was priced at a maneh, how do we know that we reckon his worth only at a maneh?

         E.   As it is said, "According to his years shall he give back the price of his redemption" (Lev. 25:52).

         F.   Now I know thus far that that is the rule for a Hebrew slave who is sold to an idolator, and who is redeemed [by his family], for his hand is on the top. How do I know that the same rule applies to an Israelite [who owns a Hebrew slave who is up for redemption]?

         G.   Scripture states, "A hired servant" in two different contexts [Lev. 25:40, a slave sold to an Israelite, and Lev. 25:50, a slave sold to an idolator], serving therefore to establish an analogy between them [and to invoke for the one the rules that govern the case of the other. The lenient ruling for the slave governs the redemption of the field].

VI.41   A.   Said Abbayye, "Lo, I am equivalent to Ben Azzai in the marketplaces of Tiberias [who challenged all comers to ask him

hard questions]." [Abbayye is challenged, B, G-V, and replies at C-
F, then W + Y-BB.]

B. *One of the rabbis [taking up the challenge] said to Abbayye, "There is the*
possibility of interpreting [the verses referring to the redemption of the
Hebrew slave] in a lenient way [favoring the redemption and making it
easy] and in a strict way. Why do you choose to do so in a lenient way? I
might propose that they should be interpreted in a strict way."

C.   "Let not the thought enter your mind, for the All-Merciful was
            lenient to [the Hebrew slave]. For it has been taught on
            Tannaite authority:

D.   "'Because he fares well with you' (Deut. 15:16). He must be
            with you [and at your status] in food and in drink, so that you
            may not eat a piece of fine bread while he eats a piece of
            coarse bread, you may not drink vintage wine while he
            drinks new wine, you may not sleep on a soft bed while he
            sleeps on the ground.

E.   "On this basis it is said that he who buys a Hebrew slave is
            like one who buys a master for himself."

F.   *"But might one not say, that pertains to what has to do with*
            eating and drinking, so as not to distress him, but, so far as
            redemption, we should impose a strict rule on him, along the
            lines of what R. Yosé b. R. Hanina said?"

G.   For it has been taught on Tannaite authority: R. Yosé bar
            Hanina says, "Come and see how harsh is the dust kicked up
            in connection with the laws of the Seventh Year. [Even if one
            violates only derivative rules, the result is severe.] If a
            person trades in produce grown in the Seventh Year, in the
            end he will have to sell his movables, as it is said, 'In this
            year of Jubilee you shall return, every man to his possession'
            (Lev. 25:13), and it is said, 'If you sell anything to your
            neighbor or buy anything from your neighbor's hand' (Lev.
            25:14). [The two verses are juxtaposed to indicate that if a
            person does the one, he will be punished by the other, so for
            selling or buying produce of the Seventh Year, he will have
            to sell his property, in this case], movables, something
            acquired from hand to hand.

H.   "If the person does not perceive [what he has done], in the
            end he will have to sell his fields, as it is said, 'If your brother
            becomes poor and has to sell some of his possessions' (Lev.
            25:25).

I.   "It is not brought home to him, so in the end he will have to
            sell his house, as it is said, 'And if a man sells a dwelling
            house in a walled city' (Lev. 25:29)" [T. Arakhin 5:9].

J.   *What is the difference between the two cases, in that, in the*
            former instance, it says, "If the person does not perceive," and
            in the latter, "It is not brought home to him"?

K.   *The answer accords with what R. Huna said.*

L.   *For R. Huna said, "Once a person has committed a*
            transgression and done it again, it is permitted to him."

M.   *"It is permitted to him" do you say?*

N. *Rather, I should say,* "It is transformed for him so that it appears to be permitted."

O. [Continuing I:] "It is not brought home to him so in the end he will sell his daughter, as it is said, 'And if a man sells his daughter to be a maidservant' (Ex. 21:7).

P. [*Abbayye continues:*] "*And even though the matter of one's selling his daughter is not mentioned in the present context, it would be better for a person to sell his daughter and not to borrow on usurious rates, for in the case of his daughter, what is owing gradually diminishes [as she works off the debt], while in the present instance, the debt grows and grows.*

Q. "Then it is not brought home to him, so in the end he will sell himself into slavery, as it is said, 'And if your brother becomes poor with you and sells himself to you' (Lev. 25:39).

R. "And not to you, but to a proselyte, as it is said, 'To the proselyte' (Lev. 25:47).

S. "And not to a sincere proselyte but to a resident alien, as it is said, 'To a resident alien' (Lev. 25:47).

T. "'A proselyte's family' refers to an idolator.

U. "When Scripture further states, 'Or to the stock,' [20B] it refers to one who sells himself to become a servant of the idol itself.'

V. *He [Abbayye, A] replied,* "But Scripture restores him [to his status]."

W. *And a member of the household of R. Ishmael repeated as a Tannaite statement,* "Since this one has gone and sold himself to an idol, [one might have thought], 'Let us throw a stone after the fallen.' Scripture therefore has said, 'After he is sold, he shall be redeemed, one of his brothers shall redeem him' (Lev. 25:48)."

X. *Might I maintain that "He shall be redeemed" means that, while he is not to be permitted to be absorbed among the idolators, as to the matter of redeeming him, we should impose a strict ruling?*

Y. *Said R. Nahman bar Isaac,* "It is written, 'If there be yet increases in the years' (Lev. 25:51) and 'If there remain but little in the years' (Lev. 25:51). Now are there years that are prolonged and years that are shortened? [Surely not.] Rather, if his value should be increased, then 'out of the money that he was bought for' he shall be redeemed, and if his value diminishes, then 'in accord with the remaining years.'"

Z. *And might I propose a different reading, namely, where he has worked two years and four remain, let him pay the four years at the rate of* "the money that he was bought for," *and if he had worked for four years, with two remaining, then let him repay two years* "according to his year"?

AA. "If that were the case, then Scripture should have stated, 'If there be yet many years.' Why does it say, 'in years'? It means, as stated above, if his value should be increased, [then his redemption shall be paid] 'out of the money that he was bought for,' and if his value decreased, then the basis of the fee for redemption will be] 'according to his remaining years.'"

BB.   *Said R. Joseph, "R. Nahman has interpreted these verses as if from Sinai."*

VI.42   A.   R. Huna bar Hinena asked R. Sheshet, "A Hebrew slave sold to a gentile – may he be redeemed by halves, or may he not be redeemed by halves? Do we derive the meaning of 'his redemption' by analogy to the rule governing redeeming a field of possession, namely, just as a field of possession cannot be redeemed by halves, so he cannot be redeemed by halves? *Or maybe we invoke that analogy to produce a lenient rule but not to produce a strict rule?"*

        B.   *He said to him, "Didn't you say in that context, he is sold whole but not by halves? So here, too, he is redeemed whole but not by halves."*

        C.   *Said Abbayye, "If you find grounds for maintaining, he may redeemed by halves, then you turn out to produce a ruling that is lenient for him and also strict for him. The leniency is, if the gentile bought him for a hundred zuz and then the slave paid back fifty, which is half his value, and then he went up in value and was worth two hundred, if you say, he can be half redeemed, he pays him another hundred and goes out a free man; but if you say, he cannot be half-redeemed, then he has to pay him a hundred and fifty."*

        D.   *But you said, "if he increased in value, he is redeemed out of the money that he was bought for"!*

        E.   *That would refer to a case in which he was valuable when he was bought then lost value then gained value.*

        F.   *"And also strict for him: If he bought him for two hundred, and the slave paid back a hundred, which was half his value, and then went down in value to a hundred – if you say he can be half-redeemed, he has to pay him fifty and go free; but if you say he cannot be redeemed by halves, then the hundred was merely a bailment held by the master, and the slave gives that to him and goes free."*

VI.43   A.   R. Huna bar Hinena asked R. Sheshet, "He who sells a house in a walled city – is the house redeemed by halves or is it not redeemed by halves? Do we derive the meaning of 'his redemption' by analogy to the rule governing redeeming a field of possession, namely, just as a field of possession cannot be redeemed by halves, so he cannot be redeemed by halves? *Or maybe where Scripture made that point explicit, it stands, but where not, it is not made explicit and so is null?"*

        B.   He said to him, "We derive the answer from the exegesis of R. Simeon that one may borrow and redeem and redeem by halves.

              For it has been taught on Tannaite authority: '"And if a man shall sanctify to the Lord part of the field of his possession, and if he that sanctified the field will indeed redeem it" (Lev. 25:52) – this teaches that one may borrow and redeem and redeem by halves. Said R. Simeon, "What is the reason? The reason is that we find in the case of one who sells a field of possession that he enjoys certain advantages. That is, if the Jubilee Year comes and the field has not been redeemed, it automatically reverts to the owner at the Jubilee Year. On the

other hand, for that very reason, he suffers the disadvantages that he may not borrow to redeem the field and he may not redeem the field in halves. But [the opposite considerations apply to] one who sanctifies a field of possession. For, on the one side, he suffers a disadvantage in that, if the Jubilee Year comes and the field has not been redeemed, it automatically goes forth to the ownership of the priests. So, by contrast, he is given an advantage, in that he may borrow in order to redeem the field and he may redeem it in halves."' *Lo, one who sells a house in a walled city, too* – since he suffers the disadvantage in that, if a complete year goes by and the field is not redeemed, it is permanently alienated; but he gains the advantage that he can borrow and redeem and redeem by halves."

C.   *An objection was raised: "And if he will indeed redeem it"* – this teaches that he can borrow and redeem and redeem by halves. For one might have supposed that logic dictates the opposite conclusion, namely: If one who sells a field of possession, who enjoys the advantage that, if the Jubilee comes and the field has not been redeemed, it reverts to its original owner in the Jubilee, but who suffers the disadvantage that he may not borrow money and redeem it and redeem it by halves, then he who sanctifies a field, who suffers the disadvantage that, if the Jubilee comes and he has not redeemed the field, the field goes out to the ownership of the priests at the Jubilee, surely it follows that he does not enjoy the advantage such that he can borrow and redeem or redeem by halves [but has not got that right].

D.   But as for the one who sells a field of possession, the reason is that the advantage he enjoys is not so strong, for he cannot redeem the field forthwith. But will you say the same of one who sanctifies a field, who enjoys a considerable advantage, in that he can redeem the field forthwith?

E.   Let the one who sells a house in a walled city prove the contrary, since his advantage is sufficiently puissant that he can redeem the field forthwith – and yet he can't borrow and redeem the field or redeem the field by halves.

F.   *There is no problem, [21A] the one represents the view of rabbis, the other, R. Simeon.* [Freedman: Sheshet's answer having been deduced from Simeon's statement; Simeon holds that the reason of a scriptural law must be sought, and when found it may modify the rule and provide a basis for other laws; rabbis disagree; Simeon argues that the disabilities require compensating privileges and finds this embodied in the laws of sanctification of a field of possession, from which the same principles are applied to analogous cases; rabbis argue that when Scripture impairs one's privileges in one direction, they are weakened in all a fortiori, the sanctification of an inherited field being explicitly excepted by Scripture.]

G.   *One Tannaite statement holds:* He who sells a house in a walled city may borrow and redeem and redeem by halves. *One Tannaite* statement holds: He who sells a house in a walled city may not borrow and redeem and redeem by halves.

H. *There is no problem, the latter represents the view of rabbis, the former, R. Simeon.*

VI.44 A. *Said R. Aha b. Raba to R. Ashi, "One may raise the following objection:* What characterizes the one who sells a house in a walled city is that he is at a disadvantage since he can never redeem it again [after the first year has passed, Lev. 25:30]. But can you say the same of one who consecrates a field, who has the power to redeem the field at any time?"

B. *Said R. Aha the Elder to R. Ashi, "Because one can say, let the argument run full circle, and invoke a proof on the basis of shared traits among otherwise different classes, namely:* One who sells a field of possession will prove the contrary, for his power is such that he can redeem the field at any time in the future, but he may not borrow and redeem the field or redeem the field by halves. But what characterizes the one who sells a field of possession is that he is at a disadvantage in regard to redeeming the field immediately. Then one who sells a house in the walled city will prove the contrary – and so we go around in circle. The definitive trait of the one is not the same as the definitive trait of the other, but what characterizes them all in common is that they may be redeemed, one may not borrow and redeem, and one may redeem them all by halves. So I introduce the case of one who sanctifies a field, which may be redeemed, but one may now borrow and redeem or redeem by halves."

C. *Said Mar Zutra b. R. Mari to Rabina, "One may raise the following objection:* What they have in common is that the owner is at a disadvantage, in that they cannot be redeemed in the second year [after the act; one who sells an inherited field can redeem it only from the third year, the seller of a house in a walled city can't redeem it after the first year has passed]. But then will you say the same of one who sanctifies a field, who has the power, after all, to redeem the field in the second year?"

D. *Said to him Rabina, "It is because one may say:* A Hebrew slave sold to a gentile will prove the contrary, for he has the advantage of being redeemed in the second year, but he may not borrow and redeem himself, nor may he be redeemed by halves."

VI.45 A. *R. Huna bar Hinena asked this question of R. Sheshet:* "He who sells a house in a walled city – may the house be redeemed by relatives or may the house not be redeemed by relatives? Do we draw a verbal analogy based on the appearance of 'his redemption' both here and with regard to a field of possession: Just as a field of possession may not be redeemed by halves but may be redeemed by relatives, *so the same would apply here, namely,* this, too, may not be redeemed by halves but may be redeemed by relatives. *Or maybe, when the word 'redemption' is stated by Scripture, it serves to establish an analogy with respect to redeeming the field by halves, but it is not stated by Scripture with regard to redemption by relatives?"*

B. He said to him, "It may not be redeemed by relatives."

C. *An objection was raised:* "'And in all the land of your possession you shall effect a redemption for the land' (Lev.

25:24) – that serves to encompass houses and Hebrew slaves [relatives may redeem these]. *Doesn't this refer to houses in walled cities?"*

D.   *No, it refers to houses in villages.*

E.   *But Scripture explicitly refers to houses in villages: "They shall be reckoned with the fields of the country" (Lev. 25:31).*

F.   *That verse serves to impose as an obligation the duty of redemption by relatives, in line with the position of R. Eliezer, for it has been stated on Tannaite authority:* "'If your brother become poor and sell some of his possessions, then shall his kinsman that is next to him come and shall redeem that which his brother has sold' (Lev. 25:25) – that is an option.

G.   "You say it is an option, but maybe it's an obligation? Scripture states, 'And if a man has no kinsman' (Lev. 25:26). Now is it conceivable that there can be an Israelite who has no [kinsmen to serve as] redeemers? Rather, this refers to one who has such but whose kinsman doesn't want to repurchase it, showing he has the option to do so," the words of R. Joshua.

H.   R. Eliezer says, "'If your brother become poor and sell some of his possessions, then shall his kinsman that is next to him come and shall redeem that which his brother has sold' (Lev. 25:25) – that is an obligation.

I.   "You say it is an obligation, but maybe it's only an option? Scripture states, 'and in all...you shall effect a redemption' (Lev. 25:26) – thus Scripture establishes it as an obligation."

J.   *Rabbis said to R. Ashi, and some say, Rabina to R. Ashi, "There is no problem for one who maintains that it serves to encompass houses in walled cities, that is in line with Scripture's statement, 'in all.' But from the perspective of the one who says that it encompasses houses in villages, what is the meaning of 'in all'?"*

K.   *That's a problem.*

L.   *Objected Abbayye, "* Why does the clause, 'he shall redeem him' occur three times [at Lev. 25:48, 49, 52]? It serves to encompass all instances of redemption, indicating that they are to be redeemed in this manner [encompassing redemption by relatives]. *Doesn't this mean houses in walled cities and Hebrew slaves?"*

M.   No, it refers to houses in villages and fields of possession.

N.   *But Scripture explicitly covers the matter of* houses in villages and fields of possession, in the language, "They shall be reckoned with the fields of the country"!

O.   *It is in line with what R. Nahman bar Isaac said, "It is to indicate that the closer the relation, the greater his priority." Here, too, it is to indicate,* the closer the relation, the greater his priority. [Freedman: It is in the same order of priority as the kinsmen enumerated at Lev. 25:48, 49.]

VI.46   A.   *In what connection is this statement of R. Nahman bar Isaac made?*

B.   *It is in connection with the question that was raised:* "A Hebrew slave sold to an Israelite – is he redeemed by relatives or is he not redeemed by relatives? *With respect to Rabbi that is not an issue, for he has said,* 'Through these he is redeemed, but not by the passage of six years.' *Therefore he cannot be redeemed. Our question addresses the view of rabbis. What is the law? Do we establish a verbal analogy on the strength of the recurrent use of the word 'hired hand,' and we do not derive a lesson from the language,* 'one of his brothers may redeem him' (Lev. 25:38)? *Or perhaps,* 'he may redeem him,' *means, him but no one else* [a Hebrew slave sold to an Israelite]?"

C.   *Come and take note:* "In all...you shall effect a redemption' – this encompasses houses and Hebrew slaves." *Doesn't that mean houses in a walled city and Hebrew slaves sold to Israelites?*

D.   No, it means a Hebrew slave sold to a gentile.

E.   *A Hebrew slave sold to a gentile is covered by an explicit statement of Scripture,* "or his uncle or his uncle's son may redeem him" (Lev. 25:49) – [21B] *that serves to make doing so obligatory, and even from the perspective of R. Joshua.*

F.   *Come and take note:* "Why does the clause, 'he shall redeem him' occur three times [at Lev. 25:48, 49, 52]? It serves to encompass all instances of redemption, indicating that they are to be redeemed in this manner [encompassing redemption by relatives]. *Doesn't this mean houses in walled cities and Hebrew slaves sold to Israelites?*"

G.   No, it refers to houses in villages and fields of possession.

H.   *But Scripture makes explicit reference to the matter of the field of possession:* "They shall be reckoned with the fields of the country"!

I.   Said R. Nahman bar Isaac, "It is to indicate that the closer the relation, the greater his priority."

VII.1 A.   The slave whose ear is pierced is acquired through an act of piercing the ear (Ex. 21:5):

B.   *For it is written,* "Then his master shall bore his ear through with an awl" (Ex. 21:6).

VIII.1 A.   And he acquires himself by the Jubilee or by the death of the master:

B.   *For it is written,* "and he shall serve him" but not his son or daughter;

C.   "forever" – until the "forever" of the Jubilee.

VIII.2 A.   *Our rabbis have taught on Tannaite authority:*

B.   "'An awl' (Deut. 15:17):

C.   "I know only that an awl is sufficient for boring the ear of the slave. How do I know that sufficient also would be a prick, thorn, borer, or stylus?

D.   "Scripture states, 'Then you shall take' (Deut. 15:12) – including everything that can be taken in hand," the words of R. Yosé b. R. Judah.

E. Rabbi says, "Since the verse says, 'an awl,' we draw the conclusion that the awl is made only of metal, and so anything that is used must be metal.

F. "Another matter: 'You shall take an awl' – teaches that a big awl is meant."

G. Said R. Eleazar, "R. Yudan b. Rabbi would expound as follows: 'When they pierce the ear, they do it only through the earlobe.'

H. "Sages say, 'A Hebrew slave of the priestly caste is not subjected to the boring of the ear, because that thereby blemishes him.'"

I. *Now if you hold that the boring is done only through the earlobe, then the Hebrew slave of the priestly caste cannot be blemished thereby, since we bore only through the top part of the ear [and in any event, boring makes a blemish, and Yosé takes the view that even a needle's point, a smaller hole than a lentil's size, constitutes maiming]!*

VIII.3 A. *What is at issue here?*

B. *Rabbi invokes the categories of an encompassing rule followed by an exclusionary particularization:*

C. "You shall take" is an encompassing rule; "an awl" is an exclusionary particularization; "through his ear into the door" reverts and gives an encompassing rule. So where you have an encompassing rule, an exclusionary particularization, and another encompassing rule, you cover under the encompassing rule only what bears the traits of the exclusionary particularization; just as the exclusionary particularization states explicitly that the object must be of metal, so must anything used for the purpose be of metal.

D. *R. Yosé b. R. Judah interprets the categories of scriptural evidences of inclusionary and exclusionary usages:*

E. "You shall take" is inclusionary; "an awl" is exclusionary; "through his ear into the door" reverts and forms an inclusionary statement. Where you have an inclusionary, an exclusionary, and an inclusionary statement, the upshot is to encompass all things.

F. *So what is excluded? An ointment.*

VIII.4 A. The master has said: "'You shall take an awl' – teaches that a big awl is meant":

B. *On what basis?*

C. It is in line with what Raba said, "'Therefore the children of Israel don't eat the sinew of the hip that is on the hollow of the thigh' (Gen. 32:33) – the right thigh; here, too, 'the awl,' means, the most special of awls."

VIII.5 A. Said R. Eleazar, "R. Yudan b. Rabbi would expound as follows: 'When they pierce the ear, they do it only through the earlobe.' Sages say, 'A Hebrew slave of the priestly caste is not subjected to the boring of the ear, because that thereby blemishes him'":

B. So let him be blemished!

C.   Said Rabbah b. R. Shila, "Said Scripture, 'And he shall return to his own family' (Lev. 25:41) – to his family's presumptive rights."

VIII.6   A.   *The question was raised:* "A Hebrew slave who is a priest – what is the law as to his master's giving him a Canaanite slave girl? *Is this an anomaly, in which case there is no distinguishing priests from Israelites? Or perhaps priests are exceptional, since* Scripture imposes additional religious duties on them?"

B.   Rab said, "It is permitted."

C.   And Samuel said, "It is forbidden."

D.   *Said R. Nahman to R. Anan, "When you were at the household of Master Samuel, you wasted your time playing chess. Why didn't you reply to him on the basis of the following:* Sages say, 'A Hebrew slave of the priestly caste is not subjected to the boring of the ear, because that thereby blemishes him'? *Now if you say his master can't give him a gentile slave girl, the law that a Hebrew slave who is a priest is not bored simply follows that we require that the slave be able to say,* 'I love my master, my wife, and my children' *and that is not possible here [cf. Ex. 21:5]."*

E.   *Nothing more is to be said.*

The foregoing uses the cited verse as a fact, without further amplification, governing a situation that is to be sorted out: either that condition is met, or nothing is to be done. In the next item, we work on yet another fact, involving not the meaning of Scripture but the implication of its fact. In this way, we read a scriptural fact as we would a Mishnah fact.

VIII.7   A.   *The question was raised:* "A priest – what is the law as to his taking 'a woman of goodly form' (Deut. 21:11)? *Is this an anomaly, in which case there is no distinguishing priests from Israelites? Or perhaps priests are exceptional, since* Scripture imposes additional religious duties on them?"

B.   Rab said, "It is permitted."

C.   And Samuel said, "It is forbidden."

D.   *With respect to the first act of sexual relations, all parties concur that it is permitted, for* the Torah spoke only with reference to the human desire to do evil. *Where there is a disagreement, it concerns* a second and later act of sexual relations.

E.   Rab said, "It is permitted."

F.   And Samuel said, "It is forbidden."

G.   Rab said, "It is permitted, *for once it is permitted, it remains so.*"

H.   And Samuel said, "It is forbidden, *for she is a proselyte, and a proselyte is not a worthy bride of a priest.*"

I.   There are those who say that with respect to the second act of sexual relations all parties concur that it is permitted, since she is a proselyte. Where there is a disagreement, it concerns the first act of sexual relations.

J.   Rab said, "It is permitted, *for* the Torah spoke only with reference to the human desire to do evil. "

K.   And Samuel said, "It is forbidden, *for in any case in which one can invoke the verse,* 'then you shall bring her home to your house' (Deut. 21:12), *we also invoke the verse,* 'and see among the captives' (Deut. 21:11), *but in any case in which one cannot invoke the verse,* 'then you shall bring her home to your house' (Deut. 21:12), *we also do not invoke the verse,* 'and see among the captives' (Deut. 21:11)."

What follows differs from the foregoing, because we now impute a sense to each of the clauses, so our reading is meant to amplify the sense of the passage, rather than expound the facts of the passage.

VIII.8   A.   *Our rabbis have taught on Tannaite authority:*

B.   ["When you take the field against your enemies, and the Lord your God delivers them into your power, and you take some of them captive, and you see among the captives a beautiful woman and you desire her and would take her to wife, you shall bring her into your house, and she shall trim her hair, pare her nails, and discard her captive's garb. She shall spend a month's time in your house lamenting her father and mother. After that you may come to her and possess her, and she shall be your wife. Then, should you no longer want her, you must release her outright. You must not sell her for money; since you had your will of her, you must not enslave her" (Deut. 21:10-14)].

C.   "...And you see among the captives":

D.   At the time of the taking of the captives.

E.   "...A [beautiful] woman":

F.   Even a married woman [Sifré Deut. CCXI:II.1-2].

G.   "...A [beautiful] woman":

H.   The Torah spoke only with reference to the human desire to do evil. It is better for the Israelites to eat meat of [22A] beasts about to die but properly slaughtered than the meat of dying animals that have perished on their own without slaughter.

I.   "And you desire" – even if she's not pretty.

J.   "Her" – but not her and her girlfriend [the soldiers get one each].

K.   "...And would take her to wife": – you have marriage rights over her.

L.   "...For yourself to wife": – that is so that you may not say, "Lo, this one is for father," "Lo, this one is for my brother" [Sifré Deut. CCXI:II.4].

M.   "And you shall bring her home" – this teaches that he must not molest her in battle.

VIII.9   A.   *Our rabbis have taught on Tannaite authority:*

B.   "But should he say to you, 'I do not want to leave you,' [for he loves you and your household and is happy with you, you shall take an awl and put it through his ear into the door, and he shall become your slave in perpetuity. Do the same with your female slave. When you do set him free, do not feel aggrieved, for in the six years he has given you double the service of a hired man. Moreover, the Lord your God will bless you in all you do]" (Deut. 15:12-17):

C.   Is it possible to suppose that this may take place one time only?

D.   Scripture says, "But should he say to you, 'I do not want to leave you,'" – unless he says so and repeats it.

E.   If he said so during the six years, but did not say so at the end of the six years, lo, this one does not have his ear pierced to the doorpost,

F.   for it is said, "I do not want to leave you" – which applies only if said at the time of his leaving.

G.   If he said so at the end of the six years, but did not say so during the six years, lo, this one does not have his ear pierced to the doorpost,

H.   for it is said, "But if the slave should say to you...,"

I.   that is, while he is yet a slave [Sifré Deut. CXXI.I.1-3].

VIII.10 A.   The master has said, "If he made the statement at the beginning of the sixth year but not at the end, he is not bored, for it is said, 'I will not go out free'" [so he has to make the statement when he is about to leave].

B.   *But we derive the law from the passage,* "I will not go out free," *why not derive the rule from the fact that he has to say,* "I love my master, my wife, and my children," *which condition is not met? Furthermore,* "If he says it at the end of the sixth year but not at the beginning, he is not bored, for it is said, 'the slave...'": *Isn't he then a slave at the end of the sixth year?*

C.   Said Raba, "The meaning is, 'at the beginning of the last penny's worthy of service, and at the end of the same.'"

VIII.11 A.   *Our rabbis have taught on Tannaite authority:*

B.   If he has a wife and children, and his master does not have a wife and children, lo, this one does not have his ear pierced to the doorpost,

C.   as it is said, "...for he loves you and your household and is happy with you." [Sifré Deut. CXXI:II.2].

D.   If his master has a wife and children and he doesn't have a wife and children, he is not bored, as it is said, "I love my master, my wife, and my children."

E.   "...For he loves you and your household and is happy with you":

F.   Since it is said, "I have loved my master" (Ex. 21:5), do I not know that "he loves you and your household and is happy with you"?

G.   On this basis, you may rule:

H.	If the slave loved the master, but the master did not love the slave,
I.	if he was beloved of his master, but he did not love his master –
J.	lo, this one does not have his ear pierced to the doorpost, as it is said, "...for he loves you and your household and is happy with you" [Sifré Deut. CXXI:II.1].
K.	"...Is happy with you":
L.	Lo, if he was sick, or his master was, lo, this one does not have his ear pierced to the doorpost [Sifré Deut. CXXI:III].
VIII.12 A.	*R. Bibi bar Abbayye raised this question: "If both of them are sick, what is the law? We require 'with thee' which pertains, or maybe we require 'because he is well with thee,' which doesn't pertain?"*
B.	*The question stands.*
VIII.13 A.	*Our rabbis have taught on Tannaite authority:*
B.	"Because he fares well with you" (Deut. 15:16). He must be with you [and at your status] in food and in drink, so that you may not eat a piece of fine bread while he eats a piece of coarse bread, you may not drink vintage wine while he drinks new wine, you may not sleep on a soft bed while he sleeps on the ground.
C.	On this basis it is said that he who buys a Hebrew slave is like one who buys a master for himself.
VIII.14 A.	*Our rabbis have taught on Tannaite authority:*
B.	"Then he shall go out from you, he and his children with him" (Lev. 25:41):
C.	Said R. Simeon, "If he was sold, were his sons and daughters sold? But on the basis of this verse, it is the fact that his master is obligated for food for his children."
D.	Along these same lines:
E.	"If he is married, then his wife shall go out with him" (Ex. 21:3):
F.	Said R. Simeon, "If he was sold, was his wife sold? But on the basis of this verse, it is the fact that his master is obligated for food for his wife."
VIII.15 A.	*And both items were required. For had we been told the fact concerning his children, it is because they are not able to work for a living, but as to a wife, who can work for her living, I might say, "Well, then, let her earn her keep." If we had the rule only concerning the wife, that might be because it is inappropriate for her to go begging, but as for the children, who may appropriately go begging, I might have thought that that is not the case. So both items were necessary.*
VIII.16 A.	*Our rabbis have taught on Tannaite authority:*
B.	[22B] If Scripture had said, "...his ear on the door," I might have thought, then let a hole be bored against his ear through the door. So it is only the door, but not his ear.
C.	"Not his ear"?! But it's written, "and his master shall bore his ear through with an awl" (Ex. 21:6).

	D.	Rather, I might have said, the ear is bored outside and then placed on the door, and a hole bored through the door opposite his ear. Therefore it is said, "and you shall thrust it through his ear into the door." How? The boring goes on until the door is reached.
VIII.17	A.	"The door":
	B.	May I then infer that that is so whether it is removed from the hinges or not?
	C.	Scripture states, "unto the door or unto the doorpost" (Ex. 21:6): Just as the doorpost must be standing in place, so the door must be standing in place.
VIII.18	A.	Rabban Yohanan ben Zakkai would expound this verse in the manner of a homer exegesis: "How come the ear was singled out of all the limbs of the body? Said the Holy One, blessed be He, 'The ear, which heard my voice at Mount Sinai at the moment that I said, "For to me the children of Israel are slaves, they are my slaves" (Lev. 25:55), nonetheless went and acquired a master for itself. So let it be pierced.'"
	B.	R. Simeon b. Rabbi would expound this verse of Scripture in the manner of a homer exegesis: "How come the door and doorpost were singled out from all other parts of the house? Said the Holy One, blessed be He, 'The door and the doorpost, which were witnesses in Egypt when I passed over the lintel and the doorposts and proclaimed, "For to me the children of Israel are slaves, they are my slaves" (Lev. 25:55), not servants of servants, now I brought them forth from slavery to freedom; yet this man has gone and acquired a master for himself – let him be bored before them in particular.'"

I.1+2-6+7-10 commence with attention to the scriptural source for the Mishnah's law. II.1, III.1, IV.1, V.1-2 all do the same, but with less elaboration. The sustained composite at VI.1-2, with a long thematic appendix at Nos. 3-5, 6+7-13, 14+15-18 utilize a clause of our Mishnah paragraph to work out a problem of its own. None of this is put together as Mishnah commentary; the whole is worked out in its own terms and parachuted down for the reason given. Only at VI.19, with its talmud at Nos. 20-21, and a Tannaite complement at No. 22, with its talmud at No. 23, and further talmud at Nos. 24-25, do we regain the Mishnah sentence that is under discussion, there complementing with a Tannaite formulation. The string of theoretical problems that extend from the original tangential discussion of the designation of a slave girl for marriage continues at No. 26, with a footnote at Nos. 27+28-29. Nos. 30+31, 32+33, 34+35-36, 37+38-39, 40+41, continue with a Tannaite formulation this sizable appendix on a tangential topic. Nos. 42-43+44, 45 with its footnote at 46, pursue the same general theme, though the strung-out character of the composite is entirely self-evident. Clearly, a rather formidable talmud had taken shape around the themes expounded here, and the whole was then preserved as a huge appendix to a rather modest discussion of a Mishnah statement. **VII.1, VIII.1** find a source for the Mishnah's rule. **VIII.2**, with a talmud at Nos. 3+4-5, with what is now the usual thematic appendix at Nos. 6-8, then addresses the topic of the Mishnah's rule. Another well-composed set, Nos. 9-18, form an appropriate, and sizable, composite on the theme of our Mishnah topic. So the rather considerable corpus of materials for **VIII.1** really does amplify the theme at hand in a relevant manner.

1:3

- A. A Canaanite slave is acquired through money, through a writ, or through usucaption.
- B. "And he acquires himself through money paid by others or through a writ [of indebtedness] taken on by himself," the words of R. Meir.
- C. And sages say, "By money paid by himself or by a writ taken on by others,
- D. "on condition that the money belongs to others."

I.1
- A. *How on the basis of Scripture do we know this fact?*
- B. As it is written, "And you shall make them [gentile slaves] an inheritance for your children after you, to possess as an inheritance" (Lev. 25:46) – Scripture thus has treated them as comparable to a field of inheritance. Just as a field of inheritance is acquired through money, writ, or usucaption, so a Canaanite slave is acquired through money, through a writ, or through usucaption.
- C. Might one then propose: Just as a field of inheritance reverts to its original owner at the Jubilee, so a Canaanite slave reverts to the original owner at the Jubilee?
- D. Scripture states, "Of them shall you take your slaves forever" (Lev. 25:46).

The foregoing is a commonplace reading of the Torah by the Talmud, as we already realize: How on the basis of Scripture do we know what the Mishnah has told us in this particular sentence?

I.2
- A. *A Tannaite statement:* Also through barter.
- B. *What about the Tannaite statement before us [which omits that medium of acquisition]?*
- C. *He has specified those modes of acquisition that do not apply to movables; but what applies to movables [and also to slaves, in that same category] he does not specify in his Tannaite formulation.*
I.3
- A. Said Samuel, "A Canaanite slave is acquired also through drawing. How so? If the purchaser grabs the slave and he goes with him, he acquires title to him; if he calls him and he goes to him, he does not acquire title to him."
- B. *What about the Tannaite statement before us [which omits that medium of acquisition]?*

C. *There is no problem in explaining the omission of drawing, for he has specified those modes of acquisition that do not apply to movables; but what applies to movables [and also to slaves, in that same category] he does not specify in his Tannaite formulation. But as to that other Tannaite authority [the one cited at No. 2], should his formulation not encompass drawing?*

D. *What he has encompassed in his Tannaite statement are modes of acquisitions that pertain to both real estate and movables, but drawing, which pertains to movables but not to real estate, he has not encompassed in his Tannaite formulation.*

I.4   A. "How so? If the purchaser grabs the slave and he goes with him, he acquires title to him; if he calls him and he goes to him, he does not acquire title to him":

B. *Well, now, he doesn't, does he? Then what about that which has been taught on Tannaite authority:*

C. How is an animal acquired through the mode of handing over [delivery]? [Slotki: Harnessing, like drawing, is one of the modes of acquiring right of ownership; the buyer takes possession of the animal by performing some act that resembles harnessing, or, in the case of other objects, obtaining full delivery.] If the buyer takes hold of the hoof, hair, saddle, saddle bag that is upon it, bit in the mouth, or bell on the neck, he has acquired title. How is it done through drawing the object? If he calls the beast and it comes, or if he strikes it with a stick and it runs before him, he acquires title as soon as it has moved a foreleg and a hind leg.

D. R. Ahi, and some say, R. Aha, says, "That takes place only if it has moved the full length of its body." [The four legs must be moved from their original position.]

E. *Say: A beast moves on its master's will, a slave on his own.*

F. Said R. Ashi, "A minor slave is classified as a beast."

I.5   A. *Our rabbis have taught on Tannaite authority:*

B. How is a slave acquired through an act of usucaption? If the slave fastened the shoe of the man or undid it, or if he carried his clothing after him to the bathhouse, or if he undressed him or washed him or anointed him or scraped him or dressed him or put on his shoes or lifted him up, the man acquires title to the slave.

C. Said R. Simeon, "An act of usucaption of this kind should not be greater than an act of raising up, since raising up an object confers title under all circumstances."

I.6   A. *What is the meaning of this statement?*

B. Said R. Ashi, "[*This is the sense of his statement:*] If the slave lifted up his master, the master acquires title, but if the master lifts up the slave, the master does not acquire ownership of the slave. Said R. Simeon, 'An act of usucaption of this kind should not be greater than an act of raising up, since raising up an object confers title under all circumstances.'" [Simon: If the master lifts up the slave, this action also confers ownership.]

I.7   A. *Now that you have said,* if the slave lifted up his master, the master acquires title, *then what about the following:* A Canaanite slave girl should be acquired through an act of sexual relations [since in that situation she lifts up the master]?

B. *When we invoke the stated rule, it is in a case in which* the one party derives pleasure, but the other party suffers anguish. *But here,* this one enjoys it and so does that one.

C. *Well, then, what about anal intercourse?*

D. Said R. Ahai bar Ada of Aha, "Who's going to tell us that both of them don't get a kick out of it? And, furthermore, the language that Scripture uses is, 'you shall not lie with mankind with the lyings of a woman' (Lev. 18:22), in which case Scripture has treated as comparable anal and vaginal sexual relations."

I.8   A. R. Judah the Hindu was a proselyte, so he had no heirs. *He fell ill. Mar Zutra came to inquire after his health. He saw that he was dying, so he said to his slave, "Take off my shoes and take them to my house for me" [so that when the proselyte died, the slave would be engaged in a service to him, and he would thereby acquire title through usucaption].*

B. *There are those who say, the slave was an adult.*

C. [23A] This one left for death and the other one [the slave] left to life.

D. *Others say, he was a minor, and this did not accord with what Abba Saul said, for it has been taught on Tannaite authority:* A proselyte who died, and Israelites grabbed his property, and among them were slaves, whether adult or minor, the slaves have acquired title to themselves as free persons. Abba Saul says, "The adults have acquired title to themselves as free persons, but the minors – whoever takes hold of them has acquired title to them."

II.1   A. "**And he acquires himself through money paid by others or through a writ [of indebtedness] taken on by himself,**" the words of R. Meir:

B. **Through money paid by others** – but not by money paid by the slave himself? *With what situation do we deal? Should we say,* without his knowledge and consent? *Then note: We have heard that* R. Meir holds, it is a disadvantage for the slave to go forth from the possession of his master to freedom, *and we have learned as a Tannaite statement in the Mishnah,* **For they act to the advantage of another person not in his presence, but they act to his disadvantage only in his presence [M. Git. 1:6F].** *So it is obvious that it is with the slave's knowledge and consent, and so we are informed that* it may be done through money paid by others – but not by money paid by the slave himself. *Then it follows that* there is no possibility for a slave to acquire title to anything without his owner's participation. *But then note what follows:* **Through a writ [of indebtedness] taken on by himself!** *So if it is taken on by himself, it is a valid medium of emancipation, but if it is taken on by others, it is not! Now if it is with his own knowledge and consent, then why can it not be validly done by third parties? And should you say, what is the meaning of,* **through a writ [of indebtedness] taken on by himself?** *It means,* even through a writ [of indebtedness] taken on by himself, *and so we are informed that* the advent of his writ of emancipation and his right to form a domain unto himself come about simultaneously, *lo, that is not how it has been taught as a Tannaite statement, for lo, it has been taught on Tannaite authority:* "**...By a writ undertaken on his own account, but not one undertaken by others,**" the words of R. Meir [T. Qid. 1:6F].

C. Said Abbayye, "In point of fact, it is not with his knowledge and consent. But a slave acquired by reason of a monetary obligation [that he is unable to meet, on account of which he is sold into slavery] is exceptional, for, since the master acquires title to him willy-nilly, the master also transfers title back to him willy-nilly."

D. If so, the same rule should pertain to a writ!

E. This sort of deed stands by itself [with its own wording] and that kind of writ stands by itself.

F. Well, then, here, too, this money stands by itself and that money stands by itself [since each is paid for its own purpose]!

G. They have the same mint mark.

H. Raba said, "As to money, when the master receives it, it effects his liberation, but as for a deed, when others receive it, it effects his liberation."

III.1   A. **And sages say, "By money paid by himself or by a writ taken on by others":**

B. If the money is paid by himself, it liberates him, but if it is paid by others, it doesn't? *Now why should this be the case? Granting that this is without his knowledge and consent, in any event notice: We know that rabbis take the position that it is to the slave's advantage to leave the master's domain for freedom, and we have learned in the Mishnah,* **For they act to the advantage of another person not in his presence, but they act to his disadvantage only in his presence [M. Git. 1:6F].** *And should you say, what is the meaning of* paid by himself? *Also money paid by himself, and so we are informed that there is every possibility for a slave to acquire title to anything without his owner's participation, if so, note what follows:* **By a writ taken on by others** – not undertaken by him himself! *And yet it is an established fact for us that the advent of his writ of emancipation and his right to form a domain unto himself come about simultaneously. And should you say, what is the meaning of* by a writ taken on by others? *Also by a writ taken on by others, and so we are informed that it is to the slave's advantage to leave the master's domain for freedom, if so, then why not blend the whole and repeat the entire matter in a single statement, namely:* With money and with a writ, whether taken on by others or taken on by himself?

C. *Rather, the sense must be:* With money, whether taken on by others or taken on by himself, or with a writ, if it is taken on by others, but not if it is taken on by the slave himself, *and the whole represents the position of R. Simeon b. Eleazar, for it has been taught on Tannaite authority:*

D. **R. Simeon b. Eleazar says, "Also by a writ when taken on by others, but not when taken on by himself" [T. Qid. 1:6F].**

E. There are three different opinions on the matter [Meir, money through others, without his knowledge, but not through his own agency, and by deed through his own agency but not that of others; Simeon b. Eleazar, both by money and deed, through the agency of others but not through his own; rabbis, both by money and by deed, through the agency of others and his own (Freedman)].

F. Said Rabbah, "What is the scriptural foundation for the position of R. Simeon b. Eleazar? He derives a verbal analogy on the basis of the same word, to her, that occurs with reference to a slave and a wife, namely, just as a woman is divorced only when the writ of divorce will be taken into a domain that does not belong to the husband, so a slave, too, is liberated only when the writ reaches a domain that is not his master's."

III.2 A. *Rabbah asked,* [23B] "From the perspective of R. Simeon b. Eleazar, what is the law on a Canaanite slave's appointing a messenger to receive his writ of emancipation from the hand of his master? *Since we derive a verbal analogy on the basis of the word 'to her' that appears both in his context and in that of a woman, he is in the status of a woman, or perhaps, as to a woman, since she has the power to receive her writ of divorce, an agent also can do so, but a slave, who has not got the power to receive his writ of emancipation, also has not got the power to appoint an agent?*"

B. *After he raised the question, he solved it: "We do deduce the verbal analogy on the basis of the common word that joins the slave to the married woman, so he is in the status of a married woman."*

C. *Then what about that which R. Huna b. R. Joshua said, namely: "The priests serve as the agents of the All-Merciful,"* for if it should enter your mind that they are our slaves, is there something that we could not do, but they have the power to do in our behalf? Well, isn't there anything? Then what about the case of a slave, for he can't accept his writ of emancipation in his own behalf, but he can appoint someone as an agent to do so!

D. But the analogy is null. For an Israelite has no relevance to the rules governing offerings at all, but a slave most certainly bears a relevance to writs of severance, *for it has been taught on Tannaite authority:* It is quite appropriate that a slave may accept a writ of emancipation in behalf of his fellow from the hand of the other's master, but not from his own.

IV.1 A. On condition that the money belongs to others:

B. *May we then say that this is what is at issue between sages and R. Meir: R. Meir takes the position that* the slave has no right of effecting title without his master's participation, and a woman has no right of effecting title without her husband's participation, *while rabbis maintain that* the slave has the right of effecting title without his master's participation, and a woman has the right of effecting title without her husband's participation?

C. *Said Rabbah said R. Sheshet, "All parties concur that* the slave has no right of effecting title without his master's participation, and a woman has no right of effecting title without her husband's participation. *And here with what case do we deal? It is one in which a stranger gave the slave a title to a maneh, with the stipulation,* 'this is on the stipulation that your master has no right to it.' *R. Meir maintains that, when the donor said to him, 'Acquire title,' the slave acquired title and so did the master, and the statement,* 'this is on the stipulation that your master has no right to it,' *is null. And rabbis maintain that once*

he said to him, 'this is on the stipulation that your master has no
right to it,' *the stipulation takes effect."*

D.   *And R. Eleazar said, "In any case such as this, all parties concur that what
the slave acquires the master acquires. Here with what situation do we
deal? With a case in which a third party gave him title to a maneh and
said to him,* 'It is on the stipulation that with this money you go forth
to freedom.' *R. Meir maintains that, when the donor said to him,*
'Acquire title,' *the slave acquired title and so did the master, and the
statement,* 'this is on the stipulation that your master has no right to
it,' *is null. And rabbis maintain that he did not accord title of it even to
the slave, for he said to him,* 'It is on the stipulation that with this
money you go forth to freedom.'"

E.   *Now there is a contrast between what R. Meir has said with another
statement of R. Meir, and likewise between what rabbis have said and
another statement of rabbis, for it has been taught on Tannaite authority:*

F.   **[24A] A woman may not redeem second tithe without adding a
fifth to its value.**

G.   **R. Simeon b. Eleazar says in the name of R. Meir, "A woman does
redeem second tithe without adding a fifth to its value"** [T. M.S.
4:7D-E]. [Freedman: When one redeems second tithe produce of his
own and turns its value into ready cash, he adds a fifth to its value,
but if he does the same for produce belonging to another, he does
not have to do so unless the owner made him his agent to do so].

H.   *Now with what situation do we deal here? If we say that the
money belongs to the husband and the produce in the status of
second tithe likewise belongs to the husband, then the wife is
just carrying out the commission of her husband [so she surely
should have to pay the added fifth]! So it must be a case in
which the money belongs to her and the produce in the status
of second tithe belongs to her husband. But what Scripture has
said is, "And if a man will redeem any of his tithe, then he
shall add thereto the fifth party" (Lev. 27:31) – he but not his
wife. So it must be a case in which a third party has given the
wife title to a maneh and said to her, "It is on the stipulation
that with it you redeem the produce in the status of second
tithe." So we infer that they hold contrary opinions [to the
ones they announce with respect to the slave's freedom.]*
[Freedman: The rights of a slave and a woman are similar:
Either they can both acquire independently or they both
cannot.]

I.   *Said Abbayye, "Big deal – so reverse the attributions."*

J.   *Raba said, "Under no circumstances reverse the attributions. Here we
deal with produce in the status of second tithe that comes to the woman
from her father's household as his heir. R. Meir is consistent with views
expressed elsewhere, for he has said,* 'Tithe is property belonging to
what has been sanctified,' *so that her husband does not acquire title to
it. And rabbis are consistent with views expressed elsewhere, for they
maintain,* 'Tithe is property belonging to the ordinary person,' *so
that her husband does acquire title to it. Therefore she does indeed carry
out the commission of her husband."*

Here is another instance in which the facts of Scripture are manipulated in their own term, for example, Scripture has made certain points, and we now wish to utilize the facts that Scripture (happens to have) supplied, as much as, in other discussions, we should utilize the facts that the Mishnah (happens to have) supplied, or taken for granted. I treat the following as a scriptural discussion not because Scripture is cited, but because facts it – and it alone – has supplied, are utilized.

IV.2   A.   *A Tannaite statement:* A gentile slave goes free through the loss of his eye, tooth, or major limbs that do not grow back [in line with Ex. 21:26-27].

       B.   *Now there is no problem understanding why that is so for the eye and tooth, since they are made explicit in Scripture, but on what basis do we know that that is the fact for the loss of the major limbs?*

       C.   *These are comparable to the tooth and eye:* Just as the loss of the tooth or eye represent blemishes that are exposed to sight and these do not grow back, so any blemishes that are exposed to sight and that are not going to grow back are covered by the same loss.

       D.   *But why not say:* The reference to "tooth" and "eye" constitute two rules that are redundant [Freedman: for the analogy could not be drawn if only one of them were mentioned], and whenever you have two verses that are redundant, they cannot be used to illuminate other cases.

       E.   *But both are required and they are not redundant, for if the All-Merciful had made reference only to the matter of the tooth, I might have supposed that even* [24B] *a milk tooth's loss would suffice; so the All-Merciful made reference to "eye" as well. And if the Merciful had made reference only to "eye," I would have supposed:* Just as the eye was created with the person himself, so that would apply to any such limb, *but the law would not cover the tooth, which grew in later on.*

       F.   *Well, why not say,* "and if a man smite" (Ex. 21:26-27) forms an encompassing generalization; "the tooth...the eye" form a particularization; in any case in which you have an encompassing generalization followed by a particularization, covered by the generalization is only what is contained in the particularization, with the result that the slave goes free for the loss of the tooth or the eye, *but nothing else.*

       G.   "He shall go free" forms another encompassing generalization, and wherever you have a sequence made up of an encompassing generalization, a particularization, and another encompassing generalization, you include under the rule what is similar to the particularization: Just as the particularization makes explicit that the slave goes free by reason of blemishes that are exposed to sight and these do not grow back, so any blemishes that are exposed to sight and that are not going to grow back are covered by the same loss and with the same outcome.

H. *Well, how about this:* Just as the particularization makes clear that a blemish that is exposed to sight, which causes the body part to cease to work, and which body part does not grow back, serves to liberate the slave, so any sort of blemish that is exposed to sight, which causes the body part to cease to work, and which body part does not grow back, serves to liberate the slave? *Then how come it has been taught on Tannaite authority:* If the owner pulled out the slave's beard and loosened his jaw, the slave is freed on that account?

I. "He shall let him go free" forms an extension of the law.

J. Well, if it's an extension of the law, then even if he hit him on his hand and it withered but is going to get better, he also should go free. *Then how come it has been taught on Tannaite authority:* If he hit him on his hand and it withered but is going to get better, he does not go free?

K. *If he did go free, then what's the point of tooth and eye?*

IV.3 A. *Our rabbis have taught on Tannaite authority:*

B. "In all these cases, a slave goes forth to freedom, but he requires a writ of emancipation from his master," the words of R. Simeon.

C. R. Meir says, "He doesn't require one."

D. R. Eliezer says, "He requires one."

E. R. Tarfon says, "He doesn't require one."

F. R. Aqiba says, "He requires one."

G. Those who settle matters in the presence of sages say, "The position of R. Tarfon makes more sense in the case of a tooth or eye, since the Torah has itself assigned him freedom on these counts, but the position of R. Aqiba is more sensible in the case of other parts of the body, because the freedom that is assigned in those cases represents an extrajudicial penalty imposed by sages on the master."

H. It is an extrajudicial penalty? *But there are verses of Scripture that are interpreted here!*

I. Rather, "Since it is an exposition of sages."

IV.4 A. *What is the scriptural basis for the position of R. Simeon?*

B. *He derives the sense of "sending her" from the use of the same word in the case of a woman: Just as the woman is sent forth by a writ, so a slave is sent forth by a writ.*

C. *And R. Meir?*

D. *If the words "to freedom" were included at the end of the verse in question, it would be as you say, but since it is written at the outset, "to freedom shall he send him away," the sense is, to begin with he is free.*

IV.5 A. *Our rabbis have taught on Tannaite authority:*

B. If the master hit the slave on his eye and blinded him, on his ear and deafened him, the slave goes forth by that reason to freedom. If he hit an object that was opposite the slave's eye, and the slave cannot see, or opposite his ear, so that he cannot hear, the slave does not go forth on that account to freedom.

IV.6 A. *Said R. Shemen to R. Ashi, "Does that bear the implication that noise is nothing? But didn't R. Ammi bar Ezekiel teach as a Tannaite statement:* A chicken that put its head into an empty glass jar and crowed and broke the jar – the owner pays full damages? And said R. Joseph,

'They say in the household of the master: A horse that neighed or an ass that brayed and broke utensils – the owner pays half-damages'!"

B. *He said to him, "Man is exceptional, for, since he is self-aware, he frightens himself [and is responsible if he is frightened by noise], for it has been taught on Tannaite authority:* He who frightens his fellow to death is exempt under the laws of humanity but liable under the laws of Heaven. How so? If he blew on the ear and deafened him, he is exempt. If he seized him and tore him on the ear and deafened him, he is liable. [In the latter case he did a deed of consequence.] [cf. T. B.Q. 9:26]."

IV.7 A. *Our rabbis have taught on Tannaite authority:*

B. If he hit his eye and impaired his eyesight, his tooth and loosened it, but he still can use them at this time, the slave does not go forth on their account to freedom, but if not, the slave does go forth on their account to freedom.

C. *It has further been taught on Tannaite authority:*

D. If the slave had poor eyesight but the master totally blinded him, or if his tooth was loose and the master knocked it out, then, if he could use them beforetimes, the slave goes free on their account, but if not, the slave does not go free on their account.

IV.8 A. *And it was necessary to state both rules, for had we been informed of only the first rule, it might have been because, to begin with, the man had healthy vision and now he has weak vision, but in this case, since, to begin with, he had weak vision, I might have said that that is not the rule. And if we had been informed only of the second case, then it might have been because now he has totally blinded him, but in that case, in which he did not totally blind him, I might have said that the slave does not go free. So both were needed.*

IV.9 A. *Our rabbis have taught on Tannaite authority:*

B. Lo, if his master was a physician, and the slave told him to paint his eye with an ointment, and the master blinded him, or to drill his tooth and he knocked it out, the slave just grins at his master and walks out free.

C. Rabban Simeon b. Gamaliel says, "'...and he destroy it' (Ex. 21:26) – only if he intends to destroy it."

IV.10 A. *So how do rabbis deal with the clause, "...and he destroy it" (Ex. 21:26)?*

B. *They require it in line with that which has been taught on Tannaite authority:*

C. *R. Eleazar says, "Lo, if the master stuck his hand into his slave girl's womb and blinded the foetus that was in her belly, he is exempt from punishment. How come? Scripture said, '...and he destroy it' (Ex. 21:26) – only if he intends to destroy it."*

D. *And the other party?*

E. *That rule he derives from the language, "and he destroy it" instead of the language, "and he destroy."*

F. *And the other party?*

G. *He derives no lesson from the language, "and he destroy it" instead of the language, "and he destroy."*

IV.11   A.   Said R. Sheshet, "If the slave's eye was blind and the master removed it, the slave goes forth to freedom on that account. How come? Because he now lacks a limb."

        B.   *And a Tannaite statement is repeated along these same lines:* Freedom from blemish and male gender are required in the case of animals for sacrifice, but not for fowl. Might one then suppose that if the wing was dried up, the foot cut off, the eye plucked out, the bird remains fit? Scripture said, "And if the burnt-offering be of fowl" (Lev. 1:14), but not all fowl.

IV.12   A.   Said R. Hiyya bar Ashi said Rab, "If the slave had [25A] an extra finger and the master cut it off, the slave goes out free."

        B.   Said R. Huna, "But that is on condition that the extra finger counts along with the hand."

IV.13   A.   *The elders of Nezonayya didn't come to the public sessions of R. Hisda. He said to R. Hamnuna, "Go, excommunicate them."*

        B.   *He went and said to him, "How come rabbis have not come to the session?"*

        C.   *They said to him, "Why should we come? For when we ask him a question, he can't answer it for us."*

        D.   *He said to them, "Well, have you ever asked me a question that I couldn't answer for you?"*

        E.   *They asked him the following:* "A slave whose master castrated him, what is the law on classifying this blemish? *Is it tantamount to one that is visible to the eye or is it not?"*

        F.   *He didn't know the answer.*

        G.   *They said to him, "So what's your name?"*

        H.   *He said to them, "Hamnuna."*

        I.   *They said to him, "It's not Hamnuna but Qarnuna."*

        J.   *He came before R. Hisda. He said to him "Well, they asked you a question that can be answered from the Mishnah, for we have learned in the Mishnah:* Twenty-four tips of limbs in man which are not susceptible to uncleanness because of quick flesh: The tips of the joints of hands and feet, and the tips of the ears, and the tip of the nose, and the tip of the penis. And the tips of the breasts which are in the woman. R. Judah says, 'Also of the man.' R. Eliezer says, 'Also the warts and the wens are not susceptible to uncleanness because of quick flesh' [M. Neg. 6:7]. *And a Tannaite statement in that connection:* And on account of the loss of all of these, a slave goes forth to freedom. Rabbi says, 'Also on account of castration.' Ben Azzai says, 'Also on account of the tongue.'"

IV.14   A.   The master has said: "Rabbi says, 'Also on account of castration'":

        B.   *Castration of what? Should I have said castration of the penis? But that is the same as loss of the penis [to which reference is explicitly made]. So it must mean, castration of the testicles.*

IV.15   A.   Rabbi says, "Also on account of castration":

        B.   *And doesn't Rabbi include in the last removal of the tongue? And by way of contrast:* If a priest was sprinkling a man made unclean by corpse uncleanness with purification water, and a sprinkle hit his mouth – Rabbi says, "This constitutes a valid act of sprinkling." And sages say, "This does not constitute a valid act of sprinkling." *Now isn't this sprinkling on his tongue* [Freedman: so Rabbi regards the tongue as an exposed limb, contradicting his exclusion of the tongue in the case of a slave]?

C. *No, it means on his lips.*

D. *Well, if it means on his lips, then that is self-evidently the rule and it hardly needs to be spelled out!*

E. *What might you otherwise have supposed, sometimes the lips are tightly pressed together? So we are informed that, one way or the other [they are regarded as exposed].*

F. *But it has been taught on Tannaite authority:* "On his tongue," *and it further has been taught on Tannaite authority:* And that, the greater part of the tongue has been removed. R. Judah says, "The greater part of the fore-tongue"!

G. *Rather, Rabbi says,* "castration, *and it is not necessary to say,* the tongue, too."

H. Ben Azzai says, "The tongue but not castration."

I. *And what is the point of saying* "also"?

J. *It refers to the first clause.*

K. *If so, then Ben Azzai's statement should have come first.*

L. *The Tannaite framer of the passage heard Rabbi's statement and set it in place, then he heard Ben Azzai's statement and repeated it,* but the initial Tannaite formulation of the Mishnah paragraph did not move from the place assigned to it.

M. Said Ulla, "All concur in regard to the tongue that, so far as issues of uncleanness are concerned, it is held to be exposed with respect to dead creeping things. *How come? The All-Merciful has said,* 'and whomsoever he who has a flux touches,' (Lev. 15:11), *and this, too, can be touched.* With respect to immersion, however, it is tantamount to a concealed part of the body. *What is the scriptural basis? The All-Merciful has said,* 'And he shall bathe his flesh in water' (Lev. 15:13) – just as the flesh is exposed, so everything that has to be touched by the water must be exposed. They differ only with respect to sprinkling in particular. *Rabbi compares it to the matter of uncleanness, and sages invoke the analogy of immersion, and both parties differ with respect to this one verse of Scripture:* 'And the clean shall sprinkle upon the unclean' (Num. 19:19) – Rabbi interprets the matter, 'And the clean shall sprinkle upon the unclean on the third day and on the seventh day and purify him,' *and rabbis read,* 'and on the seventh day he shall purify him and he shall wash his clothes and bathe himself in water' [Freedman: hence sprinkling must be on the same part that needs immersion, excluding the tongue, which doesn't]."

N. *So why don't rabbis make the comparison to the matter of uncleanness?*

O. *We seek governing analogies for matters of cleanness from matters of cleanness.*

P. And why shouldn't Rabbi invoke the analogy of immersion?

Q. "And he shall wash his clothes" *closes the subject* [Freedman: therefore "shall purify" cannot be linked with "bathe himself"].

R. *But does Rabbi really take the view that, with respect to immersion, the tongue is regarded as concealed?* But didn't Rabin bar R. Ada say R.

Isaac said, "There is the case of the slave girl of Rabbi, who immersed, and when she came up out of the water, a bone that constitutes interposition between her body and the water was found between her teeth, so Rabbi required her to immerse a second time"?

S.   *To be sure, we don't require that the water enter the spot, but we do require that there be the possibility of its entering, and that accords with what R. Zira said, for* said R. Zira, "In the case of whatever is suitable for mingling, actual mingling is not essential, and in the case of whatever is not suitable for mingling, actual mingling is indispensable." [Cashdan, *Menahot* 18B: In Zira's view the law before us is that mingling can be omitted so long as it is possible to do so if one wants, and the Mishnah's rule would mean that no oil at all was poured in.]

T.   *There is a conflict of Tannaite statements on the same matter:*

U.   "'That which has its stones bruised, crushed, torn, or cut' (Lev. 22:24) – all of them affect the testicles," the words of R. Judah.

V.   "In the stones" but not in the penis? Rather: "Also in the stones," the words of R. Judah.

W.   R. Eliezer b. Jacob says, "All of them refers to defects in the penis."

X.   R. Yosé says, "'Bruised, crushed' also can refer to the testicles, but 'torn, or cut' can refer to the penis, but in the testicles do not constitute a blemish."

I.1 finds a scripture basis for the Mishnah's rule. Nos. 2-3+4 address a further Tannaite statement on the same topic. Then we have a Tannaite complement, tacked on to the foregoing for obvious reasons, at No. 5, with its talmud at Nos. 6, 7. No. 8 illustrates the foregoing. II.1 analyzes the language of the Mishnah sentence. III.1+2 follow suit. Nos. 2-3+4, 5-6, 7-8, 9-10, 11-12, 13 then move on to a tangential theme, relevant to our topic but not to the particular rule at hand. Nos. 13+14-15 are added because of their general congruence to the foregoing, but, of course, we have moved from a supplement to an appendix.

1:4

A.   "Large cattle are acquired through delivery, and small cattle through lifting up," the words of R. Meir and R. Eleazar.

B.   And sages say, "Small cattle are acquired through an act of drawing."

I.1   A.   Rab expounded in Qimhunayya, "Large cattle are acquired through drawing the beast."

B.   *Samuel came across the disciples of Rab. He said to them, "Did Rab say that large beasts are acquired through drawing? But we have learned as the Tannaite formulation, 'through delivery'! And Rab also said that it was through delivery."*

C.   *So did Rab retract his opinion?*

D. *He made his ruling in accord with the Tannaite authority behind the following, which has been taught on Tannaite authority:* And sages say, "This and that [large, small beasts alike] are acquired through drawing." R. Simeon says, "This and that are acquired through lifting up the beast."

E. *Objected R. Joseph,* "Well, then, how in R. Simeon's opinion can an elephant be acquired [who can lift up the damn thing]!"

F. Said to him Abbayye, "Through a symbolic barter, *or also* by renting the place in which it is located [on which account the place belongs to the purchaser, along with its contents]."

G. R. Zira said, "The purchaser brings four utensils and puts them under the elephant's feet."

H. *That yields the proposition:* When the purchaser's utensils are in the domain of the seller and a commodity that has been purchased is put in them, the purchaser has acquired title to the commodity. [But that is not a settled question, so how can we be so sure?]

I. *Here with what situation do we deal? It is an alley [belonging to no private party]. [26A] Or also, it may involve bundles of twigs [of a height that serve to raise the elephant above the ground when he steps on them].*

I.1 works on the correct wording of our Mishnah rule.

1:5

A. **Property for which there is security is acquired through money, writ, and usucaption.**

B. **And that for which there is no security is acquired only by an act of drawing [from one place to another].**

C. **Property for which there is no security is acquired along with property for which there is security through money, writ, and usucaption.**

D. **And property for which there is no security imposes the need for an oath on property for which there is security.**

I.1　A.　Property for which there is security is acquired through money:

　　B.　*How on the basis of Scripture do we know that fact?*

　　C.　Said Hezekiah, "Said Scripture, 'people will acquire fields with money' (Jer. 32:44)."

　　D.　*But might one say, that is valid only unless there is a deed, since the verse goes on, "And subscribe the deeds and attest them and call witnesses" (Jer. 32:44)?*

　　E.　*If the order of the language were such that "acquire" came at the end, it would be as you maintain; but since "acquire" appears at the beginning, the meaning is, money transfers title, the deed merely attests to that fact.*

I.2　A.　Rab, "This rule was repeated only in reference to a place in which they do not write out a deed, but in a place where they did write out a deed, money by itself does not effect transfer of title."

　　B.　*But if the buyer stipulates [that either money or deed serves], that is the case.*

　　C.　*For instance, that is as in the case of R. Idi bar Abin, when he bought land, he would say, "If I want, I'll acquire it through transfer of cash, if I want,*

I'll acquire it through a deed. If I want, I'll acquire it through transfer of cash – and if you want to retract after I've paid, you can't. If I want, I'll acquire it through a deed, and if I want to retract, I can."

II.1   A.   Writ:

           B.   *How on the basis of Scripture do we know that fact?*

           C.   *Shall we say, because it is written,* "And subscribe the deeds and attest them and call witnesses" (Jer. 32:44)? *But haven't you already said,* "The deed merely attests to that fact"? *Rather, proof derives from the following:* "So I took the deed of purchase" (Jer. 32:11).

II.2   A.   Said Samuel, "This rule was repeated only in reference to a deed of gift, but as to a deed of sale, the transfer of title takes place only when the purchaser gives him the cash."

           B.   *Objected R. Hamnuna,* "'Writ: How so? If the seller wrote on a parchment or on a potsherd, themselves of no intrinsic value, "My field is sold to you, my field becomes your property," it is deemed to have been sold or given by deed'! [So the deed confers ownership, even prior to the transfer of funds.]"

           C.   *R. Hamnuna refuted his own allegation? For he added:* "That rule pertains to a case in which someone sold the field because it was really worthless" [the money therefore hardly matters, but this would not ordinarily be so (Simon)].

           D.   And R. Ashi said, "The seller really wanted to transfer the field as a gift and to give it over to him, and the reason he made the transfer in the form of a deed and in the language of a sale is so as to strengthen the hold of the donee to the title of the field."

III.1   A.   And usucaption:

           B.   *How on the basis of Scripture do we know that fact?*

           C.   Because it is written, "And dwell in the cities that you have taken" (Jer. 40:10) – how did you take them? By dwelling in them.

           D.   *A Tannaite authority of the household of R. Ishmael:* "And you shall possess it and dwell therein" (Deut. 11:31) – how shall you possess it? By dwelling therein.

IV.1   A.   And that for which there is no security [= movables] is acquired only by an act of drawing [from one place to another]:

           B.   *How on the basis of Scripture do we know that fact?*

           C.   It is written, "And if you sell anything to your neighbor or buy anything of your neighbor's hand" (Lev. 25:14) – this speaks of something that is acquired by passing from hand to hand [by drawing, that is, only movables].

           D.   *And from the viewpoint of R. Yohanan, who has said,* "By the law of the Torah, the transfer of cash serves to transfer title," *what is to be said?*

           E.   *The Tannaite authority here repeats the rule governing an ordinance deriving from rabbis.*

V.1   A.   Property for which there is no security is acquired along with property for which there is security through money, writ, and usucaption:

           B.   *How on the basis of Scripture do we know that fact?*

C. Said Hezekiah, "Said Scripture, 'And their father gave them gifts...with walled cities in Judah' (2 Chr. 21:3)." [Freedman: Thus they acquired the gifts, which were movables, in conjunction with the walled cities, that is, real estate.]

V.2 A. *The question was raised: "Do the movables have to be heaped upon the land to be transferred, or is that not the case?"*

B. *Said R. Joseph, "Come and take note: R.* Aqiba says, 'Any area of land, however minuscule, (1) is subject [to the laws of] peah, and [the laws of] first fruits, [26B] (2) [may be used as security] for writing a prosbol [which states that the Sabbatical Year will not negate the obligation to repay a loan], (3) [and may be used as collateral] for purchasing movable property with money, a contract, or usucaption' [M. Pe. 3:6]. *Now if you maintain that we require that the goods be piled up on the land, then what good is a very small piece of land?"*

C. *R. Samuel bar Bisna explained the matter in the presence of R. Joseph, "For instance, sticking a needle into it." [That would be acquired along with the land (Freedman).]*

D. *Said to him R. Joseph, "All you're doing is harassing us! Does the Tannaite authority go to so much trouble to give us a lesson about a needle?"*

E. *Said R. Ashi, "So who's going to tell us that he didn't suspend a pearl on the needle, wroth a thousand zuz?"*

F. *Come and take note:* Said R. Eleazar, "There was a case of a certain man of Meron who was in Jerusalem, who had a large volume of movables that he wanted to give away. They told him that he had no remedy except to transfer title along with a piece of real estate. What did he do? He went and he bought a land no bigger than a sela coin near Jerusalem, and he said, 'The north of this property belongs to Mr. So-and-so, and along with it go a hundred sheep and a hundred barrels of wine.' [And the same for the other directions.] When he died, the court confirmed his instructions." *Now, if you maintain that we require that the goods be piled up on the land, then what good would land the size of a sela coin ever serve under such circumstances?*

G. *Well, do you really think that it was actually land no bigger than a sela coin? What is the meaning of "sela" here? A big area. And why was it called "a sela"? Because it was hard as a rock [and the word "sela" means rock as well as sela coin].*

H. *Come and take note:* Said R. Judah said Rabbi, "There was the case of a man in Jerusalem who got sick – that is in accord with R. Eliezer – and some say, he was healthy – and that is in accord with rabbis. Now he had movables in abundance that he wanted to give away as a gift. They said to him that he had no remedy except to buy some land. What did he do? He went and purchased land of the size of a quarter-qab in the area near Jerusalem, and he stated, 'A square handbreadth of this land goes to Mr. So-and-so, and with it a hundred sheep and a hundred barrels of wine,' and then he died. Sages confirmed his instructions." *Now, if you maintain that we require that the goods be piled up on the land, then what good would land the size of a quarter-qab ever serve under such circumstances?*

I. *Here with what situation do we deal? It is in fact one in which the transfer consisted of cash. And that is a reasonable supposition, for if you should imagine that the gift really involved a hundred sheep and a hundred barrels of wine in fact, why couldn't he transfer title to him through barter?*

J. *Well, what are you thinking then, that it was money? So why couldn't he transfer title to him for the money through an act of drawing? So the sense must be: The recipient was not there to do the drawing. And here, too, the reason is that the recipient was not there to go through the process of acquiring the title as specified.*

K. *Well, then, why not transfer title to him through a third party?*

L. *He didn't want to rely on a third party, fearing that he would take off and eat up the gift!*

M. *So what's the sense of the language, he had no remedy...?*

N. *This is the sense of the matter: Because he had no confidence in a third party,* under those circumstances he had no remedy except to transfer the goods along with a piece of real estate.

O. *Come and take note:* There was the case involving Rabban Gamaliel and the elders, traveling on a ship when the time for removal of the agricultural gifts had come, requiring their transfer to their proper recipients. Said Rabban Gamaliel, "The tenth I intend to measure out and designate as first tithe is given [27A] to Joshua [who is a Levite], and the place in which it is located is rented to him. The other tenth which I intend to remove and designate as poor man's tithe is given to Aqiba ben Joseph, who will make it available to the poor, and the place in which it is located is rented to him" [M. M.S. 5:9C]. *Now this surely proves that the goods must be heaped up on the real estate.*

P. *No, this case is exceptional, for he didn't want to put them to any trouble.*

Q. *Come and take note of what* Rabbah bar Isaac said Rab said, "There are two classifications of deeds. If someone says, 'Take possession of the field in behalf of Mr. So-and-so [as my gift to him], and also write a deed for him,' he may retract on the deed [Slotki: if the donor, having given instructions to the witnesses, desires to have no written confirmation of the gift, he may recall the deed at any time before it reaches the donee], but he may not retract on the gift of the land. If he says, 'Take possession of the field on condition that you write a deed for him,' he may retract both the deed and the field." And R. Hiyya bar Abin said R. Huna said, "There are three classifications of deeds, *the two that we have said just now, and the following:* If the seller prior to the sale went ahead and wrote a deed, [Slotki: being anxious to sell, and in order to expedite the transaction on obtaining the consent of the buyer, he requests a scribe to prepare the deed before he knows whether the person to whom he wishes to sell would consent to buy], in line with that which we have learned in the Mishnah: They write a writ of sale to the seller, even though the buyer is not with him. But they do not write a writ of sale for the purchaser, unless the seller is with him [M. B.B. 10:3H-I]. Then, once the buyer has taken possession of the land, he acquires the deed as well, without regard to the location of the deed." *That proves that we do not require that the goods be piled up on the land.*

R.   *The case of a deed is exceptional, since it has a bearing on the land itself.*

S.   *But lo, in that regard there is a Tannaite statement:* And that is in line with what we have learned: "Movable property may be acquired along with landed property through transfer of money, deed, and exercising a right of possession."

T.   *That is decisive proof.*

V.3   A.   *The question was raised: "Do we require the explicit statement that the movables are acquired* by virtue of *the acquisition of the land, or do we not require such an explicit statement?"*

B.   *Come and take note of the Tannaite formulation, using the word "all," but the Tannaite formulation of the transaction does not require use of the words "by virtue of...."*

C.   *Well, from your viewpoint, is the language, "let him acquire it" stated as part of the Tannaite formulation [though we know that that has to be articulated]? Rather, the meaning is, he certainly must make use of the language, "let him acquire it," and here, too, he has to articulate the language, "by virtue of...."*

D.   *And the decided law is, we do not require that* the movables be piled up on the real estate, *but we do require that the language be used, "in virtue of...," and "let him acquire it."*

V.4   A.   *The question was raised: "What if the field is transferred through sale, but the movables are transferred as a gift?" [Are the movables then transferred along with the real estate?]*

B.   *Come and take note:* The tenth I intend to measure out and designate as first tithe is given to Joshua [who is a Levite], and the place in which it is located is rented to him.

C.   *That's decisive proof [the tithe was a gift, the place rented, which is like a sale].*

V.5   A.   *The question was raised:* If the field went to one party and the movables to another, what is the rule?

B.   *Come and take note:* The other tenth which I intend to remove and designate as poor man's tithe is given to Aqiba ben Joseph, who will make it available to the poor, and the place in which it is located is rented to him. *Now what is the meaning of "rented"? It is, rented for the tithe [so the locus was rented to Aqiba, but the tenth was for the poor (Freedman)]. If you prefer, I shall say: The case of R. Aqiba is exceptional, since he was serving in the agency of the poor.*

V.6   A.   Said Raba, "The rule that movables are acquired along with land applies only if the purchaser had paid money for all of the movables. But if he had not paid money for them all, he acquires only the movables that are covered by his money."

B.   *It has been taught on Tannaite authority in accord with the position of Raba:* Greater is the power of a document than the power of money, and greater is the power of money than the power of a document. [T.: For a document allows one to collect from indentured property, which is not the case with money.] Greater is the power of money, for money serves for the redemption of things that have been given as Valuations and as herem to the sanctuary, things that have been sanctified, and second tithe,

which is obviously not the case with a document [T. Ket. 2:1M-O].
[B.:] Greater is the power of a document, for a document removes
an Israelite woman from a marriage, which is not the case with
money. And greater is the power of both of them than the power
of usucaption, and greater is the power of usucaption than the
power of both of them. Greater is the power of both of them, that
both of them serve to acquire title to a Hebrew slave, which is not
the case with usucaption. And greater is the power of usucaption,
for usucaption serves if one has sold to the other ten fields in ten
provinces, so that, once the purchaser has acquired one of them
by usucaption, he has acquired all of them. [27B] Under what
circumstances? If he gave him the cash price for all of them. But
if he didn't give him the cash for all of them, he has acquired title
to only what his money has paid for [T. Ket. 2:1P-S].

V.7   A.   *That supports the position of Samuel, for* said Samuel, "If one has sold
             to the other ten fields in ten provinces, so that, once the purchaser
             has acquired one of them by usucaption, he has acquired all of
             them."

        B.   Said R. Aha b. R. Iqa, "You may know that that is the case, for if he
             had given him ten beasts tied by one cord and said to him, 'Acquire
             them,' wouldn't he acquire all of them?"

        C.   *He said to him, "But are the cases comparable? There the cord is in hand
             [tying all the beasts together], but in the case of the land, there is no cord
             that binds them all in the hand of the purchaser!"*

        D.   *There are those who say,* said R. Aha b. R. Iqa, "You may know that he
             does not as a matter of fact acquire them all, for if he had given him
             ten beasts tied by one cord and said to him, 'Acquire them,' would
             he acquire all of them?"

        E.   *But are the cases comparable? There the beasts are distinct entities, but
             here, the earth forms a single block.*

VI.1   A.   And property for which there is no security imposes the need
             for an oath on property for which there is security:

        B.   Said Ulla, "How on the basis of the Torah do we derive the
             rule of the superimposed oath [by which, if one is required to
             take an oath on one count, he may be forced to extend the
             oath to other counts]? As it is said, 'And the woman shall
             say, Amen, Amen,' *and we have learned in the Mishnah:* To
             what does she say, Amen, Amen?...'Amen that I have not
             gone aside while betrothed, married, awaiting levirate
             marriage, or wholly taken in Levirate marriage' [M. Sot. 2:5A-
             D]. *Now as this reference to her having been betrothed, what
             can it possibly mean? If we say that he expressed his warning
             of jealousy to her when she was betrothed, and then she went
             aside with the alleged lover, and is now made to drink the
             bitter water while still betrothed, then is a woman who has
             been merely betrothed required to undergo the ordeal of
             drinking the bitter water as a woman accused of adultery? Lo,
             we have learned in the Mishnah:* A betrothed girl and a
             deceased childless brother's widow awaiting levirate
             marriage neither undergo the ordeal of drinking the bitter
             water nor receive a marriage contract, since it is written,

'When a wife, being subject to her husband, goes astray' (Num. 5:29) – excluding the betrothed girl and the deceased childless brother's widow awaiting levirate marriage [M. Sot. 4:1A-C]. *And if it is proposed that she was warned when betrothed, then went aside with the alleged lover, and now has to drink that she has been married, do the waters test her under these conditions? Has it not been taught on Tannaite authority:* 'And the man shall be free from iniquity, and the woman shall bear her iniquity' (Num. 5:31). [The sense of the foregoing verse of Scripture is that] when the man is free of transgression, the water puts his wife to the test, [and] if the man is not free of transgression, the water does not put his wife to the test? *Rather, the oath can be imposed [to cover the specified matter] only because it is superimposed."*

C. *Well, we have found that the superimposed oath pertains in the case of the wife accused of adultery, which involves a prohibition of a religious nature. But how do we know that it applies to monetary matters?*

D. *A Tannaite statement of the household of R. Ishmael:* "It is based on an argument a fortiori, namely: If an accused wife [28A] who has not been subjected to an oath on the evidence of one witness, nonetheless is subject to a superimposed oath, a monetary claim, which can be brought on the strength of a single witness so that an oath has to be taken, surely will be subject to an oath on which other matters are superimposed!

E. *Well, we have found that the superimposed oath pertains in a case in which the claim is certain; what about one that is subject to doubt?*

F. *It has been taught on Tannaite authority:* R. Simeon b. Yohai says, "There is a statement concerning the taking of an oath outside of the Temple court [all oaths except the one taken by the accused wife are administered outside of the Temple court], and there is a statement covering the taking of an oath within the Temple court. Just as in the case of an oath taken inside the Temple court, the law has treated a case of doubt as equivalent to a case of certainty, so an oath that is imposed outside of the Temple court is such that the law has treated a case of doubt as equivalent to a case of certainty."

VI.2 A. Then to what extent is a superimposed oath carried?

B. Said R. Judah said Rab, "Even if he imposes the demand: 'Take an oath to me that you're not my slave.'"

C. *But in such a case we would excommunicate that character! For it has been taught on Tannaite authority:* He who calls his fellow a slave – let him be excommunicated. If he called him a mamzer, he is flogged with forty stripes. If he calls him wicked, he may take action against the slanderer's livelihood [cf. Freedman].

D. Rather, said Raba, "'Swear to me that you were not sold to me as a Hebrew slave.'"

E.   *Well, that's a perfectly honorable claim – he owes him money [and is claiming his service in payment for the money, so why should that be regarded as a superimposed oath]?*

F.   *Raba is consistent with his views expressed elsewhere, for said Raba, "A Hebrew slave is acquired as to his very body."*

G.   *Well, if so, then what we have is nothing other than a claim as to real estate!*

H.   *What might you have supposed? Only in the case of land is it common for people to make a sale in secret, so if he had sold the land, it would not be broadly known, but as for a case such as this, if he had sold himself, it would have been known? So we are informed that that is not the case.*

I.1 finds a scriptural basis for the rule of the Mishnah, so, too, II.1, III.1, IV.1, V.1. I.2, and II.2-6 qualify the rule at hand. Nos. 6+7 then continue the tangential inquiry. VI.1-2 find a scriptural foundation for the Mishnah's fact and extend the amplification of that fact.

1:6A-F

A.   Whatever is used as payment for something else –
B.   once this one has effected acquisition [thereof]
C.   the other has become liable for what is given in exchange.
D.   How so?
E.   [If] one exchanged an ox for a cow, or an ass for an ox,
F.   once this one has effected acquisition, the other has become liable for what is given in exchange.

I.1 A.   [Whatever is used as payment for something else:] *What is subject to barter? Money.* [Freedman: It is assumed that the language, Whatever is used as payment for something else includes money. Hence the point is: If A exchanges a cow for B's money, the money not being given as payment but as barter, just as an ox might be given, then as soon as A gets the money, B accepts liability for whatever happens to the cow, which is now subject to his title; that is the case even though if the money had been given as payment, the receipt of the money by A would not have transferred title of the cow to B.] *That then proves* money may be treated as an object of barter.

B.   *Said R. Judah, "This is the sense of the passage:* Whatever may be assessed as the value of another object, [excluding money, which, by definition, requires no assessment, since its value is explicit], [28B] once one party has taken possession of that object, the other becomes liable for what is given in exchange. *And that reading is reasonable, for lo, the passage proceeds as follows:* How so? If one has exchanged an ox for a cow or an ass for an ox [once one party has taken possession of that object, the other becomes liable for what is given in exchange]."

C.   *That's decisive proof.*

D.   *And with respect to what we originally imagined, which is that* money may serve as an object of barter, *what is the meaning of the language,* How so?

E.   *This is the sense of the matter:* Produce, too, can serve to effect a barter. How so? If one has exchanged an ox for a cow or an ass for an ox [once one party has taken possession of that object, the other becomes liable for what is given in exchange].

F.   *Well, that reading poses no problem to R. Sheshet, who does indeed maintain that produce may serve for the purposes of barter. But from the viewpoint of R. Nahman, who has maintained that produce cannot effect a barter, what is the sense of the matter?*

G.   *This is the sense of the matter:* Money may sometimes serve as a medium of barter. How so? If one has exchanged an ox for a cow or an ass for an ox [once one party has taken possession of that object, the other becomes liable for what is given in exchange].

H.   *And what's the operative consideration in his mind?*

I.   *He shares the viewpoint of R. Yohanan, who has said,* "By the law of the Torah, the transfer of cash serves to transfer title."

J.   Then how come they have said that only drawing a beast transfers title?

K.   It is a precautionary decree, lest the other say to him, "Your grain has burned up in the silo."

L.   *Rabbis made a precautionary decree only to cover what is commonplace, but not for what is uncommon* [and therefore biblical law pertains (Freedman)].

M.   *And from the perspective of R. Simeon b. Laqish, who* has said, "The medium of acquiring title through drawing a beast is explicitly required by the Torah," *then there is no problem if he concurs with R. Sheshet's view that produce can effect a barter, for the matter can be explained as does R. Sheshet. But if he concurs with R. Nahman, that produce cannot effect a barter, while money does not transfer title at all, then how is the matter to be worked out?*

N.   *You really have to say that he concurs with R. Sheshet.*

I.1 investigates the relationship between our case and a general rule, finding in our case proof of the prevailing principle.

1:6G-H

G.   **The right of the Most High is effected through money, and the right of ordinary folk through usucaption.**

H.   **One's word of mouth [dedication of an object] to the Most High is equivalent to one's act of delivery to an ordinary person.**

I.1   A.   *Our rabbis have taught on Tannaite authority:*

B.   How is the right of the Most High...effected through money? If the Temple treasurer handed over money for a beast, even if the animal is located on the other side of the world, he acquires title to it, but an ordinary person acquires title only by performing the act of drawing the beast.

C.   How is it so that one's word of mouth [dedication of an object] to the Most High is equivalent to one's act of delivery to an ordinary person? He who says, "This ox is a burnt-offering," "This house is sanctified," even if they are at the other side of the world, the sanctuary acquires title. In the case of an ordinary person, he acquires title only [29A] by performing an act of drawing or usucaption.

D. If a common person performed the act of drawing when the beast was worth a maneh but did not suffice to redeem the beast, paying the money, until the price rose to two hundred zuz, he must pay the two hundred. How come? Scripture says, "And he will pay the money and depart," meaning, if he has given the money, lo, these belong to him, but if not, they do not belong to him. If he performed the act of drawing when it was worth two hundred zuz but did not suffice to redeem it before the price fell to a maneh, he still has to pay two hundred zuz. How come? So that the rights of a common person should not be stronger than those of the sanctuary. If he redeemed it when it was worth two hundred but did not suffice to draw the beast before the price went down to a maneh, he has to pay the two hundred zuz. How come? Scripture says, "And he will pay the money and depart." If he redeems it at a maneh and did not suffice to perform the act of drawing before it went up to two hundred zuz, what he has redeemed is redeemed, and he pays only a maneh [T. Ar. 4:4A-G].

E. *Why? Here, too, should we not just say, So that the rights of a common person should not be stronger than those of the sanctuary?*

F. *But doesn't an ordinary person have to submit to the curse, "He who punished the generation of the blood will punish him who does not stand by his word"?*

I.1 provides a Tannaite complement, spelling out the rule of the Mishnah paragraph.

1:7

A. For every commandment concerning the son to which the father is subject – men are liable, and women are exempt.

B. And for every commandment concerning the father to which the son is subject, men and women are equally liable.

C. For every positive commandment dependent upon the time [of year], men are liable, and women are exempt.

D. And for every positive commandment not dependent upon the time, men and women are equally liable.

E. For every negative commandment, whether dependent upon the time or not dependent upon the time, men and women are equally liable,

F. except for not marring the corners of the beard, not rounding the corners of the head (Lev. 19:27), and not becoming unclean because of the dead (Lev. 21:1).

I.1   A.   *What is the meaning of For every commandment concerning the son to which the father is subject...? Should we say, from every religious duty that the son is required to do for the father, women are exempt? But hasn't it been taught on Tannaite authority: "Every man his mother and his father you shall fear" (Lev. 19:27) – I know only that that applies to the man. How do I know that it applies to the woman? When*

Scripture says, "his mother and his father you shall fear," lo, both of them are included?

B. *Said R. Judah, "This is the sense of the statement:* For every commandment concerning the son to which the father is subject to do for his son – men are liable, and women are exempt."

I.2 A. *Thus we learn as a Tannaite statement here that which our rabbis have taught on Tannaite authority:*

B. The father is responsible with respect to his son to circumcise him, to redeem him, to teach him Torah, to marry him off to a woman, and to teach him a trade.

C. And there are those who say, also to teach him to swim.

D. R. Judah says, "Anyone who does not teach his son a trade is as though he trains him to be a gangster" [T. Qid. 1:11F-H].

I.3 A. ...To circumcise him: *How on the basis of Scripture do we know that he must do so?*

B. *As it is written,* "And Abraham circumcised Isaac, his son" (Gen. 21:4).

C. *And how do we know that if his father did not circumcise him, the court is liable to circumcise him?*

D. *As it is written,* "Every male among you shall be circumcised" (Gen. 17:10).

E. *And how do we know that if the court did not circumcise him, he is liable to circumcise himself?*

F. *As it is written,* "And the uncircumcised male who will not circumcise the flesh of his foreskin, that soul shall be cut off" (Gen. 17:14).

G. *And how do we know that his mother is not liable to do so?*

H. *As it is written,* "And Abraham circumcised his son...as God had commanded him" (Gen. 21:4) – him, not her.

I. *So we have shown on the basis of Scripture that that was the rule governing that time, but how do we know that it is the rule for all time?*

J. *A Tannaite authority of the household of R. Ishmael:* "Wherever the language, 'command,' is used, the sole purpose is to encourage obedience both at that time and for all generations: As for encouragement, "But charge Joshua and encourage him and strengthen him" (Deut. 3:28); both at that time and for all generations: "From the day that the Lord gave commandment and onward throughout your generations" (Num. 15:23).

I.4 A. To redeem him: *How on the basis of Scripture do we know that he must do so?*

B. *As it is written,* "And all the firstborn of man among your sons you shall redeem" (Ex. 13:13).

C. *And whence do we know that if the father did not redeem him, he is liable to redeem himself?*

D. *As it is written,* "Nevertheless the firstborn of man you shall surely redeem" (Num. 18:15).

E. *And how do we know that his mother is not liable to do so?*

F.　　As it is written, "you shall redeem" which through a shift in vowels may be read, "you shall redeem yourself," so, one who is charged with redeeming himself is liable to redeem others, while one who is not obligated to redeem herself is not obligated to redeem others.

G.　　*So how do we know that she is not required to redeem herself?*

H.　　As it is written, "you shall redeem" which through a shift in vowels may be read, "you shall redeem yourself," thus: One whom others are commanded to redeem is commanded to redeem himself, one whom others are not commanded to redeem is not commanded to redeem herself.

I.　　*So how do we know that others are not commanded to redeem her?*

J.　　As it is written, "And all the firstborn of man among your sons shall you redeem" (Ex. 13:13) – your sons, not your daughters.

I.5　　A.　*Our rabbis have taught on Tannaite authority:*

　　　B.　[M. Bekh. 8:6M-P: If a man who was firstborn son had a firstborn son and was told that he had not been redeemed so that [he is] to redeem himself and [he is] to redeem his son, he comes before his son. R. Judah says, "His son comes before him. For the requirement of redeeming him [the father] falls upon *his* father, while the requirement of redeeming his son falls on him."] If he was to be redeemed and his son was to be redeemed, he takes precedence over his son.

　　　C.　R. Judah says, "His son takes precedence over him, for the religious duty pertains to his father, and the religious duty involving the son pertains to the father."

　　　D.　*Said R. Jeremiah, "All parties concur* [29B] *that in a case in which there are only five selas in hand, he takes precedence over his son. What is the reason? The religious duty involving himself is of greater importance. Where there is a disagreement, it concerns a case in which there are five selas worth of encumbered property, and five selas worth of unencumbered property. R. Judah takes the view that* a debt that derives from what is written in the Torah is classified within the same category as one that is obligated in a note, and therefore the five selas due for himself does the priest go and seize from encumbered property, and with the five selas of unencumbered property he redeems his son. Rabbis take the position that a debt that derives from what is written in the Torah is not classified within the same category as one that is obligated in a note [but is treated only as a verbal loan], and therefore the religious duty of redemption pertaining to the father takes precedence."

I.6　　A.　*Our rabbis have taught on Tannaite authority:*

　　　B.　If a man was obligated to redeem his son and to make a pilgrimage for the festival, he first redeems his son and then makes the pilgrimage for the festival.

　　　C.　R. Judah says, "He makes the pilgrimage for the festival and then he redeems his son, for the former is a religious duty that will pass with the passage of time, but the other is a religious duty that will not pass with the passage of time" [T. Bekh. 6:10A-C].

	D.	*Now there is no problem understanding the position of R. Judah, for he has stated the operative consideration in so many words, but what is the source in Scripture for the view of rabbis?*
	E.	Scripture said, "All the firstborn of your sons shall you redeem" (Ex. 34:20), and only then it is stated, "And none shall appear before me empty-handed" (Ex. 34:20).
I.7	A.	*Our rabbis have taught on Tannaite authority:*
	B.	How do we know that of a man had five firstborn sons by five wives, he is required to redeem all of them?
	C.	Scripture states, "All the firstborn of your sons shall you redeem" (Ex. 34:20).
	D.	*Well, what else is new? Obviously, Scripture has invoked as the criterion, the one that opens the womb first!*
	E.	*What might you otherwise have supposed? We should establish a verbal analogy between the meaning of firstborn here and that in the matter of inheritance, so that, just as in that case, the sense is, "the beginning of his strength" (Deut. 21:17), the same meaning applies here, too. So we are informed that that is not the case.*
I.8	A.	To teach him Torah: *How on the basis of Scripture do we know that fact?*
	B.	"And you shall teach them to your sons" (Deut. 11:19).
	C.	*And that in a case in which his father did not teach him, he is liable to teach himself?*
	D.	"And you shall study" (Deut. 5:1).
	E.	*And that she is not liable to do so?*
	F.	"You you shall teach" can be read "and you shall study," with the consequence: Whoever is commanded to study is commanded to teach, and whoever is not commanded to study is also not commanded to teach.
	G.	*And how do we know that she herself is not obligated to teach herself?*
	H.	"And you shall teach" can be read, "And you shall learn": One whom others are commanded to teach is commanded to teach himself, and one whom others are not commanded to teach is not commanded to teach herself.
	I.	So how do we know that others are not commanded to teach her?
	J.	Because it is written, "And you shall teach them to your sons" – not your daughters.
I.9	A.	*Our rabbis have taught on Tannaite authority:*
	B.	If he had to study Torah and his son likewise, he takes precedence over his son.
	C.	R. Judah says, "If his son was an eager student, gifted and retentive, his son takes precedence over him" [T. Bekh. 6:10F-H].
I.10	A.	*That is in line with the case of R. Jacob b. R. Aha bar Jacob, whose father sent him to Abbayye. When he came home, his father observed that his traditions were not very sharp. He said to him, "I'm better than you are. So you stay here, and I'll go."*

B. *Abbayye heard that he was coming. Now there was a certain demon in the household of rabbis that Abbayye consulted, so when only two disciples came in to study, even in daylight, they were harmed. Abbayye ordered,* "Nobody rent him a room [so he'll have to sleep in the schoolhouse], maybe there'll be a miracle."

C. *So he came and spent the night in the schoolhouse. The demon appeared to him like a seven-headed dragon. Every time he fell on his knees, one head fell off. But the next day he rebuked them:* "So if there weren't a miracle, you would have endangered my life."

I.11   A. *Our rabbis have taught on Tannaite authority:*

       B. **If someone had to study the Torah and get married, let him study the Torah and then get married. But if he can't live without a wife, let him get married and then study the Torah [T. Bekh. 6:10D-E].**

I.12   A. Said R. Judah said Samuel, "The law is: One marries a wife and then studies Torah."

       B. R. Yohanan said, "With a millstone around his neck, is he going to study much Torah?"

       C. *But there is really no disagreement. The one refers to us, the other to them [in the Land of Israel].*

I.13   A. R. Hisda praised R. Hamnuna before R. Huna as a major authority. He said to him, "When he comes to hand, bring him to me."

       B. *When he came, he saw that he wasn't wearing a head covering. "Why don't you have a head covering?" he asked.*

       C. *He said to him, "Because I'm not married."*

       D. *He turned his face away: "See that you don't come before me until you are married."*

       E. *R. Huna was consistent with views expressed elsewhere, for he said,* "Someone twenty years of age and not married spends his whole day in sin."

       F. *Do you really think, in sin?! Rather: Spends his whole day thinking about sin.*

I.14   A. *Said Raba, and so did a Tannaite authority of the household of R. Ishmael:* "Until someone is twenty years old, the Holy One, blessed be He, sits and looks forward to when a man will marry a wife. But once he reaches the age of twenty and has not married, he says, 'Blast be his bones.'"

I.15   A. *Said R. Hisda, "The fact that I am better than my fellows is because I got married at sixteen, and if I'd married at fourteen, [30A] I'd be able to say to Satan, 'An arrow in your eye.'"*

I.16   A. *Said Raba to R. Nathan bar Ammi, "While your hand is still on your son's neck, marry him off, that is, between sixteen and twenty-two." Others say, "Eighteen and twenty-four."*

I.17   A.   *There is a conflict of Tannaite statements on the same matter:*

       B.   *"Raise up a youth in the way he should go" (Prov. 22:6):*

       C.   *R. Judah and R. Nehemiah –*

       D.   *One said, "[Youth means] from sixteen to twenty-two."*

       E.   *The other: "From eighteen to twenty-four."*

I.18   A. To what extent is a man obligated to teach his son Torah?

B. Said R. Judah said Samuel, "The exemplary case is Zebulun b. Dan, whose grandfather taught him Scripture, Mishnah, talmud analysis, law and lore."

C. *An objection was raised:* If he taught him Scripture, he need not teach him Mishnah, and said Raba, "Scripture refers to Torah, as in the case of Zebulun b. Dan, but also not as in the case of Zebulun b. Dan: As in the case of Zebulun b. Dan, whose grandfather taught him, but not as in the case of Zebulun b. Dan, *for in that case involved were lessons in Scripture, Mishnah, talmud analysis, laws and lore, but here involved is only Scripture alone."*

D. *And is the grandfather so obligated? And hasn't it been taught on Tannaite authority:* "And you shall teach them to your sons" (Deut. 11:19) – and not to your grandsons. And how am I to interpret, "And you shall make them known to your sons and your sons' sons" (Deut. 4:9)? This lets you know that whoever teaches his son Torah is regarded by Scripture as though he had taught not only him but also his son and his son's son to the end of all generations.

E. *He made his statement in line with the position of the following Tannaite authority, as has been taught on Tannaite authority:* "And you shall teach them to your sons": I know only that this applies to your sons. How do I know that it applies to your sons' sons? It is said, "And you shall make them known to your sons and your sons' sons." Then why say, " "And you shall teach them to your sons"? To teach: Your sons but not your daughters.

I.19 A. Said R. Joshua b. Levi, "He who teaches his grandson Torah is credited by Scripture as though he had received [Torah] from Mount Horeb. For it is said, 'And you shall make them known to your children and your children's children' (Deut. 4:9), and, juxtaposed next, it is written, 'The day that you stood before the Lord your God in Horeb' (Deut. 4:10)."

B. *R. Hiyya bar Abba came across R. Joshua b. Levi, wearing a plain cloth on his head [not a kerchief indicative of his status as a major authority] and bringing a child to the house of assembly. He said to him, "So what's going on?"*

C. *He said to him, "So is it such a small thing that is written in Scripture, 'And you shall make them known to your children and your children's children' (Deut. 4:9), and, juxtaposed next, it is written, 'The day that you stood before the Lord your God in Horeb' (Deut. 4:10)?"*

D. *From that time onward R. Hiyya bar Abba didn't taste breakfast sausage before hearing a child review his lesson and adding a verse to it.*

E. *Rabbah bar R. Huna didn't taste breakfast sausage before he brought a child to the schoolhouse.*

I.20 A. *Said R. Safra said R. Joshua b. Hananiah,* "What is the meaning of the verse, 'and you shall teach them diligently to your children' (Deut. 6:7)? Read the letters to yield not 'repeat' but rather 'divide into three,' so that a person should

always divide years into three parts: a third for Scripture, a
third for Mishnah, a third for talmud."

B.   *So does someone know how many years he will live?*

C.   *The teaching is required for days [not years].*

What follows is of a different order; it is another instance in which
the sense or usage of Scripture is clarified in its own terms, and not with
the purpose of showing the origin of law or yielding details of law.

I.21   A.   Therefore the early masters were called scribes [those who
numbered], because they would count up all the letters in the
Torah. For they would say, "The W in the word belly (gahon)
[Lev. 11:42: "whatever goes on the belly"] is the midpoint
among all of the letters of a scroll of the Torah. The words
'diligently enquire' [at Lev. 10:16] mark the midpoint among
the words; the word 'he shall be shaven' (Lev. 13:33) marks
half the verses; in the verse, 'the boar out of the wood does
ravage it' (Ps. 80:14), the ayin of the word for forest marks the
midpoint of the Psalms; 'but he, being full of compassion,
forgives their iniquity' (Ps. 78:38) marks the midpoint of all
of the verses [of Psalms]."

I.22   A.   *R. Joseph raised this question: "Is the W in the word belly
assigned to the first half or the second half?"*

         B.   *They said to him, "Let's get a scroll of the Torah and count
them up. Didn't Rabbah bar R. Hannah state, 'They didn't
move from the spot until they brought a scroll of the Torah
and counted them up?'"*

         C.   *He said to them, "Well, they were experts in the matter of the
defective and full spellings of words, but we're not [so even if
we counted, we wouldn't know]."*

I.23   A.   *R. Joseph raised this question: "Is the word 'he shall be
shaven' (Lev. 13:33) assigned to the former half or the latter
half?"*

         B.   *Said to him Abbayye, "As to the count of the verses, in any
event, we certainly can bring a scroll and count them up."*

         C.   *As to counting up the verses, we're no experts, for when R. Aha
bar Ada came, he said, "In the West the following verse is
divided into three parts, each counted on its own: 'And the
Lord said to Moses, Lo, I come to you in a thick cloud' (Ex.
19:9)."*

I.24   A.   *Our rabbis have taught on Tannaite authority:* There are 5,888
verses in the Torah; the Psalms are longer by eight,
Chronicles are less by eight.

I.25   A.   *Our rabbis have taught on Tannaite authority:*

         B.   ["And you shall teach them diligently to your children"
(Deut. 6:7)]: "[That is to say, 'Impress them upon your
children':]

         C.   [The meaning of "impressing," or "repeating," is that] the
teachings of the Torah should be so sharp in your mouth that
when someone asks you something, you should not stammer.

         D.   But you should give a reply forthwith.

E. So Scripture says, [30B] "Say to wisdom, 'you are my sister,' and call understanding your kinswoman" (Prov. 7:4).

F. "Bind them on your fingers, write them on the table of your heart" (Prov. 7:3).

G. "Your arrows are sharp" (Ps. 45:6).

H. "The peoples fall under you, they sink into the heart of the king's enemies" (Ps. 45:6).

I. "As arrows in the hand of a mighty man, so are the children of one's youth" (Ps. 127:4).

J. And concerning these children: "Happy is the man who has his quiver full of them, they shall not be put to shame when they speak with their enemies in the gate" (Ps. 127:5) [Sifré Deut. XXXIV:I.1-2].

K. *What is the meaning of* their enemies in the gate?

L. Said R. Hiyya bar Abba, "Even father and his son, master and his disciple: When they are engaged in Torah study in the same topic, they turn into mutual enemies, but they don't leave the spot until they come to love one another, as it is said, 'Wherefore it is said in the book of the wars of the Lord, love is at the end' (Num. 21:14)."

I.26 A. *Our rabbis have taught on Tannaite authority:*

B. "Therefore impress these my words upon your very heart; [bind them as a sign on your hand and let them serve as a symbol on your forehead; and teach them to your children, reciting them when you stay at home and when you are away, when you lie down and when you get up, and inscribe them on the doorposts of your house and on your gates, to the end that you and your children may endure in the land that the Lord swore to your fathers to assign to them, as long as there is a Heaven over the earth]" (Deut. 11:18-21):

C. This use of the word [impress, which can be read to sound like "medicine, ointment"] indicates that words of Torah are compared to a life-giving medicine.

D. The matter may be compared to the case of a man [Sif. Deut.: king] who grew angry with his son and gave him a severe blow, but then put a salve on the wound and said to him, "My son, so long as this bandage is on the wound, eat whatever you like, drink whatever you like, and wash in either warm or cold water, and nothing will do you injury. But if you remove the bandage, the sore will immediately begin to produce ulcers."

E. So the Holy One, blessed be He, said to Israel, "My children, I have created in you an impulse to do evil, than which nothing is more evil.

F. "'Sin crouches at the door and to you is its desire' (Gen. 4:7).

G. "Keep yourselves occupied with teachings of the Torah, and [sin] will not control you.

H. "But if you leave off studying words of the Torah, lo, it will control you, as it is said, 'and to you is its desire' (Gen. 4:7).

I.   "And not only so, but all of its undertakings concern you. But if you want, you will control it, as it is said, 'But you may rule over it' (Gen. 4:7)."

J.   And Scripture says, "And if your enemy is hungry, give him bread to eat, and if he is thirsty, give him water to drink, for you will heap coals of fire upon his head" (Prov. 25:21-22) [Sifré Deut. XLVI.I.2].

Here the verse of Scripture provides information, rather than requiring amplification in its own terms:

I.27   A.   *Our rabbis have taught on Tannaite authority:*

       B.   So formidable is the lust to do evil that even its creator has called it evil, as it is written, "For that the desire of man's heart is evil from his youth" (Gen. 8:21).

       C.   Said R. Isaac, "The desire to do evil renews itself daily against a person: 'Every imagination of the thoughts of his heart was only evil every day' (Gen. 6:5)."

       D.   And said R. Simeon b. Levi, "A man's inclination [to do evil] prevails over him every day and seeks to kill him. For it is said, 'The wicked watches the righteous and seeks to slay him' (Ps. 37:32). And if the Holy One, blessed be He, were not there to help him, he could not withstand it. For it is said, 'The Lord will not leave him in his hand nor suffer him to be condemned when he is judged' (Ps. 37:32)."

I.28   A.   *A Tannaite statement of the household of R. Ishmael:* "If that vile one meets you, drag it to the house of study. If it is a stone, it will dissolve. If it is iron, it will be pulverized. If it is a stone, it will dissolve," as it is written, "Lo, everyone who is thirsty, come to water" (Isa. 55:1). And it is written, "The water wears down stones" (Job 14:19). "If it is iron, it will be pulverized," as it is written, "Is not my word like fire, says the Lord, and like a hammer that breaks the rock into pieces" (Jer. 23:29).

By contrast to the foregoing, the following appeals to Scripture as a source of facts pertinent to the Mishnah's rules (or other Tannaite rules).

I.29   A.   To marry him off to a woman:

       B.   *What is the source in Scripture?*

       C.   Because it is said in Scripture, "Take wives for yourselves and produce sons and daughters, and take wives for your sons and give your daughters to husbands" (Jer. 29:6).

       D.   *Well, there's no problem about marrying off a son, the decision is his. But as regards the daughter, does the matter depend on him? [You have to find the husband, too.]*

       E.   *This is the sense of Jeremiah's statement: "Give her a dowry, clothes, ornaments, so men will come looking for her."*

I.30   A.   And to teach him a trade:

       B.   *What is the source in Scripture?*

C. Said Hezekiah, "Said Scripture, 'See to a livelihood with the wife whom you love' (Qoh. 9:9)."

D. If this refers literally to a wife, then, just as the father is obligated to find a wife for him, so he is obligated to teach him a trade. If the meaning of "wife" is as a metaphor for Torah, then just as he is obligated to teach him Torah, so he is obligated to teach him a trade.

I.31 A. And there are those who say, also to teach him to swim:

B. *How come?*

C. *Because it can save his life.*

I.32 A. R. Judah says, "Anyone who does not teach his son a trade trains him to be a gangster":

B. *Can you imagine, to be a gangster?! Rather, is as though he trains him to be a gangster.*

C. And what's at issue here?

D. *At issue here is training him in commerce [Judah rejecting commerce].*

II.1 A. And for every commandment concerning the father to which the son is subject, men and women are equally liable:

B. *What is the definition of for every commandment concerning the father to which the son is subject? Should we say, for all of the religious duties that a father is obligated to do for his son, women are obligated as well? But hasn't it been taught on Tannaite authority:* The father is responsible with respect to his son to circumcise him, to redeem him – the father, not the mother.

C. *Said R. Judah, "This is the sense of the statement:* For every commandment concerning the father to which the son is subject, men and women are equally liable. *Thus we learn the Tannaite statement in line with that which our rabbis have taught on Tannaite authority:* '"You shall fear every man his father and his mother" (Lev. 19:3) – I know that that is so only for a man. How do I know it applies to a woman? Scripture states, "you shall fear," covering both. Then why state "man"? A man has the possibility of carrying this out, but a woman doesn't, since she is subject to the authority of a third party."'

What makes the foregoing of interest is that it shows us what is by now a recurrent pattern, that is, a citation of a verse, a paraphrase of its sense, and extension of its range of application.

D. Said R. Idi bar Abin said Rab, "If she was divorced, however, both of them are equally obligated."

II.2 A. *Our rabbis have taught on Tannaite authority:*

B. It is said, "Honor your father and your mother" (Ex. 20:12), and it is further said, "Honor the Lord with your wealth" (Prov. 3:9).

C. Scripture thereby establishes an analogy between the honor of father and mother and the honor of the Omnipresent.

D. It is said, "He who curses his father or his mother will certainly die" (Prov. 20:20), and it is said, "Any person who curses his God will bear his sin" (Lev. 24:15).

E.   Scripture thereby establishes an analogy between cursing
      father and mother and cursing the Omnipresent.

F.   But it is not possible to refer to smiting Heaven [in the way in
      which one is warned not to hit one's parents].

G.   And that is entirely reasonable, for all three of them are
      partners [in a human being] [Sifra Qedoshim CXCV:II.3].

II.3   A.   *Our rabbis have taught on Tannaite authority:*

       B.   Three form a partnership in the creation of a human being, the Holy
            One, blessed be He, one's father and one's mother. When someone
            honors father and mother, said the Holy One, blessed be He, "I
            credit it to them as though I had lived among them and they
            honored me."

II.4   A.   *It has been taught on Tannaite authority:*

       B.   Rabbi says, "It is perfectly self-evident to the One who spoke and
            brought the world into being that the son honors his mother more
            than his father, because [31A] she influences him with kind words.
            Therefore the Holy One, blessed be He, gave precedence to
            honoring the father over honoring the mother. But it also is
            perfectly self-evident before the One who spoke and brought the
            world into being that the son fears the father more than the mother,
            because he teaches him Torah. Therefore the Holy One, blessed be
            He, gave priority to fear of the mother over fear of the father."

II.5   A.   *A Tannaite authority repeated before R. Nahman:* "When someone gives
            anguish to his father or his mother, said the Holy One, blessed be
            He, 'I did well in not living among them, for if I lived among them,
            they would have given me anguish, too.'"

II.6   A.   Said R. Isaac, "Whoever secretly carries out a transgression is
            as though he stepped on the feet of the Presence of God:
            'Thus said the Lord, the heaven is my throne, and the earth is
            my footstool' (Isa. 66:1)."

II.7   A.   Said R. Joshua b. Levi, "It is forbidden to walk about stiffly
            erect, even for four cubits, for it is written, 'The whole earth
            is full of his glory' (Isa. 6:3)."

       B.   R. Huna b. R. Joshua wouldn't walk four cubits bareheaded.
            He said, "The Presence of God is above my head."

II.8   A.   A widow's son asked R. Eliezer, "If father says, 'Give me a glass of
            water,' and mother says, 'Give me a glass of water,' to which of
            them do I give precedence?"

       B.   He said to him, "Ignore the honor owing to your mother and carry
            out the act of respect owing to your father, for you and your mother
            are equally obligated to pay respect to your father."

       C.   He came before R. Joshua, who said the same to him.

       D.   "My lord, if she is divorced, what is the law?"

       E.   He said to him, "From the character of your eyelids, it's obvious
            that you're a widow's son. Pour out some water for them in a basin
            and cackle for them like chickens."

II.9   A.   *Ulla the elder gave this exposition at the gate of the patriarch:*
            "What is the meaning of Scripture, 'All the kings of the earth
            shall praise you, Lord, for they have heard the words of your
            mouth' (Ps. 138:4)? What is stated is not, 'the word of your
            mouth,' but 'the words of your mouth.' So when the Holy

One, blessed be He, said, 'I am the Lord your God' 'you shall have no other Gods before me,' (Ex. 20:2-3), said the nations of the world, 'All he wants is his own self-aggrandizement.' When he said, 'Honor your father and your mother' (Ex. 20:12), they retracted and confessed to the validity of the first statements as well."

B.   *Raba said, "From the following verse [the same point can be drawn, namely:] 'The beginning of your word is true' (Ps. 119:160) – the beginning but not the end? But what comes at the end of your word – the truth of the beginning of your word is understood."*

II.10   A.   *They asked R. Ulla, "To what extent is one obligated to honor father and mother?"*

B.   He said to them, "Go and observe how a certain gentile has treated his father in Ashkelon, and Dama b. Netinah is his name. On one occasion sages wanted to do business with him in the amount of six hundred thousand but the keys were lying under his father's pillow, and he would not disturb him."

C.   Said R. Judah said Samuel, "They asked R. Eliezer, to what extent is one obligated to honor one's father and one's mother? He said to them, 'Go and observe how a certain gentile has treated his father in Ashkelon, and Dama b. Netinah is his name. On one occasion they wanted to buy from him precious stones for the ephod, in the amount of six hundred thousand *(R. Kahana repeated as the Tannaite version,* eight hundred thousand) but the keys were lying under his father's pillow, and he would not disturb him. Another year the Holy One, blessed be He, gave him his reward, for a red cow was born to him in his corral, and sages of Israel came to him. He said to them, "I know full well of you that if I should demand of you all the money in the world, you will give it to me. But now I ask of you only that sum of money that I lost in honor of my father."'"

D.   And said R. Hanina, "Now if someone who is not subject to commandments acts in such a way, then if someone who is subject to the commandment acts in such a way, all the more so! For said R. Hanina, 'Greater is he who is commanded and acts on that account than he who is not commanded and acts on that account.'"

II.11   A.   *Said R. Joseph, "To begin with, I thought that if someone said to me, the decided law accords with R. Judah, that a blind person is exempt from the obligation of the commandments, I should have made a big party for all the rabbis, since I'm not obligated to do them but I do them anyhow. But now that I've heard the statement of R. Hanina, 'Greater is he who is commanded and acts on that account than he who is not commanded and acts on that account,' to the contrary, if someone will tell me that the decided law is not in accord with R. Judah, I'll make a big party for all the rabbis."*

II.12   A.   When R. Dimi came, he said, "Once [Dama] was dressed in a gold embroidered silk coat, sitting among the Roman nobles, and his mother came along and tore it from him and hit him on the head and spat in his face, but he did not in any way answer back to her."

II.13   A.   *A Tannaite statement of Abimi b. R. Abbahu:* There is he who feeds his father pheasant to eat but this drives the son from the world, and there is he who binds his father up to the grinding wheel, [31B] and this brings the son into the world to come. [Someone fed the father pheasants but when the father asked how he could afford them, said, "It's none of your business, chew and eat." By contrast, someone was grinding on a mill and the father was summoned for the corvée, so the son said to the father, "You grind for me and I'll go in your place."]

II.14   A.   Said R. Abbahu, "For instance, my son Abimi carried out in an exemplary manner the religious duty of honor of parents."

      B.   *Abimi had five ordained sons when his father was yet alive, but when R. Abbahu came and called at the gate, he ran and opened for him, saying, "Coming, coming," until he got there.*

      C.   *Once he said to him, "Bring me a glass of water." Before he got there, the father dozed off. So he bent over him until he woke up. This brought it about that Abimi succeeded in explaining "a song of Asaph" (Ps. 79:1).*

The foregoing is little more than a casual allusion to a phrase, without any further amplification thereof, on the one side, or demonstration therefrom, on the other.

II.15   A.   *Said R. Jacob bar Abbuha to Abbayye, "How about someone like me? For when I come home from the household of the master, father pours a cup for me, and mother mixes – what am I supposed to do?"*

      B.   *He said to him, "Well,* take it from your mother but not from your father, *since he, too, is obligated to study the Torah, it may be an insult to him."*

II.16   A.   *R. Tarfon's mother – whenever she wanted to get into bed, he would bend down and let her climb up on his back, and when she wanted to get out, she would step down on him. He went and praised himself in the schoolhouse.* They said to him, "So you still haven't got to half the honor that is owing: Has she thrown down a money bag in your presence into the sea, without your answering back to her?"

II.17   A.   *R. Joseph – when he heard the sound of his mother's steps, he said, "Let me arise before the Presence of God, who approaches."*

II.18   A.   Said R. Yohanan, "Happy is he who never knew his parents [since it is so hard properly to honor them]."

II.19   A.   R. Yohanan – when his mother was carrying him, his father died, and when his mother bore him, she died.

      B.   The same is so of Abbayye.

      C.   *But how can that be so,* when he was always saying, "Mother told me"?

      D.   *That was his stepmother.*

II.20   A.   *R. Assi had an aged mother. She said to him, "I want some jewelry." So he made it for her.*

      B.   *"I want a man."*

      C.   *"I'll go looking for someone for you."*

      D.   *"I want a man as handsome as you."*

      E.   *At that he left her and went to the Land of Israel. He heard that she was coming after him. He came to R. Yohanan and asked him,* "What is the law on my leaving the Land and going abroad?"

F. He said to him, "It is forbidden."

G. "What is the law as to going to greet my mother?"

H. He said to him, "I don't know."

I. *He waited a bit and then went and came back.* He said to him, "Assi, you obviously want to go. May the Omnipresent bring you back here in peace."

J. *Assi came before R. Eleazar. He said to him, "God forbid! Maybe he was mad?"*

K. *"What did he say to you?"*

L. "May the Omnipresent bring you back here in peace."

M. *He said to him, "Well, if he had been angry, he wouldn't have given you a blessing."*

N. *In the meanwhile he heard that it was her coffin that was coming. He said, "If I had known that, I wouldn't have gone out."*

II.21 A. *Our rabbis have taught on Tannaite authority:*

B. The child must honor the parent in life and after death.

C. In life: How so? If one is obeyed somewhere because of his father, he shouldn't say, "Let me go for my own sake," "Wish me Godspeed for my own sake," "Free me for my own sake," but only, "For my father's sake."

D. And after death: How so? If one was saying something he had heard from his father's own mouth, he should not say, "This is what my father said," but rather, "This is what my father, my teacher, for whose resting place may I be an atonement, said."

E. *But that is the rule* only during the first twelve months after his death. From that point onward, he says only, "of blessed memory, for the life of the world to come."

II.22 A. *Our rabbis have taught on Tannaite authority:*

B. A sage changes the name of his father and the name of his teacher, but the interpreter doesn't change the name of his father or the name of his teacher. [The sage when using an interpreter to give a teaching he heard from his father does not refer to his father by name but by the formula, "my father and my teacher," but the interpreter doesn't do that (Freedman).]

C. *Whose father? Should I say, the father of the interpreter? Isn't the interpreter obligated to honor his parents?*

D. Rather, said Raba, "The name of the sage's father or the name of the sage's teacher."

E. *That would be like the case of Mar b. R. Ashi; when he gave an exposition in the assembly, he would say to the interpreter, "This is what my father, my teacher said," and the interpreter would say, "This is what R. Ashi said."*

II.23 A. *Our rabbis have taught on Tannaite authority:*

B. What is the form of reverence that is owing?

C. The son should not sit in his place, speak in his place, contradict him.

D. What is the form of honor that is owing?

E. The son should feed him, give him drink, dress him, cover him, bring him in and take him out [Sifra CXCIX.I.5].

II.24 A. *The question was raised:* [32A] "At whose expense [must he feed him and so on]?"

B.   R. Judah said Samuel said, "The son's."

C.   R. Nathan bar Oshayya said, "The father's."

D.   *Rabbis gave a ruling to R. Jeremiah, some say, to the son of R. Jeremiah, in accord with him who said, "The father's."*

E.   *An objection was raised:* "Honor your father and your mother" (Ex. 20:12), and further, "Honor the Lord with your property" (Prov. 3:9) – just as the latter means, at one's own expense, so the former has the same meaning. *But if you say that it is at the father's expense, then what does it cost the son?*

F.   It costs him time off from his own work.

G.   *Come and take note:* **Two brothers, two partners, a father and a son, a master and his disciple redeem one another's second tithe; and feed one another with the tithe set aside for the poor [T. M.S. 4:7A].** But if you say that it is at the son's expense, then it will turn out that this fellow is paying off his debt out of what belongs to the poor.

H.   *This speaks only of what is excess [over and above the father's needs, over and above what is ordinarily expected].*

I.   *If so, then what's the point of the continuation of the Tannaite formulation:* Said R. Judah, "May a curse come upon someone who feeds his father tithe set aside for the poor?" *Now if it speaks only of what is excess [over and above the father's needs, over and above what is ordinarily expected], then what difference does it make?*

J.   *It's a disgrace for the father.*

K.   *Come and take note:* They asked R. Eliezer, "To what extent does the obligation of honoring father and mother extend?" He said to them, "To the extent that he might take a money bag and toss it into the sea in his presence, and the child will not yell at him." *Now if you maintain that the money belongs to the father, what difference does it make to the son?*

L.   It is a case in which the son is supposed to inherit the father's estate.

M.   *That would be like the case of Rabbah b. R. Huna. For R. Huna tore up silk in the presence of Rabbah his son. He said, "I will go and see whether he gets mad or not."*

N.   *But if he got mad, then wouldn't he violate the commandment,* "You shall not put a stumbling block before the blind" (Lev. 19:14) *[by baiting the son to treat him disrespectfully]?*

O.   *He renounced the honor owing to him.*

P.   *But didn't [Huna] violate the commandment,* "You shall not destroy the trees thereof" (Deut. 20:19) *[wasting property]?*

Q.   *He did it in the seam.*

R.   *So maybe that's why he didn't lose his temper.*

S.   *He did it when he was already upset about something [and yet he didn't insult the father].*

II.25   A.   **If those to be stoned were confused with those to be burned [M. San. 9:3D]:** *R. Ezekiel repeated the passage at hand for Rami, his son, as follows:* "'If those to be burned were confused with those to be stoned, R. Simeon says, "They are judged to be executed by stoning, for burning is the more severe of the two modes of execution" [M. 9:3E].'"

B. *Said R. Judah to him, "Father, do not repeat it in this way. Why give as the reason, 'Because burning is more stringent'? Rather, derive the fact that the larger number of those who are put to death are put to death through stoning.* [Freedman, p. 536, n. 3: For 'if criminals condemned to burning became mixed up with others condemned to stoning' implies that the latter were in the majority, as the smaller number is lost in the larger.] *Instead, this is how it should be repeated:* If those to be stoned were confused with those to be burned, R. Simeon says, 'They are judged to be executed by stoning, for burning is the more severe of the two modes of execution' [M. 9:3D-E]."

C. *He said to him, "Then take up the concluding clause:* But sages say, 'They are adjudged to be executed by burning, for stoning is the more severe mode of execution of the two' [M. 9:3F]. *Why invoke the criterion that stoning is the more severe penalty? But derive that point from the simple fact that the greater number of those who are put to death are put to death through burning?"*

D. *He said to him, "In that case, it is rabbis who frame matters so as to state to R. Simeon, 'In accord with your view, for you maintain that burning is more severe,' but to the contrary,* stoning is the more severe [Freedman, p. 536, n. 4: but their ruling could be deduced from the fact that the majority are to be executed through burning]."

E. *Said Samuel to R. Judah, "Sharp one! Do not say things in this way to your father! This is what has been taught on Tannaite authority:* Lo, if one's father was violating the teachings of the Torah, he should not say to him, 'Father, you have violated the teachings of the Torah.' Rather, one should say to him, 'Father, this is what is written in the Torah.'"

F. *Still, he's giving him grief!*

G. Rather, he says to him, "Father, there is a verse of Scripture that is written in the Torah, and this is what it says. [He does not state the law directly but lets the father draw his own inference (Freedman, p. 536, n. 8)]."

II.26 A. Eleazar b. Matthias says, "If father says, 'Give me a drink of water,' and I have a religious duty to carry out, I ignore the honor owing to father and I carry out the religious duty, for both father and I are obligated to carry out religious duties."

B. Issi b. Judah says, "If it is possible for the religious duty to be done by someone else, then let it be done by someone else, and he should go and carry out the honor owing to his father."

C. Said R. Mattenah, "The decided law is in accord with Issi b. Judah."

II.27 A. Said R. Isaac b. Shila said R. Mattenah said R. Hisda, "If a father renounced the honor that is coming to him, the honor that is coming to him is validly renounced. If the master renounced the honor that is coming to him, the honor that is coming to him is not renounced."

B. And R. Joseph said, "Even if a master renounced the honor that is owing to him, the honor that is owing to him is renounced: 'And the Lord went before them by day' (Ex. 13:21)."

C.   Said Raba, "But how are the cases comparable? In that case, the Holy One, blessed be He – the world is his, and the Torah is his, so he can well renounce the honor that is owing to him. [32B] But in this case, does the Torah belong to the master [that he can renounce the honor owing to it]?"

D.   Said Raba, "Yessiree, the Torah belongs to him, for it is written, 'And in his Torah he meditates day and night' (Ps. 1:2)."

E.   Well, is that so! For Raba was serving drinks at the celebration of his son's wedding, and when he offered a cup to R. Pappa and R. Huna b. R. Joshua, they arose in his honor; when he offered it to R. Mari and R. Phineas b. R. Hisda, they didn't get up in his honor, so he got mad and said, "Are these rabbis rabbis, but those rabbis not rabbis?"

F.   Furthermore, R. Pappa was serving drinks at the wedding celebration of Abba Mar his son, and he offered a cup to R. Isaac b. R. Judah and he didn't arise in his honor, and he got mad.

G.   Nonetheless, they ought to have paid him respect.

II.28 A.   Said R. Ashi, "Even from the perspective of him who has said, 'The master who has renounced the honor coming to him – the honor coming to him is renounced,' nonetheless, the patriarch who has renounced the honor coming to him – the honor coming to him is not renounced."

B.   An objection was raised: There was the case concerning R. Eliezer, R. Joshua, and R. Sadoq, who were reclining at the banquet of the son of Rabban Gamaliel, and Rabban Gamaliel was standing and pouring drinks for them. He gave the cup to R. Eliezer, and he did not take it. He gave it to R. Joshua and he accepted it. Said to him R. Eliezer, "What's going on, Joshua! Should we recline while Rabban Gamaliel is standing and serving drinks to us?"

C.   He said to him, "We find that a greater one than he served as a waiter, namely, Abraham, the greatest one of his generation, did so, and concerning him it is written, 'And he stood over them' (Gen. 18:8). And should you say, they appeared to him as ministering angels [on which account he acted as he did], they appeared to him only in the guise of Arabs. So in our case, shouldn't the majestic Rabban Gamaliel stand and pour drinks for us?"

D.   Said to them R. Sadoq, "How long are you going to ignore the honor owing to the Omnipresent and concentrate only on the honor owing to mortals? The Holy One, blessed be He, brings back the winds and causes the mists to ascend, rain to fall, earth to yield, so setting a table before every single person, and, as to us, shouldn't the majestic Rabban Gamaliel stand over us and pour?"

E.   Rather, if there was such a statement, this is what the statement actually said:

F.   Said R. Ashi, "Even from the perspective of him who has said, 'The patriarch who has renounced the honor coming to him – the honor coming to him is renounced,' the king who has renounced the honor coming to him – the honor coming to him is not renounced, for it is said, 'You shall surely set a king over you' – his authority shall be over you."

II.29 A.   Our rabbis have taught on Tannaite authority:

B. "You shall rise up before the hoary head" (Lev. 19:32):

C. Might one suppose that one is obligated to rise up even before a malefactor?

D. Scripture says, "elder."

E. An "elder" is only a sage,

F. as it is said, "Collect for me seventy men of the elders of Israel" (Num. 11:16).

G. R. Yosé the Galilean says, "An 'elder' is only one who has acquired wisdom, as it is said, 'The Lord created me at the beginning of his way' (Prov. 8:22)."

H. Might one suppose that one should rise up before him only from a distance?

I. Scripture says, "and honor the face of an elder."

J. If then it is to "honor the face of an elder," might one suppose that one should honor him with money?

K. Scripture says, "rise up...and honor...."

L. Just as "rising up" does not involve an expenditure of money, so "honoring" does not involve an expenditure of money.

M. Might one suppose that he has to rise up before him in the toilet or bathhouse?

N. Scripture says, "You shall rise up and you shall honor": I have commanded you to rise up only in a place in which that confers honor.

O. Might one suppose that if one saw him, one may close his eyes as though he had not seen him?

P. Lo, the matter is handed over to the heart, for it is said, "You shall fear your God, I am the Lord" –

Q. in connection with anything that is handed over to the heart, the fear of God is invoked.

R. R. Simeon b. Eleazar says, "How do we know that an elder should not make trouble for others?

S. "Scripture says, 'an elder and you shall fear your God'" [Sifra CCIV:III.1].

T. Issi b. Judah said, "You shall rise up before the hoary head' means, any hoary head [not only a master]."

II.30   A. *What R. Yosé the Galilean says is the same as what the first Tannaite authority says!*

B. *At issue between them is a youngster who is a sage. The first Tannaite authority maintains that a youngster who is a sage is not included, while R. Yosé the Galilean maintains that he is.*

C. *What's the operative reading of Scripture behind the position of R. Yosé the Galilean?*

D. *If matters were otherwise, Scripture should have written, "Before the hoary head of an old man you should rise up and pay respect." How come the All-Merciful treated these categories separately? To teach that one hoary head is not the same as the other, and vice versa. This proves that even a sage who is a younger is included.*

E. *And the first Tannaite authority?*

F. *The reason that matters are formulated as they are is that Scripture wanted to keep "old man" together with "and you shall fear."*

G. *And the first Tannaite authority – what is the scriptural basis for his position?*

H. *If it should enter your mind that matters are as R. Yosé the Galilean claims, then the All-Merciful should have written,* [33A] *"You shall rise up before and honor the hoary head, you shall rise up before and honor the old man." But since that is not how matters are written out, it proves that the two categories are one and the same.*

II.31 A. The master has said: "Might one suppose that one should honor him with money? Scripture says, "rise up...and honor...." Just as "rising up" does not involve an expenditure of money, so "honoring" does not involve an expenditure of money":

B. *But as to rising, is there never monetary consideration? Wouldn't it even speak of one who is involved in piercing pearls, and, if he rises up before him, he will be disturbed in his work?*

C. Rather, Scripture compares rising to honoring: Just as honoring involves an interruption in one's work, so rising, too, would involve an interruption in one's work.

D. Why not compare honoring to rising in this way: Just as rising involves no monetary costs, so honoring should involve no monetary cost? So on that basis sages have said, Craftsman are not permitted to rise before disciples of sages when the craftsman are engaged in doing their work.

E. *Well aren't they now? And haven't we learned in the Mishnah: And all the craftsmen of Jerusalem stand before them and greet them, [saying], "Brothers, men of such and such a place, you have come in peace" [M. Bik. 3:3]]?*

F. Said R. Yohanan, "Before such as those mentioned here they arise, but before disciples of sages they don't arise."

G. Said R. Yosé bar Abin, "Come and see how valued is a religious duty done at the proper time. For lo, 'Before such as those mentioned here they arise, but before disciples of sages they don't arise.'"

H. *But maybe the case there is exceptional, since you may otherwise make them stumble in the future [deciding not to come to Jerusalem with the first fruits].*

II.32 A. Said the master, "Might one suppose that he has to rise up before him in the toilet or bathhouse? Scripture says, "You shall rise up and you shall honor": I have commanded you to rise up only in a place in which that confers honor:

B. *But don't we rise up under those circumstances? And lo, R. Hiyya was seated in a bathhouse, when R. Simeon b. Rabbi went by and he did not rise before him. The other was angered and came and told his father, "I taught him two of the Five Parts of the Book of Psalms, and he doesn't stand before me!"*

	C.	*And furthermore, Bar Qappara, and some say, R. Samuel bar R. Yosé, was sitting in a bathhouse. R. Simeon b. Rabbi came in and went by, and the other did not rise before him. The other was angered and came and told his father,* "Two-thirds of a third of the Torah of the Priests [Leviticus] I taught him, and he didn't rise before me!"
	D.	He said to him, "But maybe he was sitting and reflecting on them."
	E.	*So the operative consideration is that he was sitting and reflecting on them, lo, otherwise, it would not be proper?*
	F.	*No problem, the one speaks of inner rooms, the other, outer rooms [in the inner rooms people have no clothes on so they don't rise, in the outer rooms they are clothed and show respect].*
	G.	*That moreover stands to reason, for* said Rabbah bar bar Hannah said R. Yohanan, "In every place it is permitted to reflect on Torah teachings except for the bathhouse and the toilet."
	H.	*But it may be exceptional if [reflecting on one's Torah study under such circumstances] is involuntary.*
II.33	A.	Might one suppose that if one saw him, one may close his eyes as though he had not seen him? Lo, the matter is handed over to the heart, for it is said, "you shall fear your God, I am the Lord" – in connection with anything that is handed over to the heart, the fear of God is invoked:
	B.	*So are we dealing with genuinely wicked people?*
	C.	Rather: Might one suppose that he may shut his eyes *before the time at which the obligatory greeting comes about, so that, when the obligation takes effect, he will not see him to stand up before him?*
	D.	Scripture said, "You shall rise up and you shall fear."
II.34	A.	*A Tannaite statement:* What is the rising up that expresses honor? One must say, it is in the space of four cubits [when the sage comes that close, in which case it is only in the sage's honor that one has arisen].
	B.	Said Abbayye, "We have made that rule only in the case of his master who was not his principal teacher, but in the case of his master who was his principal teacher, it should be from as far a distance as he can see."
	C.	*As to Abbayye, when he saw the ear of the ass of R. Joseph, he would get up.*
	D.	*Abbayye was riding on an ass and going along the bank at the Sagya Canal. R. Mesharshayya and others were sitting on the other side and didn't arise in his presence. He said to them, "Am I not your principal master?"*
	E.	*They said to him, "We weren't thinking about it."*
II.35	A.	R. Simeon b. Eleazar says, "How do we know that an elder should not make trouble for others? Scripture says, 'an elder and you shall fear your God'":
	B.	*Said Abbayye, "We hold in hand the tradition that if the sage took a circuitous route, he will have a long life."*

C.   *Abbayye took a circuitous route. R. Zira took a circuitous route. Rabina took a circuitous route. Rabina was sitting before R. Jeremiah of Difti; a certain man went by and didn't cover his head. He said, "What gall that man has!"*

D.   *He said to him, "Well, maybe he's from Mata Mehassaya, where people treat rabbis arrogantly."*

II.36   A.   Issi b. Judah said, "You shall rise up before the hoary head' means, any hoary head [not only a master]":

B.   Said R. Yohanan, "The decided law accords with Issi b. Judah."

C.   *R. Yohanan would rise before gentile sages, saying, "How many troubles have washed over these."*

D.   *Raba, while he would not get up, did pay them respect.*

E.   *Abbayye would give his hand to the aged.*

F.   *Raba would send his messengers.*

G.   *R. Nahman would send his bodyguards, saying, "But for the Torah that I know, how many Nahman bar Abbas are there in the market."*

The massive construction just now surveyed forms a response to Scripture in two ways. First, as we see, the pertinent verse of Scripture is analyzed and amplified. But second, the entire composite forms an essay on the theme and language and proposal of Scripture. This is a case in which the Torah not only takes a place in the Talmud but defines the work of the Talmud itself. And, we realize, when that happens, then the Talmud forms a sustained essay on (a theme, a proposition, a proposal) of Scripture, not as exegesis but as thematic exposition. And yet the form is very simple and the expansion follows lines of no particular complexity.

II.37   A.   Said R. Aibu said R. Yannai, [33B] "A disciple of a sage is allowed to stand up before his master only morning and night, so that the honor accruing to the master is no more than the honor owing to Heaven."

B.   *An objection was raised:* R. Simeon b. Eleazar says, "How do we know that an elder should not make trouble for others? Scripture says, 'an elder and you shall fear your God'"! *Now if you say that it is only morning and night, why should he not trouble people? It would be an obligation. So it would follow that one would have to rise any time during the day.*

C.   *No, it is morning and evening only, yet even so, so far as people, one should not impose on people.*

II.38   A.   Said R. Eleazar, "Any disciple who does not arise before his master is called wicked and will not live a long time, and his learning will be forbidden: 'But it shall not be well with the wicked, neither shall he prolong his days which are as a shadow, because he doesn't fear God' (Qoh. 8:13). Now I don't know the meaning of this 'fear,' but when Scripture says, 'you shall rise up before the hoary head...and fear your God' (Lev. 19:32), then 'fear' means 'rising.'"

	B.	*But why not say:* Fear of usury or dishonest weights?
	C.	*R. Eleazar forms a verbal analogy between the two matters since the word "before" occurs in both instances.*
II.39	A.	*The question was raised:* If his son was also his master, what is the law about his standing before his father?
	B.	*Come and take note of what Samuel said to R. Judah, "Smartass, get up before your father."*
	C.	*R. Ezekiel was exceptional, since he also had good deeds to his credit, for even Mar Samuel would arise before him.*
	D.	*Then what is the sense of the statement that he made to him?*
	E.	*This is the sense of the statement that he made to him: Sometimes he may come up behind me. Then you rise before him, and don't worry about the honor owing to me.*
II.40	A.	*The question was raised:* What if his son was his master, should his father stand before him?
	B.	*Come and take note that* said R. Joshua b. Levi, "As for me, it is not appropriate for me to stand up before my son, but it is because of the honor that is owing to the household of the patriarch." *So the operative consideration is that I am his teacher, but if he were my teacher, I would rise before him.*
	C.	*This is the sense of his statement:* "As for me, it is not appropriate for me to stand up before my son, *even if he were my master, since I am his father,* but it is because of the honor that is owing to the household of the patriarch."
II.41	A.	*The question was raised:* Is riding equivalent to walking [so the disciples stand when the master rides by], or is that not the case?
	B.	*Said Abbayye "Come and take note:* **The unclean [person] stands under the tree, and the clean person passes – he is unclean. The clean person stands under the tree, and the unclean passes – he is clean. And if the unclean person sat down, the clean person is unclean. And so with the stone which is afflicted with plague – he is clean. And if he put it down, lo, this one is unclean [M. Neg. 13:7]. And said R. Nahman bar Kohen, "That is to say, 'Riding equivalent to walking.'"**
	C.	*That settles the question.*

I do not catalogue the next item or mark it as a "Scripture pericope," but, of course, the composition depends on Scripture for its sense and context; it is not exegetical, it is surely scriptural – and in a profound sense, the same is to be said of our Talmud in all its parts.

II.42	A.	*The question was raised:* What is the law about rising before a scroll of the Torah?
	B.	R. Hilqiah, R. Simon, and R. Eleazar say, "It is an argument a fortiori: If people stand up before those who study the Torah, shouldn't they stand up before the Torah itself?!"
	C.	*R. Ilai and R. Jacob bar Zabedi were sitting when R. Simeon b. Abba passed by. He said to them, "First of all, you are sages and I am merely an associate; second, should the Torah rise before its students? [So you shouldn't have paid me that respect.]"*

D.   *He concurs with* R. Eleazar, who said, "A disciple of a sage is not permitted to rise before his master when he is engaged in study of the Torah."

E.   *Abbayye cursed that teaching.*

II.43   A.   "And when Moses went into the tent, all the people rose up and stood and looked after Moses until he was gone into the tent" (Ex. 33:8):

B.   R. Ammi and R. Isaac Nappaha –

C.   One said, "It was derogatory."

D.   The other said, "It was a compliment."

E.   *As to the one who said it was derogatory, that is as is [Moses was disparaged, but we're not going to say so].*

F.   *As to the view of the one who said it was to pay a compliment,* said Hezekiah, "Said to me R. Hanina b. R. Abbahu said R. Abbahu said R. Abdimi of Haifa, 'When a sage passes, one has to rise before him at a distance of four cubits, and when he has passed by for a distance of four cubits, he sits down; when a principal of a court passes, one stands up before him when he comes in sight and as soon as he has gone on four cubits, he may sit down; when the patriarch passes, one rises when he comes into sight and sits down only after he has taken his seat: "And when Moses went into the tent, all the people rose up and stood and looked after Moses until he was gone into the tent."'"

III.1   A.   For every positive commandment dependent upon the time [of year], men are liable, and women are exempt:

B.   *Our rabbis have taught on Tannaite authority:*

C.   What is the definition of a positive commandment dependent upon the time [of day or year]? Building a tabernacle at the festival of Tabernacles, carrying the palm branch on that festival, sounding the ram's horn, wearing show fringes, [34A] putting on phylacteries. And what is the definition of a positive commandment not dependent upon time? The fixing of an amulet to the doorpost, the erection of a parapet (Deut. 22:8), returning lost property, sending forth the dam from the nest [T. Qid. 1:10A-C].

III.2   A.   *Is this an encompassing generalization here?* But what about unleavened bread, rejoicing on the festivals, and assembly on the Festival of Sukkot in the Seventh Year (Deut. 31:12) [which include women, but which] depend on a particular time, and for which women are obligated! *And furthermore:* What about study of the Torah, procreation, and the redemption of the firstborn, which are not religious duties that depend on a particular time, and yet women are exempt from these?

B.   Said R. Yohanan, "We may not establish analogies resting on encompassing principles, and that is so even though exceptions are explicitly stated, *for we have learned in the Mishnah:* With any [food] do they prepare an erub and a shittuf [partnership meal], except for water and salt [M. Er. 3:1A]. *Now aren't there any other exceptions? Lo, there is the matter of mushrooms and truffles. So it must follow,* We may not establish analogies resting on encompassing principles, and that is so even though exceptions are explicitly stated."

IV.1   A.   **For every positive commandment dependent upon the time [of year], men are liable, and women are exempt:**

       B.   *How do we know this rule?*

       C.   We derive an analogy from the matter of phylacteries: Just as women are exempt from the requirement to put on phylacteries, so they are exempt from every positive commandment dependent upon the time of day or year.

       D.   And the rule in respect to phylacteries itself derives from the matter of study of the Torah: Just as in the case of study of the Torah, women are exempt, so in the case of phylacteries, women are exempt.

       E.   *But why not draw an analogy to the mezuzah from phylacteries [exempting a woman there as well]?*

       F.   Phylacteries are treated as comparable to study of the Torah in both the first and the second sections [Deut. 6:4-9, Deut. 11:13-21], but they are not comparable to the mezuzah in the second section.

       G.   *But why not draw an analogy to the mezuzah from study of the Torah [exempting a woman there as well]?*

       H.   *Don't let it enter your mind, for it is written, "That your days may be long" (Deut. 11:21) – so do men need a long life but not women?*

IV.2   A.   **What about the building of the tabernacle, which is a positive commandment dependent upon the time of year?**

       B.   **Scripture says, "You shall dwell in booths for seven days" (Lev. 23:42).** *Now the reason for women's being exempt from this obligation is that Scripture referred to "the homeborn" [males, not females], but otherwise, women would be liable!*

       C.   *Said Abbayye, "It is necessary to make that exclusion explicit. I might have thought, since it is written, 'You shall dwell in booths for seven days,' 'you should dwell' is comparable to 'you should live in a house,' and just as normal living in a house involves a husband and wife together, so the sukkah must be inhabited by husband and wife together."*

       D.   *And Raba said, [34B] "It is necessary to make that exclusion explicit. I might have thought, we should establish a verbal analogy involving the fifteenth of the month from another holiday in which there is the requirement that it be on the fifteenth of the month. Just as in that other holiday, that is, Passover, women are subject to the obligation, so here, too, women are subject to the obligation. So it was necessary."*

IV.3   A.   **But what about the pilgrimage, which is a positive commandment dependent upon the time of year?**

       B.   *Now the reason that a woman is exempt is that Scripture said, "Three times in the year all your males shall appear" (Ex. 23:17) – excluding women. But if it were not for that fact, women would be liable!*

       C.   *It is necessary to make that exclusion explicit, for otherwise I would have thought that we derive the rule governing the*

	appearance on the festival from the rule governing assembling once in seven years, which a woman is obligated to do.
D.	*Well, then, instead of deriving an exemption from phylacteries, why not deduce that she is obligated based on the requirement of participation in the rejoicing of a festival [which a woman is obligated to do by Deut. 16:14]?*
E.	Said Abbayye, "As to a woman, the obligation is on her husband to provide for her rejoicing."
F.	*So what are you going to say of a widow?*
G.	It would speak of the one with whom she is living.
H.	*Why not derive the obligation of a woman from the religious duty of assembling every seven years on Tabernacles?*
I.	The reason is that the obligation to eat unleavened bread on Passover and the obligation of assembling are two verses of Scripture that go over the same matter, and where you have a case in which two verses of Scripture go over the same matter, they do not establish an analogy for other cases [but the rule is limited to those explicit cases].
J.	*If that's so, then phylacteries and the pilgrimage also are two verses that go over the same matter and these two cannot serve to establish an analogy governing other matters!*
K.	*Both matters are required. For if the All-Merciful had made reference to phylacteries but not made reference to the pilgrimage, I might have thought we should establish an analogy between the meaning of the pilgrimage and the requirement of assembling every seven years. If the All-Merciful had made reference to pilgrimage but not phylacteries, I might have supposed: Let the matter of phylacteries be treated as comparable to the mezuzah. So both are required.*
L.	*If so, then why shouldn't we say that it was necessary for Scripture to make reference to both the requirement of eating unleavened bread and also to gathering once in seven years. [Then these two are not items that go over the same matter, as we originally alleged.]*
M.	*Well, then, what are they required to show us? For if the All-Merciful had made reference to assembling every seven years, but not to the requirement of eating unleavened bread on Passover, it would make the latter unnecessary, for I would maintain, deduce the rule governing a holiday on the fifteenth from the feast of Tabernacles on the fifteenth. But if the All-Merciful had written unleavened bread, with the reference to assembling needless, I would have reasoned: If it is required for children, all the more so, women. So it really is a case of two verses that go over the same matter, and they cannot serve to establish a generative analogy.*
N.	*Well, now, that poses no problems from the perspective of him who maintains that they cannot serve to establish a generative analogy. But from the perspective of him who has said they can serve to establish a generative analogy, what is to be said? And furthermore, as to the fact that for every*

positive commandment not dependent upon the time, women are liable – *how do we know that fact?*

O. *We derive that fact from the matter of fear of parents:* Because women as much as men are required to fear their parents (Lev. 19:3): Just as fearing parents is required for women, so for every positive commandment not dependent upon time women are liable.

P. *But why not draw your generative analogy from the matter of study of Torah?*

Q. Because the study of Torah and the requirement of procreation are two verses of Scripture that go over the same matter, and wherever there are two verses of Scripture that cover the same matter, they cannot serve to establish a generative analogy.

R. [35A] *Well, from the perspective of* R. Yohanan b. Beroqa, who has said, "The religious duty applies to them both: 'And God blessed them...be fruitful and multiply,' (Gen. 1:28)" *what is to be said?*

S. *Well, the reason is that* study of the Torah and redeeming the firstborn are two verses of Scripture that go over the same matter, and wherever there are two verses of Scripture that cover the same matter, they cannot serve to establish a generative analogy.

T. *And then, also, from the perspective of R. Yohanan b. Beroqa,* the commandment concerning procreation and the commandment concerning fear of parents are two verses of Scripture that go over the same matter, and wherever there are two verses of Scripture that cover the same matter, they cannot serve to establish a generative analogy.

U. *In point of fact, those two matters both had to be spelled out [and do not therefore fall into the classification of two verses of Scripture that go over the same matter]. For if the All-Merciful had made reference to fear of parents but not to procreation, I might have supposed that when Scripture referred to* "and conquer it" (Gen. 1:28), *Scripture spoke of man, whose nature it is to conquer, and not to woman, whose nature it is not to conquer, so she would be omitted. And if Scripture had spoken of procreation but not of fear of parents, I might have thought that a man, who has the capacity to carry out such a requirement, would be covered by that requirement, but a woman, who has not got the means to carry out that commandment, since she has not got the means to do it, would be exempt from that requirement in any way at all. So it was necessary.*

V. *Well, now, that poses no problems from the perspective of him who maintains that* two verses of Scripture that go over the same matter cannot serve to establish a generative analogy. *But from the perspective of him who has said, they can serve to establish a generative analogy, what is to be said?*

W. *Said Raba, "The Papunian knows the reason for this item, and who might that be? It is R. Aha bar Jacob: 'Said Scripture,*

"And it shall be a sign for you upon your hand and for a memorial between your eyes, that the Torah of the Lord may be in your mouth" (Ex. 13:9) – Thus the whole of the Torah is treated as analogous to phylacteries. Just as the rules governing phylacteries are an affirmative action dependent on a particular time, from which women are exempt, so are women exempt from all affirmative actions dependent upon a particular time. And, since women are exempt from all affirmative actions dependent on a particular time, it must follow that they also are subject to all of those affirmative actions that are not limited to a particular time.'"

X.   *Well, now that poses no problem to those who maintain that* phylacteries *are an affirmative action that depends on a particular time, but from the perspective of him who maintains that* wearing phylacteries *is an affirmative action that does not depend upon a particular time, what is to be said?*

Y.   *Whom have you heard who takes the view that* wearing phylacteries is an affirmative action that does not depend upon a particular time?

Z.   *It is R. Meir, and R. Meir takes the position that* there are two verses that go over the same matter and these do not generate an analogy serving other cases.

AA.   And from the perspective of R. Judah, who has said, "Two verses that go over the same matter do establish a generative analogy for other cases, and, further, that wearing phylacteries is an affirmative action that does not depend upon a particular time," *what is to be said?*

BB.   Since eating unleavened bread, rejoicing on the festivals, and assembling every seven years on Tabernacles represent three verses that go over the same matter [namely, positive duties, dependent on a particular time, but binding on women (Freedman)], as such, they do not generate an analogy governing any other case.

The foregoing dispute depends upon different principles on how Scripture is to be read, also on facts supplied by Scripture, also on the exegesis of various verses – the entire repertoire of the Talmud's analysis, in fact, responds to Scripture's entire legacy: specific statements, general themes, modes of wording, and the like.

V.1   A.   And for every positive commandment not dependent upon the time, men and women are equally liable. For every negative commandment, whether dependent upon the time or not dependent upon the time, men and women are equally liable:

      B.   *What is the scriptural basis for this rule?*

      C.   R. Judah said Rab said, *and so, too, did the Tannaite authority of the household of R. Ishmael state:* "'When a man or a woman shall commit any sin that men commit' (Num. 5:6) – in this way Scripture has treated women as equal to men in regard to all penalties that are in the Torah."

D. *The household of R. Eleazar repeated as its Tannaite formulation:* "'Now these are the ordinances that you shall set before them' (Ex. 21:1) – in this language, Scripture has treated the woman as comparable to the man for the purpose of all the laws that are imposed by the Torah."

E. *The household of Hezekiah and R. Yosé the Galilean presented as a Tannaite formulation,* "Said Scripture, 'It has killed a man or a woman' (Ex. 21:1) – in this language, Scripture has treated the woman as comparable to the man for the purpose of all the forms of the death penalty that are specified in the Torah.

F. *And all three proofs are required to make the point. For had we heard only the initial one, we might have thought that it is in that area in particular that the All-Merciful has taken pity on a woman, so that she will have a means of atonement, but so far as civil laws in general, a man, who is engaged in business transactions, would be subject to the law, but I might have thought that a woman is not.*

G. *And had we been given the rule concerning the civil law, I might have thought that that is so that a woman should have a way of making a living, but as to atonement, since a man is responsible to carry out the religious duties, he would be given the means of making atonement for sin, but a woman, who is not responsible for keeping [all] religious duties, is not under the law.*

H. *And had we been given these two, the one because of making atonement, the other because of making a living, but as to the matter of manslaughter, a man, who is subject to the religious duty of paying a ransom in the case of manslaughter,* [35B] *would be subject to the law, but a woman would not.*

I. *And had we been given the matter of ransom, it might have been thought because in that matter, it is because a soul has perished, but as to these other matters, in which there is no issue of a soul's having perished, I might have thought that that was not the case. So all of them are required.*

VI.1 A. ...Except for not marring the corners of the beard, not rounding the corners of the head (Lev. 19:27), and not becoming unclean because of the dead (Lev. 21:1):

B. *There is no problem understanding the exception of defiling oneself to bury a corpse, since it is explicitly written that this applies only to males:* "Speak to the priests, the sons of Aaron: No one shall defile himself for the dead among his people" (Lev. 21:1) – *the sons of Aaron, not the daughters of Aaron. But how on the basis of Scripture do we know that the same pertains to not marring the corners of the beard, not rounding the corners of the head?*

C. "You shall not round the corner of your heads nor mar the corners of your beard" (Lev. 19:27) – anyone who is subject to the prohibition of marring the corners of the beard is covered by the prohibition of rounding, *but women, who obviously are not subject to the prohibition of marring the corners of the beard, also are not subject to the prohibition of rounding.*

D.   *So how do we know that women are not subject to the prohibition against marring the beard?*

E.   *Well, friend, if you want, I'll just say it's a matter of common sense, since they don't have beards. Or, if you need it, I'll cite a verse of Scripture:* "You shall not rend the corner of your heads, nor shall you mar the corner of your beard" (Lev. 19:27) – since Scripture has varied its usage, moving from the you plural to the you singular, [clearly the latter does not apply to both genders]. *Otherwise, the All-Merciful should speak of* "the corner of your beards." Why "your beard"? *It means,* "your beard, but not your wife's beard."

F.   *So is the woman's beard not covered? But hasn't it been taught on Tannaite authority:* A woman or a eunuch's beard that produced hair – lo, they are classified as an ordinary beard for all purposes affecting them? *Doesn't this mean, in respect to marring the beard?*

G.   Said Abbayye, "*Well, now, you can't say that it is in regard to marring, for we derive the verbal analogy out of the rule governing the 'corner' of that of the sons of Aaron:* Just as there women are exempt from the commandment, so here, too."

H.   *Yes, but if we take for granted that the language,* "sons of Aaron," *is stated with regard to everything covered in this section* [Israelites in general: "Nor shall you mar the corner of your beard," priests in particular: "Neither shall they shave off the corner of their beard," with "sons of Aaron" governing the whole section], *then let Scripture fall silent, and we should produce the same result by an argument a fortiori. For this is what I might propose:* If in the case of priests, for whom Scripture has provided an abundance of religious duty, yield the argument, "sons of Aaron" and not daughters of Aaron, then a fortiori the same rule should apply to ordinary Israelites!

I.   *But if it were not for the verbal analogy, I might have said that the matter is interrupted* [so that "sons of Aaron" does not refer to "they shall not shave"]. *So here, too, why not say that the matter is interrupted, and, so far as the argument resting on the verbal analogy, it is required for another purpose altogether, namely, for that which has been taught on Tannaite authority:*

J.   "Neither shall the priests shave off the corner of their beard" (Lev. 21:5):

K.   Might one suppose that he is liable even if he shaved it off with scissors?

L.   Scripture says, "Neither shall you mar..." (Lev. 19:27).

M.   Might one suppose if one removed it with tweezers or pincers he is liable?

N.   Scripture says, "Neither shall you mar" – which involves destruction.

O. How so? It must be a kind of shaving that involves destruction, and that is with a razor.

P. *If it were the case that the verbal analogy covers only shaving and marring but not those to whom these acts apply, Scripture should have said, "You shall not round the corner of your heads nor should you mar that of your beard." Why say, "the corner of your beard"? It is to yield both points.*

Q. *Well, then, what about that which has been taught on Tannaite authority: A woman or a eunuch's beard that produced hair – lo, they are classified as an ordinary beard for all purposes affecting them? What purpose does this law serve?*

R. Said Mar Zutra, "It pertains to the uncleanness brought on by the skin ailment" (Lev. 13:1-17, 29-37.) [Freedman: If a woman or eunuch grows a beard, though normally their chins are free of hair, the test of the skin ailment are the symptoms of hair, not those of skin.]

S. *But the symptoms of uncleanness brought on by the skin ailment so far as these affect skin or hair are explicitly stated by Scripture: "If a man or a woman have a mark of the skin ailment on head or beard (Lev. 13:29)."*

T. Rather, said Mar Zutra, "These serve to indicate the marks of purification from the skin ailment." [Freedman: When a woman becomes clean from the marks of skin ailment of the beard, she must undergo the same ritual as a man.]

U. *Well, that, too, is a pretty obvious point since she can become unclean, she obviously can be made clean!*

V. *It was necessary to make the point nonetheless, for without this statement, I might have assumed that it covers distinct subjects, that is, "If a man or a woman has a mark of the skin ailment on the head," while when reference is made to "or the beard," it would revert to the man alone; so we are informed to the contrary.*

VI.2 A. *Isi taught as a Tannaite statement: "So, too, are women exempt from the prohibition of baldness" (Lev. 21:5).*

B. *What is the scriptural basis for Isi's view?*

C. *This is how he expounds the matter: "'You are sons of the Lord your God, you shall not cut yourselves nor make any baldness between your eyes for the dead, for you are a holy people to the Lord your God' (Deut. 14:1) – sons, but not daughters, in the matter of baldness.*

D. "You maintain that it is in respect to baldness. But maybe it is in respect to cutting yourselves?

E. "When Scripture says, 'for you are a holy people to the Lord your God,' cutting is covered. So how do I interpret the sense of 'sons,' but not daughters? It is in respect to baldness.

F. "Well, why do you prefer to extend the law to cutting and to exclude from the law the matter of baldness?

G. "I extend the law to cutting, which is possible both where there is hair and where there is none, but I exclude the matter of baldness, which pertains only instead of hair."

H. *But why not say:* "sons and not daughters" in regard to both baldness and cutting, and the phrase, "for you are a holy people to the Lord your God," pertains to an incision [Lev. 21:5: Priests are not to make any incision]?

I. *Isi takes the view that* incisions and cuttings [36A] *are the same thing.*

J. *Said Abbayye, "This is the scriptural basis for the position of Isi: He derives a verbal analogy from the appearance in both contexts of the phrase, 'sons of Aaron,' in regard to baldness [both at Deut. 14:1-2, for Israelites, and Lev. 21:5, for priests]. Just as in the one case, women are exempt, so in the other, women are exempt."*

K. *But if we assume that Scripture refers to the entire matter in making reference to* "the sons of Aaron," *then let Scripture just fall silent, and the exemption of women I would derive from an argument a fortiori, as follows:* If in the case of priests, for whom Scripture has provided an abundance of religious duty, yield the argument, "sons of Aaron" and not daughters of Aaron, then a fortiori the same rule should apply to ordinary Israelites!

L. *But if it were not for the verbal analogy, I might have said that the matter is interrupted* [so that "sons of Aaron" does not refer to "they shall not shave"]. *So here, too, why not say that the matter is interrupted, and, so far as the argument resting on the verbal analogy, it is required for another purpose altogether, namely, for that which has been taught on Tannaite authority:*

M. "They shall not make tonsures [upon their heads, nor shave off the edges of their beards, nor make any cuttings in their flesh]":

N. Might one suppose that for making four or five tonsures, one should be liable only on one count?

O. Scripture refers to "tonsure" in the singular, so imposing liability for each cut.

P. "Upon their heads":

Q. What is the point of Scripture here?

R. Since it is said, "[You are the sons of the Lord your God: You shall not cut yourselves nor make any baldness on your foreheads for the dead" (Deut. 14:1),

S. one might have thought that liability is incurred only for a cut on the forehead.

T. How do we know that the prohibition extends to the entire head?

U. Scripture says, "upon their heads,"

V. to encompass the entire head.

W. Might one suppose that in the case of priests, for whom Scripture has specified numerous supererogatory commandments, liability extends to each cut and also to the entire head,

X. while for ordinary Israelites, for whom Scripture has not specified supererogatory commandments, liability should be incurred only on one count for however many cuts and only for a cut on the forehead?

Y. Scripture refers to "tonsure" in several passages [here and at Deut. 14:1, here speaking of the priests, there speaking of Israelites as well], so establishing grounds for the following analogy:

Z. Just as in the case of "cutting" stated with reference to priests, liability is incurred for each cut and is incurred for a cut on any part of the head as much as on the forehead, so for "cut" spoken of in connection with an Israelite, liability is incurred for each cut and is incurred for a cut on any part of the head as much as on the forehead.

AA. And just as "cutting" stated with reference to an Israelite imposes liability only if it is made for a deceased, so "cutting" stated with reference to priests imposes liability only if it is made for a deceased [Sifra CCXII:I.1-3].

BB. [Abbayye responds:] *"If so, Scripture should write "baldness" [in abbreviated form. Why say "baldness" in a fully spelled out form]? It is to yield both points."*

CC. *Said Raba, "This is the scriptural basis for the position of Isi: He derives how the consideration of the phrase 'between your eyes' applies from the case of phylacteries. Just as in the latter case, women are exempt, so here, too, they are exempt."*

DD. *And how come Raba doesn't state matters as does Abbayye?*

EE. *Because he doesn't see any point in the variation of spellings of the word for baldness.*

FF. *And how come Abbayye doesn't state matters as does Raba?*

GG. *He will say to you, "The matter of phylacteries themselves derives from this very passage, namely: Just as in that context 'between the eyes' means, a place where a bald spot can be made, which is the upper part of the head, so here, too, the place at which phylacteries are located is the upper part of the head."*

HH. *Now in regard to both Abbayye and Raba, how do they deal with the phrase, "you are sons" [since they make the same point on the basis of other language altogether]?*

II. *They require it in line with that which has been taught on Tannaite authority:*

JJ. "You are children of the Lord your God. You shall not gash yourselves or shave the front of your heads because of the dead. For you are a people consecrated to the Lord your God: The Lord your God chose you from among all other peoples on earth to be his treasured people" (Deut. 14:1-2):

KK. R. Judah says, "If you conduct yourselves in the way good children do, then you are children, and if not, you are not children [of the Lord your God]."

LL. R. Meir says, "One way or another, 'You are children of the Lord your God.'"

MM. And so Scripture says, "Yet the number of the children of Israel shall be as the sand of the sea...it shall be said to them, 'You are the children of the living God'" (Hos. 2:1) [B.'s version: "They are sottish children" (Jer. 4:22); "They are children in whom is no faith" (Deut. 32:20), "A seed of evil doers, sons that deal corruptly" (Isa. 1:4, then Hos. 2:1)] [Sifré Deut. XCVI:IV.1].

NN. *Why all these further verses?*

OO. *If you should reply, then only when they are foolish are they classified as sons, but not when they lack faith, come and take note:* "They are children in whom is no faith" (Deut. 32:20).

PP. *If you should reply, then only when they have no faith they are classified as sons, but when they serve idols they are not classified as sons, then come and hear:* "A seed of evil doers, sons that deal corruptly" (Isa. 1:4).

QQ. *And should you say, well, they're called sons that act corruptly, but not good sons, then come and hear:* "Yet the number of the children of Israel shall be as the sand of the sea...it shall be said to them, 'You are the children of the living God'" (Hos. 2:1).

I.1+2, supplied with its talmud and appendix on the theme of the talmud, at Nos. 3-32, begin with the required exegesis of the Mishnah's reference. II.1+2-43 then go through the same inquiry as I.1, with the usual anthology of thematically pertinent compositions, formed into an enormous composite. III.1-2 explain the rule of the Mishnah by appeal to a Tannaite complement. IV.1-2+3 go over the same sentence, now providing a scriptural basis for the rule. V.1, VI.1 ask for the scriptural basis for the rule of the Mishnah. No. 2 continues the exposition of the law of the Mishnah, now extending its coverage.

1:8

A. [The cultic rites of] laying on of hands, waving, drawing near, taking the handful, burning the fat, breaking the neck of a bird, sprinkling, and receiving [the blood] apply to men and not to women,

B. except in the case of a meal-offering of an accused wife and of a Nazirite girl, which they wave.

I.1	A.	Laying on of hands:
	B.	*For it is written,* "Speak to the sons of Israel...and he shall lay his hand upon the head of the burnt-offering" (Lev. 7:29-30) –
	C.	The sons of Israel, not the daughters of Israel do it.
II.1	A.	Waving:
	B.	*For it is written,* "Speak to the sons of Israel...the fat...may be waved" (Lev. 6:7).
	C.	The sons of Israel, not the daughters of Israel do it.
III.1	A.	Drawing near:
	B.	*For it is written,* "And this is the law of the meal-offering: The sons of Aaron shall offer it –
	C.	The sons of Aaron, not the daughters of Aaron do it.
IV.1	A.	Taking the handful:

	B.	*For it is written,* "And he shall bring it to Aaron's sons, the priests, and he shall take out of it his handful of the fine flour" (Lev. 2:2) –
	C.	The sons of Aaron, not the daughters of Aaron do it.
V.1	A.	Burning the fat:
	B.	*For it is written,* "And Aaron's sons shall burn it" (Lev. 2:2).
	C.	The sons of Aaron, not the daughters of Aaron do it.
VI.1	A.	Breaking the neck of a bird, sprinkling:
	B.	*For it is written,* "And he shall wring off his head and burn it on the altar" –
	C.	*Treating as comparable wringing the neck and burning the fat.*
VII.1	A.	And receiving [the blood]:
	B.	*For it is written,* "And the priests, the sons of Aaron," and a master has said, [36B] "'And they shall bring' refers to receiving the blood."
VIII.1	A.	Sprinkling:
	B.	*Sprinkling what? If it is the blood of the red cow, "Eleazar" [the priest] is written in that connection. And if it is the blood that is sprinkled in the inner sanctum of the Temple [for example, on the veil and golden altar], then* the anointed priest *is required for that [for example, Lev. 4:5].*
	C.	*It is the sprinkling of the blood of fowl, deriving a fortiori from the case of the beast: If* an animal, for slaughter of which a priest is not specified, has to have a priest for sprinkling its blood, then fowl, for the wringing of the neck of which a priest is required, surely should have to have a priest for sprinkling the blood.
IX.1	A.	Except in the case of a meal-offering of an accused wife and of a Nazirite girl, which they wave:
	B.	*Said R. Eleazar to R. Josiah, his contemporary, "You may not take your seat until you explain the following matter: How do we know that the meal-offering of the accused wife had to be waved?"*
	C.	*[He replied,] "How do we know indeed! It is written, 'And he shall wave' (Num. 5:25)!"*
	D.	[No, the question is,] "How do we know that it must be done by the owner [explaining why the priest puts the woman's hand on the utensil of service, along with his own, so that she may wave the offering as he does]?"
	E.	"The proof derives from the appearance of the word 'hand' both in the present context and in the setting of the peace-offerings. *Here it is written,* 'And the priest will take from the hand of the woman' (Num. 5:25) *and in that other connection it is written,* 'His own hands shall bring...' (Lev. 7:30). Just as, in the present instance, it is the priest who does the waving, so, in that other instance, it is the priest who does the waving. Just as, in that other context, the owner joins in, so here, too, the owner joins in. How so? The priest puts his hand under the hand of the owner and waves [the meal-offering] [M. Sot. 3:1B]."
	F.	*So we have found the case of the accused wife. How about the Nazirite woman?*

G.   We derive the sense of "palm" from the meaning in connection with the accused wife.

I.1-VII provide scriptural foundations for the Mishnah's details. VIII.1 clarifies the rule of the Mishnah. IX.1 reverts to the established inquiry.

1:9

A.   Every commandment which is dependent upon the Land applies only in the Land,

B.   and which does not depend upon the Land applies both in the Land and outside the Land,

C.   [37A] except for orlah [produce of a fruit tree in the first three years of its growth] and mixed seeds [Lev. 19:23, 19:19].

D.   R. Eliezer says, "Also: Except for [the prohibition against eating] new [produce before the omer is waved on the sixteenth of Nisan] [Lev. 23:14]."

I.1   A.   *What is the meaning of,* which is dependent upon, *and what is the meaning of,* which does not depend upon? *If I say that the sense of* which is dependent upon *pertains where the language,* "entering the Land" *is used, and the sense of* which does not depend upon *pertains where the language,* "entering the Land" *is not used, then what about the matters of* phylacteries and the disposition of the firstling of an ass, which pertain both in the Land of Israel and abroad, *even though the language* "entering the Land" *is used in their connection?*

B.   *Said R. Judah, "This is the sense of the statement:* Every religious duty that is an obligation of the person applies whether in the Land or abroad, but if it is an obligation that is incumbent upon the soil, it applies only in the Land."

I.2   A.   *What is the scriptural basis for that rule?*

B.   *It is in line with what our rabbis have taught on Tannaite authority:*

C.   ["These are the laws and rules that you must carefully observe to do in the land that the Lord, God of your fathers, is giving you to possess, as long as you live on earth. You must destroy all the sites at which the nations you are to dispossess worshiped their gods, whether on lofty mountains and on hills or under any luxuriant tree. Tear down their altars, smash their pillars, put their sacred posts to the fire, and cut down the images of their gods, obliterating their name from that site" (Deut. 12:1-3)]:

D.   "These are the laws":

E.   This refers to the midrash exegeses.

F.   "And rules":

G.   These are the laws.

H.   "...That you must carefully observe":

I.   This refers to studying.

J.   "...To do":

K.   This refers to doing the deeds.

L. "...In the Land [that the Lord, God of your fathers, is giving you to possess, as long as you live on earth]":

M. Might one suppose that all of the religious duties without exception pertain abroad?

N. Scripture says, "to do in the Land."

O. Might one suppose that all of the religious duties without exception pertain solely in the Land [and not abroad]?

P. Scripture says, "...as long as you live on earth."

Q. After Scripture has stated matters in encompassing language, Scripture has further stated matters in limiting language, on which account we learn from the stated context.

R. In context, it is stated, "You must destroy all the sites at which the nations you are to dispossess worshiped their gods."

S. Just as the matter of idolatry is singular in that it is a religious duty pertaining to one's person and not dependent upon one's being situated in the Land, thus pertaining both in the Land and also abroad, so all religious duties that are incumbent upon the person and do not depend upon one's being located in the Land apply both in the Land and abroad [Sifré Deut. LIX:I.1-2].

II.1   A. Except for orlah [produce of a fruit tree in the first three years of its growth] and mixed seeds (Lev. 19:23, 19:19). R. Eliezer says, "Also: Except for [the prohibition against eating] new [produce before the omer is waved on the sixteenth of Nisan] (Lev. 23:14)":

B. *The question was raised: Is the dissenting opinion of R. Eliezer meant to yield a lenient ruling or a strict ruling?*

C. *It is meant to yield a strict ruling, and this is the sense of the passage: The initial authority says, except for orlah and mixed seeds, these deriving from a traditional law; that is so, even though one might argue, to the contrary, these represent an obligation that is connected with the soil, but the consideration of the use of new produce only after the waving of the barley sheaf is practiced only in the Land but not overseas. How come? "Dwelling" means, after taking possession and settling down [Lev. 23:14: "It shall be a statute throughout your generations in all your dwellings," and that might mean, even outside of the Land; but even in the Land this rule came into force only after the Israelites had settled down, not while they were fighting for and dividing up the country (Freedman)]. And then R. Eliezer comes along to say: Also the consideration of the use of new produce only after the waving of the barley sheaf is practiced in the Land but not overseas. How come? "Dwelling" means, anywhere where you dwell.*

D. *Well, maybe his ruling is meant to yield a lenient ruling, and this is the sense of the passage: The initial authority says, except for orlah and mixed seeds, these deriving from a traditional law – and all the more so does the rule governing not eating new produce prior to the waving of the barley sheaf*

of new grain, for the sense of the word "dwelling" is,
anywhere where you dwell. *And then R. Eliezer comes along*
to say: Also the consideration of the use of new produce only
after the waving of the barley sheaf is practiced only in the
Land but not overseas. How come? "Dwelling" refers to the
situation that prevailed only after the Israelites had settled
down, not while they were fighting for and dividing up the
country.

E.   *And what is the reference point of* also *here [in this theory of*
     matters]?

F.   *It refers to the first clause only* [the consideration of not
     eating new grain before the waving of the sheaf of barley is
     included in the general principle that all precepts...
     (Freedman)].

G.   *Come and take note, for said Abbayye, "Who is the Tannaite*
     authority who differs from R. Eliezer? It is R. Ishmael, for it
     has been taught on Tannaite authority:

H.   ["When you come into the Land of your dwellings, which I
     give to you, and will make an offering burnt by fire to the
     Lord, then shall he who offers offer a meal-offering and
     libations" (Num. 15:2ff):] "This serves to teach you that
     wherever the word 'dwelling' appears, it refers only to the
     period after taking possession and settling down in the
     Land," the words of R. Ishmael.

I.   Said to him R. Aqiba, "Lo, there is the matter of the Sabbath,
     concerning which 'dwellings' occurs, and that applies both in
     the Land and abroad."

J.   He said to him, "The matter of the Sabbath derives from an
     argument a fortiori: If there are less important religious
     duties that apply both in the Land and abroad, the Sabbath,
     which is a weighty commandment, all the more so."

K.   *Well, now, since said Abbayye, "Who is the Tannaite authority*
     who differs from R. Eliezer? It is R. Ishmael," it must follow
     that R. Eliezer's dissenting opinion is meant to yield a strict
     ruling.

L.   *It certainly does prove the point.*

M.   *Well, to what does R. Ishmael make reference? It is to*
     libations. But in connection with libations, [37B] *the language*
     "coming into the Land" *and also* "dwelling" *are used.*
     [Freedman: Maybe only "dwelling" extends the law to all
     places only when it stands alone, but here, used along with
     "coming," it limits the applicability of the law to the Land of
     Israel.]

N.   *This is the sense of the statement:* "This serves to teach you
     that wherever the words 'coming' and 'dwelling' appear,
     Scripture refers only to the period after the inheritance and
     settlement of the Land," the words of R. Ishmael.

O.   *If so, then the language we have is inappropriate, namely:* Said
     to him R. Aqiba, "Lo, there is the matter of the Sabbath,
     concerning which 'dwellings' occurs, and that applies both in
     the Land and abroad." He said to him, "The matter of the

Sabbath derives from an argument a fortiori: If there are less important religious duties that apply both in the Land and abroad, the Sabbath, which is a weighty commandment, all the more so." *Rather, what should be said is this: "I was referring to 'coming' and 'dwelling'"!*

P. *The force of his statement was, first – and furthermore, namely: "I was referring to 'coming' and 'dwelling,'" and, furthermore, as to your statement, "Lo, there is the matter of the Sabbath, concerning which 'dwellings' occurs" – The matter of the Sabbath derives from an argument a fortiori.*

II.2 A. *What is at issue between them?*

B. *Whether or not they offered libations in the wilderness. R. Ishmael takes the view that they didn't offer libations in the wilderness, and R. Aqiba maintains that they did offer libations in the wilderness.*

C. *Said Abbayye, "This Tannaite authority of the household of R. Ishmael differs from another Tannaite authority of the household of R. Ishmael, for a Tannaite authority of the household of R. Ishmael [stated], 'Since there are unspecified "comings"* stated in the Torah, but Scripture also has qualified the meaning of one of them, indicating that it refers to the time after the Land was inherited and the people settled down, so all other references are to the period after inheriting and settling down in the Land.'"

D. *And as to the other Tannaite authority?*

E. *It is because the rules governing the king and the presentation of first fruits represent two verses of Scripture that go over the same matter, and wherever there are two verses of Scripture that go over the same matter, they do not generate an analogy governing other matters [but the rule is limited to the case].*

F. *And as to the other Tannaite authority?*

G. *Both verses are required to make the same point. For if the All-Merciful had made reference only to the king but not to first fruits, I would have supposed, since in the case of first fruits, the obligation is immediate [upon entry into the Land, prior to settling down], for there is immediate enjoyment of the crop. [So the rule is special to the case.] But if the case of the first fruits were stated and not that of the king, I might have supposed, since the king's nature is to go out and conquer, he has to be appointed immediately on entering the Land, but the obligation to present first fruits comes only when the people will have settled down.*

H. *And as to the other Tannaite authority?*

I. *Let Scripture specify the case of the king and it would be needless to give the rule for first fruits, for I would have reasoned as follows: If a king, who by nature goes out and conquers, is appointed only after inheriting and settling down in the Land, then how much are first fruits obligatory only when people have inherited and settled down in the Land.*

J. *And as to the other Tannaite authority?*

K. *Had Scripture laid that matter out in such a way, I would have thought that first fruits are governed by the analogy supplied by the dough-offering [which was obligatory as soon as they had entered the Land]. So we are told that that is not the case.*

II.3 A. *Now that you have taken the position,* Every religious duty that is an obligation of the person applies whether in the Land or abroad, [but if it is an obligation that is incumbent upon the soil, it applies only in the Land,] *then what is the point of "dwelling" that the All-Merciful spelled out in connection with the Sabbath?*

B. *It was indeed required. For it might have entered your mind to maintain, since it is written in connection with the passage on festivals, therefore it requires an act of sanctification as do the festivals [which require an act of sanctification of the new month of the month in which they occur, and that is done by a sanhedrin]. So we are informed to the contrary.*

II.4 A. *And what is the point of "dwelling" that the All-Merciful spelled out in connection with the forbidden fat and blood [at Lev. 3:17]?*

B. *It was indeed required. For it might have entered your mind to maintain, since it is written in connection with the passage on sacrifices, then, so long as sacrifices are carried out, the forbidden fat and blood are not to be used, but since the sacrifices are not carried out, there is no further prohibition. So we are informed to the contrary.*

II.5 A. *And what is the point of "dwelling" that the All-Merciful spelled out in connection with unleavened bread and bitter herbs for Passover [at Ex. 12:20]?*

B. *It was indeed required. For it might have entered your mind to maintain, since it is written,* "They shall eat the Paschal Lamb with unleavened bread and bitter herbs" (Num. 9:11), *that pertains only where the Passover sacrifice is offered, not otherwise. So we are informed to the contrary.*

II.6 A. *And what is the point of "dwelling" that the All-Merciful spelled out in connection with the phylacteries and the firstling of an ass [which are not limited to the Land of Israel]?*

B. *That is required in connection with that which a Tannaite authority of the household of R. Ishmael [stated]:* "Carry out this religious duty, on account of which you will enter the Land."

II.7 A. *Now from the viewpoint that "dwelling" means, wherever you live, there are no problems; that is in line with the statement,* "And they ate of the new produce of the Land on the day after the Passover" (Josh. 5:11). *They ate on the day after Passover, but not before, and that proves [38A] that the sheaf of first barley was offered and then they ate. But from the perspective of him who maintains that "dwelling" means, after the inheritance and settling down on the Land, why did they not eat the new produce forthwith?*

B. *Well, as a matter of fact, they didn't need to, for it is written,* "And the children of Israel ate the manna forty years, until they came to a land inhabited; they ate the manna until they came to the borders of the land of Canaan" (Ex. 16:35). It is not possible to take literally the statement, "until they came into the land inhabited," since it is said, "until they came to the borders of the land of Canaan." And it is not possible to take literally the language, "unto the borders of the land of Canaan," since it is said, "until they came to a land inhabited." So how hold the two together? Moses died on the seventh of Adar, the manna stopped coming down, but they used what they had in hand until the sixteenth of Nisan [Freedman: so "until they came to a land inhabited" refers to the actual period of eating it, but it descended only "until they came to the border," where Moses died].

We come now to a different kind of Scripture composition, namely, an explanation of the sense of a statement of Scripture:

II.8   A.   *It has further been taught on Tannaite authority:*
       B.   "And the children of Israel ate the manna forty years, until they came to a land inhabited; they ate the manna until they came to the borders of the land of Canaan" (Ex. 16:35):
       C.   Well, did they really eat it for forty years? Didn't they eat it for forty years less thirty days?
       D.   But this is to teach you that they could taste the taste of manna even in the cakes that they had brought with them from the land of Egypt.

The next is similarly free-standing, different from the foregoing. Now we ask Scripture to demonstrate a fact.

II.9   A.   *It has further been taught on Tannaite authority:*
       B.   "On the seventh of Adar, Moses died, and on the seventh of Adar, he was born.
       C.   How do we know that on the seventh of Adar, Moses died? "So Moses the servant of the Lord died there" (Deut. 34:5); "And the children of Israel wept for Moses in the plains of Moab thirty days" (Deut. 34:8); "Moses my servant is dead, now therefore arise, go over this Jordan" (Josh. 1:2); "Pass through the midst of the camp and command the people saying, Prepare you food for within three days you are to pass over this Jordan" (Josh. 1:11); "And the people came up out of the Jordan on the tenth day of the first month [Nisan]." Deduct from the tenth of Nisan the prior thirty-three days, and you learn that on the seventh of Adar, Moses died.
       D.   How do we know that on the seventh of Adar, he was born?
       E.   "And he said to them, I am a hundred and twenty years old this day, I can't go out and come in" (Deut. 31:2) – 'this day' is hardly required, so why does Scripture say it? It is to teach you that the Holy One, blessed be He, goes into session and fills out the years of the righteous from day to day and month to month: "The number of your days I will fulfill" (Ex. 23:26)

[so he was exactly a hundred and twenty years old when he
died, so he was born on that day, too (Freedman)].

II.10   A. *It has been taught on Tannaite authority:*

           B. R. Simeon b. Yohai says, "Three religious duties were assigned to
Israel when they entered the Land, and they apply both to the Land
and abroad:

           C. "And it is logical that they should apply:

           D. "If the consideration of new grain [to be eaten only after the waving
of the sheaf of barley on the fifteenth of Nisan], which is not
forbidden forever [but only until that rite], and from which it is not
forbidden to derive any kind of benefit whatsoever, and from which
the prohibition can be raised [through the rite], applies both in the
Land of Israel and abroad, then the prohibition of mixed seeds, the
prohibition of which is permanent, and the prohibition of which
extends to deriving any sort of benefit from the crop, and from
which it is not possible to raise the prohibition, surely should apply
both in the Land and abroad; and the same logic on two grounds
applies also to orlah fruit."

II.11   A. R. Eleazar b. R. Simeon says, [38B] "Every commandment for
which the Israelites became liable before they entered the Land
applies in the Land and abroad, and every commandment for
which the Israelites became liable only after they came into the
Land applies only in the Land, except for the forgiveness of debts,
the redemption of fields that have been sold, and the sending
forth free of the Hebrew slave in the Seventh Year. For even
though they became liable to them only after they had come into
the Land, they do apply in the Land and abroad" [T. Qid. 1:12A-
C].

II.12   A. Except for the forgiveness of debts: But that's a personal duty [and
applies even before entry into the Land]!

           B.   *It had nonetheless to be made articulate because of that which
has been taught on Tannaite authority, for it has been taught
on Tannaite authority:* Rabbi says, "'This is the manner of
release: Release [by every creditor of that which he has lent
his neighbor' (Deut. 15:2) – it is of two different acts of
release that Scripture speaks, one, the release of lands, the
other, the release of debts. When you release lands you
release debts, and when you do not release lands, you do not
release debts."

           C.   *But why not say:* In a place in which you have to remit
ownership of the land, you release debts, but in a place in
which you do not remit ownership of the land, which is to
say, abroad, you also do not release debts?

           D.   Scripture says, "Because the Lord's release has been
proclaimed" (Lev. 25:10) – under all circumstances.

II.13   A. The sending forth free of the Hebrew slave in the Seventh Year:
But that's a personal duty [and applies even before entry into the
Land]!

           B. *It might have entered your mind to think,* since Scripture states, "and
you shall proclaim liberty throughout the Land," that requirement

applies only in the Land but not abroad; therefore Scripture says, "It is a Jubilee" – under all circumstances.

C. Then why does Scripture make reference to "the Land"?

D. When the emancipation of slaves applies in the Land, it applies abroad; when it does not apply in the Land, it does not apply abroad.

II.14 A. *We have learned in the Mishnah:* [Consumption] in any locale [of] new produce, that is, that on behalf of which the omer has not yet been offered, is forbidden by Scripture. And the [prohibition against eating produce which is] orlah [that is, deriving from fruit trees in the first three years of their growth] applies outside of the Land of Israel] by law. And [the prohibition against planting together] diverse kinds [in a vineyard applies outside of the Land of Israel] by authority of the scribes [M. Orl. 3:9Kff.].

B. [With reference to the clause, and the [prohibition against eating produce which is] orlah [applies outside of the Land of Israel] by law], *what is the meaning of* by law?

C. Said R. Judah said Samuel, "It means, a law practiced in the province [as matter of local custom]."

D. Ulla said R. Yohanan [said], "It is a law given to Moses at Sinai."

E. *Said Ulla to R. Judah, "From my perspective, in maintaining that* it is a law given to Moses at Sinai, *there is no problem in distinguishing between orlah that is subject to doubt and mixed seeds' produce that is subject to doubt, in line with what we have learned in the Mishnah:* [Fruit about which there is] a doubt [whether or not it is in the status] of orlah – [if it is] in the Land of Israel [the fruit in question] is forbidden [deemed to have the status of orlah]. But in Syria [the fruit] is permitted [not in the status of orlah]. And outside of the Land [of Israel], one may go down [to the orchard] and purchase [such fruit], provided that he does not see him [the seller] pick [the fruit] [M. Orl. 3:9A-D], *while with respect to mixed seeds, we have learned in the Mishnah:* [As to] a vineyard which was planted with vegetables [which are of diverse kinds], and outside of [this vineyard] vegetables [of like kinds] are sold – [if it is] in the Land of Israel [the produce] is forbidden [under the law of diverse kinds]. But in Syria, it is permitted. And outside of the Land [of Israel], one may go down and buy [this produce], provided that he [the Israelite] does not pick [it] with his hand [M. Orl. 3:9F-J]. *But, by contrast, from your perspective,* [39A] *the Tannaite formulation should present in both cases:* Either this party [the Israelite] may enter the field and make a purchase, or that party [the gentile] may enter the field and gather the produce [since produce in both classifications falls into the same classification, neither one resting on the law of the Torah]."

F. *Well, didn't Samuel say to R. Anan, "Repeat as the Tannaite formulation:* 'Either this party [the Israelite] may enter the field and make a purchase, or that party [the gentile] may enter the field and gather the produce'?"

G. *Mar b. Rabana repeated this rule to yield a lenient result:* "Either this party [the Israelite] may enter the field and make a purchase, or that party [the gentile] may enter the field and gather the produce, provided that he [the Israelite] does not pick [it] with his hand."

II.15   A.   *Said Levi to Samuel, "Your eminence, provide me with produce that may or may not be orlah fruit and I'll eat it."*

        B.   *R. Avayya and Rabbah bar R. Hanan supplied one another with produce that may or may not be orlah fruit.*

        C.   *Say the sharpest wits in Pumbedita,* "The prohibition of orlah produce does not apply outside of the Land of Israel."

        D.   *R. Judah sent word to R. Yohanan reporting this ruling, to which he sent word in reply, "Shut away the rule governing produce that may or may not be orlah fruit, suppress the rule as it concerns produce that certainly are orlah fruit, and announce that produce in this classification must be stored away and not eaten. And whoever takes the view,* the prohibition of orlah produce does not apply outside of the Land of Israel – may he have no children or grandchildren 'that shall cast the line by lot in the congregation of the Lord' (Mic. 2:5)."

        E.   *Well, then, in accord with which authority do the sharpest wits in Pumbedita make their decision?*

        F.   *They make their ruling in accord with the following, which has been taught on Tannaite authority:* R. Eleazar b. R. Yosé says in the name of R. Yosé b. Durmasqah, who made the statement in the name of R. Yosé the Galilean, who made the statement in the name of R. Yohanan b. Nuri, who made the statement in the name of R. Eliezer the Elder: "The prohibition of orlah produce does not apply outside of the Land of Israel [T. Orl. 1:8P]."

        G.   *Isn't there now! And haven't we learned in the Mishnah:* R. Eliezer says, "Also: Except for [the prohibition against eating] new [produce before the omer is waved on the sixteenth of Nisan] (Lev. 23:14)"?

        H.   *Repeat the Tannaite formulation as:* Except for the prohibition against eating new produce.

II.16   A.   Said R. Assi said R. Yohanan, "The prohibition of orlah produce abroad derives from a law revealed to Moses at Sinai."

        B.   *Said R. Zira to R. Assi, "But haven't we learned in the Mishnah:* [Fruit about which there is] a doubt [whether or not it is in the status] of orlah – [if it is] in the Land of Israel [the fruit in question] is forbidden [deemed to have the status of orlah]. But in Syria [the fruit] is permitted [not in the status of orlah]. And outside of the Land [of Israel], one may go down [to the orchard] and purchase [such fruit], provided that he does not see him [the seller] pick [the fruit] [M. Orl. 3:9A-D]?"

        C.   *He was struck dumb for the moment, but then he said to him, "Maybe this is how the law was formulated:* Produce that may or may not be subject to the prohibition of orlah is permitted in the diaspora; produce that certainly is orlah fruit is forbidden."

II.17   A.   Said R. Assi said R. Yohanan, "By the ruling of the Torah, violators of the prohibition of mixed seeds [in the exile] are flogged."

        B.   *Said to him R. Eleazar b. R. Yosé, "But lo, we have learned in the Mishnah:* And [the prohibition against planting together] diverse kinds [in a vineyard applies outside of the Land of Israel] by authority of the scribes [M. Orl. 3:9M]?"

C. *No problem, the one speaks of mixed seeds in a vineyard, the other speaks of grafting heterogeneous trees.*

D. *That accords with Samuel, for* said Samuel, "Scripture states, 'You shall keep my statutes...' (Lev. 19:19), meaning 'the statutes that I have already ordained for you,' hence: 'You shall not let your cattle breed with a diverse kind; you shall not sow your field with mixed seed' (Lev. 19:19). Just as for your beast, the prohibition is against hybridization, so in respect to your field, the prohibition is against hybridization. Just as the prohibition applies to your beast whether in the Land or outside of the Land, so with respect to your field, the prohibition applies whether it is in the Land or outside of the Land."

E. *But isn't the word "your field" written [meaning, what belongs to you alone, hence in the Land of Israel]?*

F. *That serves to exclude from the prohibition the planting of mixed seeds outside of the Land of Israel.*

II.18 A. *R. Hanan and R. Anan were engaged in discussion and walking along the way. They saw someone sowing mixed seeds together. He said to him, "Well, will the master join me in excommunicating him?"*

B. *He said to him, "You don't see this matter clearly."*

C. *Then again they saw someone who was sowing wheat and barley among vines. He said to him, "Well, will the master join me in excommunicating him?"*

D. *He said to him, "Don't we accept as established what R. Josiah said, for he said, 'The law of diverse kinds is not violated unless one has sowed a wheat seed, barley seed, and grape kernel, with one and the same throw'?"*

II.19 A. *R. Joseph would mix seeds and sow them.* Said to him Abbayye, "But haven't we learned in the Mishnah, And [the prohibition against planting together] diverse kinds [in a vineyard applies outside of the Land of Israel] by authority of the scribes [M. Orl. 3:9M]?"

B. *He said to him, "No problem, the rule just cited speaks of mixed seeds in the vineyard, but what I'm doing is mixing seeds. Mixed seeds in the vineyard, of which all benefit, are forbidden by the authority of rabbis outside of the Land; mixing other seeds, of which in the Land benefit is not forbidden, is not forbidden by the rule of rabbis outside of the Land."*

C. *But then R. Joseph retracted, saying, "What I said is nonsense. For Rab sowed the garden patches for the household of Rab in separate beds. How come? Obviously, to avoid mixing seeds."*

D. *Said to him Abbayye, "Well, there is no problem if we had in hand the tradition that [39B], he sowed four distinct species on four sides of the bed and one in the middle [thus keeping the species distinct]. But here, he did so only because it would look pretty or to save work for the worker."*

I.1-2 explain the meaning of the Mishnah sentence's language, and No. 2 moves on to discover the scriptural foundations for the stated rule.

II.1-2 clarify the intent of the dispute in the Mishnah. In the context of the discussion of No. 2, Nos. 3-7, with an appendix at Nos. 8-9, then take up the conclusion concerning the sense of the Mishnah language that **I.1** established, which certainly proves that the entire, huge composite is in fact a composition worked out under uniform auspices and for a single purpose. Nos. 10-11, with its talmud at Nos. 13, 14, then proceed to Tannaite complements. Following the familiar logic of the document, Nos. 15+16, 17-18, ending up with concrete cases at Nos. 19-20, move on to the intersecting rules pertinent to our Mishnah problem.

1:10A-D

A. Whoever does a single commandment – they do well for him and lengthen his days.
B. And he inherits the Land.
C. And whoever does not do a single commandment – they do not do well for him and do not lengthen his days.
D. And he does not inherit the Land.

I.1   A. *By way of contradiction:* These are things the benefit of which a person enjoys in this world, while the principal remains for him in the world to come: [Deeds in] honor of father and mother, [performance of] righteous deeds, and [acts which] bring peace between a man and his fellow. But the study of Torah is as important as all of them together [M. Peah 1:1C-E]. [Freedman: Thus only for these is one reward in this world, while the Mishnah says that that is so of any precept.]

    B. *Said R. Judah, "This is the sense of the matter:* Whoever does a single commandment – over and above the advantage deriving from his inherited merits – they do well for him, and he is as though he had carried out the entire Torah."

    C. *Then does it follow that for these other deeds, one is rewarded even for a single one [with no other deeds to one's credit]?*

    D. Said R. Shemaiah, "It is to say that if there is an equal balance, then that one deed tips the scale in his favor."

I.2   A. *But is it really true that* if there is an equal balance, then that one deed tips the scale in his favor? *And by way of contradiction:* In the case of anyone whose merits are more than his sins, they punish him, and it is as though he had burned the entire Torah, leaving of it not even a single letter, and whoever's sins outnumber his merits – they do good for him, and it is as though he observed the entire Torah, and did not leave out a single letter of it [so he gets his reward in this world and suffers in the world to come]?

    B. *Said Abbayye, "The Mishnah paragraph before us means, they make for him a happy day and a miserable day."* [Freedman: The Mishnah means he is punished in this world, the punishment being a happy day for him, since he thereby wholly enjoys the next.]

    C. *Raba said, "Lo, who is the authority behind this ruling? It is R. Jacob, who has said, 'There is no reward in this world for carrying out the religious duties. For it has been taught on*

Tannaite authority: R. Jacob says, "You have not got a single religious duty that is written in the Torah, the reward of which is not specified alongside, that does not depend for its fulfillment on the resurrection of the dead. For example, with reference to honor of father and mother, it is written, 'That your days may be prolonged and that it may go well with you' (Deut. 5:16); with regard to sending forth the dam out of the nest: 'that it may be well with you and that you may prolong your days' (Deut. 22:6). Now, if someone's father said to him, 'Climb up into the loft and bring me the pigeons,' and he went up to the loft, sent away the dam and took the young, and climbing down, fell and was killed – what are we to make of this one's 'happiness' and 'length of days'"? But the language, "in order that it may be well with you" refers to a day that is wholly good; and "in order that your days may be long" means, on the day that is entirely long.'"

D. *But maybe such a thing never really happened?*

E. *R. Jacob saw such an incident.*

F. *Well, maybe the victim was thinking about doing a sin [at the time of the accident].*

G. A wicked thought the Holy One, blessed be He, does not join with a virtuous deed.

H. *Well, maybe the victim was thinking about idolatry [at the time of the accident,] and it is written, "That I may take the house of Israel in their own heart" (Ezek. 14:5)?*

I. *That is precisely what he meant to say: "If you ever imagine that the reward of a religious duty comes in this world, then how come keeping the religious duties didn't protect him from being led to such wicked meditations?"*

J. But lo, said R. Eleazar, "Those who are engaged in carrying out a religious duty are not harmed."

K. *There, while they are en route to carry out the religious duty, it is different [but here, he was climbing back down, having done the duty].*

L. But lo, said R. Eleazar, "Those who are engaged in carrying out a religious duty are not harmed – coming or going."

M. *It was a rickety ladder, so the possibility of an accident was ready at hand, and wherever the possibility of accident is ready at hand, there is no relying on miracles, for it is written, "And Samuel said, how can I go? If Saul hears it, he'll kill me" (1 Sam. 16:2).*

I.3 A. *Said R. Joseph, "If the Apostate [Elisha b. Abbuya] had interpreted this verse of Scripture in the way that R. Jacob, the son of his daughter, did, he would never have fallen into sin."*

B. *So what's the story with the Apostate?*

C. *There are those who say that he saw an incident like this one, and there are those who say, he saw the tongue of Huspit the Interpreter being dragged by a pig. He said, "Should the tongue that brought forth pearls lick the dust?" He apostatized and so sinned.*

I.4 A. *R. Tobi bar R. Qisna contrasted for Raba the following rules: "We have learned in the Mishnah, whoever does a single commandment – they* do well for him. *So if he does it, that is so, but if not, not, and by contrast:* If one sits and does not transgress, they give him a reward like that going to one who does a religious duty!"

B.   *He said to him, "The latter speaks of a case in which* an opportunity to sin comes to hand and he is saved from it."

C.   *It is like the case of R. Hanina bar Pappi, whom a certain Roman lady propositioned. He said something that brought up boils and scabs over his whole body. She did something that healed him. He ran away and hid in a bathhouse where, even if two people came in together, even by day, they would suffer harm [from the local demon, but he wasn't injured]. The next day, the rabbis said to him, "So who protected you?"*

D.   He said to them, "Two [40A] of Caesar's armor bearers guarded me all night long."

E.   They said to him, "Maybe you had a chance to score and you were saved from it? *For we have learned as a Tannaite statement:* Whoever has a chance to score and is saved from it – they do a miracle for him."

I am not sure how to classify the following, where a contemporary is adduced as an illustration of a verse of Scripture.

I.5   A.   **"Bless you the Lord, you messengers of his, you mighty in strength, who fulfill his word, obeying the voice of his word" (Ps. 103:20): For example, R. Sadoq and his companions.**

    B.   *A Roman lady propositioned R. Sadoq. He said to her, "I feel faint and I can't do it, maybe you've got something to eat?"*

    C.   *She said to him, "Well, there's something unclean."*

    D.   *He said to her, "So what conclusion am I supposed to draw, that someone who does this sin can eat that?"*

    E.   *She was lighting the oven to put the meat in it, but he went and sat in the oven. She said to him, "So what's going on?"*

    F.   *He said to her, "Someone who does this [act you want of me is so punished that he] falls into that [oven]."*

    G.   *She said to him, "If I'd known it was such a big deal for you guys, I wouldn't have bothered you."*

I.6   A.   *R. Kahana was selling baskets. A certain Roman lady propositioned him. He said to her, "I'll go and get ready." He went up to the roof and threw himself down, but Elijah came along and caught him.*

    B.   *He said to him, "You made me rush four hundred parasangs to do this!"*

    C.   *He said to him, "So what made it happen? Isn't it poverty [that makes me go sell baskets to women]?"*

    D.   *He gave him a basketful of denars.*

I.7   A.   *Raba pointed out to R. Nahman the following contrast: "We have learned in the Mishnah:* These are things the benefit of which a person enjoys in this world, while the principal remains for him in the world to come: [Deeds in] honor of father and mother, [performance of] righteous deeds, and [acts which] bring peace between a man and his fellow. But the study of Torah is as important as all of them together [M. Pe. 1:1C-E]. And with respect to honor of parents, it is written, 'that your days may be long and that it may go well with you' (Deut. 5:16); of performance of righteous deeds: 'He who pursues righteousness and loving kindness finds life, righteousness, and honor' (Prov. 21:21). As to bringing peace, it is said, 'seek peace and pursue it' (Ps. 34:15), and said R. Abbahu, 'We learn by verbal analogy the meaning of pursuing in two distinct passages; here, 'seek peace and pursue it,' and elsewhere, 'he who pursues after righteousness and loving kindness' (Prov. 21:21). As to study of the Torah: 'For that is your life and the length of your days' (Deut. 30:20). But as to sending forth the dam from the nest it is written, 'that it may be well with you and that you may prolong your days' (Deut. 22:7). *So why not add this item to the list?"*

B.   *"The Tannaite authority has left out some appropriate items."*

C.   *"Yes, but he's used the language,* These [in particular] are things, *and you maintain, The Tannaite authority has left out some appropriate items!?"*

D.   *Said Raba, "R. Idi explained it to me in these terms: '"Say you of the righteous when he is good that they shall eat the fruit of their doings" (Isa. 3:10) – so is there a righteous man who is good and a righteous man who isn't? But he who is good to Heaven and good to people is a righteous man who is good, but good to Heaven and not good to human beings – that's a righteous person who's not good. So too: "Woe to the wicked man who is evil, for the reward of his hands shall be given to him" (Isa. 3:11) – so is there a wicked person who is wicked and a wicked person who isn't? But one who is wicked to Heaven and wicked to people is a wicked person who is wicked; and one who is wicked to Heaven but not wicked to people is a wicked person who is not wicked.'"*

I.8   A.   Merit has both principal and interest: "Say you of the righteous when he is good that they shall eat the fruit of their doings" (Isa. 3:10).

B.   Wickedness has principal but no interest: "Woe to the wicked man who is evil, for the reward of his hands shall be given to him" (Isa. 3:11).

C.   So how do I interpret the language, "Therefore shall the wicked eat of the fruit of their own way and be filled with their own devices" (Prov. 1:31)?

D.   A transgression that produces results has results, but one that does not produce results has no results.

I.9   A.   Good intention joins with deeds: "Then they that feared the Lord spoke with one another, and the Lord listened and heard and a book of remembrance was written before him for those who feared the Lord and who thought about his name" (Mal. 3:16).

B.   *What is the meaning of* and who thought about his name?

C.   Said R. Assi, "Even if a person has given thought to doing a religious duty but was prevented from doing it, Scripture credits him as though he had done it."

D. As to bad intention, the Holy One does not join it together with a deed, as it is said, "If I regarded iniquity in my heart, the Lord would not hear" (Ps. 66:18).

E. Then how do I interpret the verse, "Lo, I bring evil upon this people, even the fruit of their intentions" (Jer. 6:19)?

F. In the case of intention that bears fruit the Holy One, blessed be He, combines the intention with action; in the case of intention that does not bear fruit, the Holy One, blessed be He, does not join intention with action.

G. Then how do I interpret the verse, "That I may take the house of Israel in their own heart" (Ezek. 14:5)?

H. *Said R. Aha bar Jacob, "That is written with reference to idolatry. For a master has said, 'The sin of idolatry is so weighty that one who denies idolatry is as though he had confessed to the entirety of the whole Torah.'"*

I. *Ulla said, "It is in line with what R. Huna said, for said R. Huna, 'Once a man has committed a transgression and gone and repeated it, it is permitted to him.'"*

J. "It is permitted to him" – *can you possibly imagine it?*

K. Rather: "It is treated as though it were permitted."

I.10   A. Said R. Abbahu in the name of R. Hanina, "It is better for someone to transgress in private but not profane the Name of Heaven in public: 'As for you, house of Israel, thus says the Lord God: Go, serve every one his idols, and hereafter also, if you will not obey me; but my holy name you shall not profane' (Ezek. 20:39)."

B. Said R. Ilai the Elder, "If someone sees that his impulse to sin is overpowering him, he should go somewhere where nobody knows him and put on ordinary clothing and cloak himself in ordinary clothing and do what he wants, but let him not profane the Name of Heaven by a public scandal."

C. *Is that so now! And hasn't it been taught on Tannaite authority:* Whoever has no concern for the honor owing to his Creator is worthy of not having come into the world. *And what would be such a case?* Rabbah says, "This refers to someone who stares at a rainbow." R. Joseph says, "This refers to someone who commits a transgression in secret."

D. *There is no contradiction, the one speaks of a case in which he can control his urge, the other, a case in which he cannot control his urge.*

I.11   A. *We have learned in the Mishnah there:* They do not allow credit in connection with profaning the name of God, whether it was done unwittingly or intentionally. *What is the meaning of* They do not allow credit?

B. Said Mar Zutra, "They don't keep books like a shopkeeper [and give credit; they exact the penalty immediately]."

C. Mar b. Rabana said, "It is to say that if one's account of sin and merit is in balance, then profaning God's name tips the scale."

I.12   A. *Our rabbis have taught on Tannaite authority:*

B. One should always [40B] see himself as if he is half meritorious and half guilty. If he did a single commandment, happy is he, for he has inclined the balance for himself to the side of merit. If he committed a single transgression, woe is he, for he has inclined the balance to the side of guilt. Concerning this one it is said, "One sinner destroys much good" (Qoh. 9:18), for on account of a single sin that he commits, much good is lost to him.

C. R. Eleazar b. R. Simeon says, "For the world is judged by the conduct of the majority in it, and an individual is judged by the majority of the deeds that he has done; if he did a single commandment, happy is he, for he has inclined the balance for himself and for the world as well to the side of merit. If he committed a single transgression, woe is he, for he has inclined the balance to the side of guilt for himself and for the world, for it is said, 'One sinner destroys much good' (Qoh. 9:18) – for on account of a single sin that he commits, much good is lost to him and to the whole world."

D. R. Simeon b. Yohai says, "If a man was righteous his entire life but at the end he rebelled, he loses the whole, for it is said, 'The righteousness of the righteous shall not deliver him in the day of his transgression' (Ezek. 33:12). And even if one is completely wicked all his life but repents at the end, he is not reproached with his wickedness, for it is said, 'And as for the wickedness of the wicked, he shall not fall thereby in the day that he turns from his wickedness' (Ezek. 33:12)" [T. Qid. 1:13-15].

E. Well, why not regard the case of the righteous one who rebels at the end as one that is half transgression and half merit?

F. *Said R. Simeon b. Laqish, "It is a case of his regretting his former, good deeds."*

I.1+2-3, 4 work out the expected interest in intersecting Mishnah rulings. A sequence of thematically pertinent compositions form a large composite as an appendix, Nos. 5-6. Once the secondary materials are added, Nos. 7+8-12 then bring us to a secondary expansion on the intersecting Mishnah passage cited at the outset, another example of the closely woven character of the composite.

1:10E-G

E. Whoever has learning in Scripture, Mishnah, and right conduct will not quickly sin,

F. since it is said, "And a threefold cord is not quickly broken" (Qoh. 4:12).

G. And whoever does not have learning in Scripture, Mishnah, and right conduct has no share in society.

I.1 A. Said R. Eliezer bar Sadoq, "To what are the righteous compared in this world? To a tree that is standing in a clean place, with its foliage extending from it to an unclean place. What do people say? 'Cut off the foliage from the tree so that the whole of it may be clean, as is its character.'

B.   "Thus the Holy One, blessed be He, brings suffering upon the righteous in this world so that they will inherit the world to come: 'And though your beginning is small, yet the latter end shall greatly increase' (Job 8:7).

C.   "To what are the wicked compared in this world? To a tree that is standing in an unclean place, with its foliage extending from it to a clean place. What do people say? 'Cut off the foliage from the tree, so that the whole of it may be unclean, as is its character' [Avot deR. Nathan XXXIX.X.1].

D.   "Thus the Holy One, blessed be He, brings prosperity on the wicked in this world, so as to destroy them and throw them out to the nethermost rung: 'There is a way that seems right to man, but at the end of it are the ways of death' (Prov. 14:12)."

I.2   A.   Once R. Tarfon and the elders were reclining at a banquet in the upper room of the house of Nitezeh in Lud. This question was raised for them: "Is study greater or is action greater?"

B.   T. Tarfon responded: "Action is greater."

C.   R. Aqiba responded: "Study is greater."

D.   All responded, saying, "Study is greater, for study brings about action."

I.3   A.   *It has been taught on Tannaite authority:*

B.   R. Yosé says, "Great is study, for it preceded the commandment to separate dough-offering by forty years, the commandments governing priestly rations and tithes by fifty-four years, the commandments covering remission of debts by sixty-one years, the commandment concerning the Jubilee Year by one hundred and three years." [Freedman: The Torah was given to Israel two months after the Exodus from Egypt, but liability to dough-offering came into force forty years later, and so throughout.]

C.   ...One hundred and three years? *But it was a hundred and four.*

D.   *He takes the view that* the Jubilee effects the release of slaves and land at the outset.

E.   And just as study of the Torah came prior to the actual practice of it, so judgment on that account takes precedence over judgment concerning practice of the Torah.

F.   *That accords with R. Hamnuna, for* said R. Hamnuna, "The beginning of a person's judgment comes with the issue of study of Torah, for it is said, 'The beginning of judgment concerns the letting out of water' (Prov. 17:14) [and water stands for Torah]."

G.   And just as judgment concerning study takes priority over judgment concerning practice, so, too, the reward for studying the Torah takes priority over the reward for practice: "And he gave them the lands and nations, and they took the labor of the people in possession, that they might keep his statutes and observe his laws" (Ps. 105:44-45).

II.1   A.   And whoever does not have learning in Scripture, Mishnah, and right conduct has no share in society:

B.   Said R. Yohanan, "And he is invalid to give testimony."

II.2   A.   *Our rabbis have taught on Tannaite authority:*

B. He who eats out in the marketplace – lo, he is like a dog.

C. And there are those who say, "He is invalid to give testimony."

D. Said R. Idi bar Abin, "The decided law is in accord with the view of those who say."

II.3 A. Expounded Bar Qappara, "A temperamental person [41A] gets nothing but his anger. To a good man they feed the good taste of the fruit of his deeds.

B. "And whoever does not have learning in Scripture, Mishnah, and right conduct – forbid yourself by a vow from having any good from him: 'Nor sits in the seat of the scorners' (Prov. 1:1) – such a person is the very seat of the scorners."

I.1 adds a Tannaite complement. Nos. 2-3 pursue the theme invited by the statement of the Mishnah. II.1 provides a minor gloss for the Mishnah's rule, and No. 2, a Tannaite complement to No. 1. No. 3 provides a secondary expansion on the Mishnah sentence's language.

3

The Torah in the Talmud of Babylonia: An Overview

I. A Survey of the Principal Results

Let us survey the chapter before us, to find out whether we may generalize about how Scripture serves the framers of this Talmud. A few simple questions, repeated throughout, will give us our answer: Does a verse of Scripture provoke the formation of a composition? That is to say, if the author of a composition has identified in Scripture in particular the problem that concerns him and leads him to set forth his syllogism and evidence and argument, then Scripture has taken an active role in the formation of his composition. He has opened Scripture and written his composition. If, on the other hand, Scripture proves inert, simply providing a piece of information in a discussion framed in terms otherwise autonomous of the Torah, then we shall conclude that Scripture serves only episodically, instrumentally, not generatively, not autonomously, not independently. In the former case, Scripture forms an independent source of thought and argument, flowing into the pages of the Talmud as a mighty source of inquiry. In the latter, Scripture subordinates itself to a program of thought that is shaped elsewhere than in its pages. Not only so, but we must not ignore the question of where Scripture plays no role at all and ask, if a composition does not make reference to the Torah, then why is that the case? So in this review, we have two complementary questions in mind: Why, but also, why not? And, of course, so what?

Rather than specify a variety of questions flowing from that basic one, let me turn to our review of Bavli Qiddushin Chapter One's Scripture compositions and composites.[1]

1:1 I.1-4, 6. What is important here is that Scripture does not define the first concern of the framer of our Talmud. One fundamental question will be, what is the (scriptural) source of this statement? The question is asked only when the answer can, and will, be, "As it is said...." Scripture is assumed to be the sole source of facts that the Mishnah invokes but does not generate on its own. Now the one question is, does Scripture's source for the Mishnah facts take pride of place, and the answer is, sometimes, sometimes not. Why not here? Because the framer of the passage has another issue in mind, with no relevance to the source of the facts at hand. And yet, we see immediately, at I.1.C, Scripture is a ubiquitous presence, always at hand. Here, we take for granted that the usage of Scripture governs word choices in the Mishnah. Has Scripture generated this passage? Of course not. Scripture is not ignored, but it also is hardly a principal player in our composition. The same judgment pertains to 1:1 I.2.D. And that results in a secondary development of the composition at No. 2, since we have contradictory usages of words in Scripture, and these have to be sorted out. The interest in the same matter accounts for the contribution of Scripture at Nos. 3, 4. Here again, we need to make some sense out of how Scripture uses certain words. The upshot is, Scripture serves as a source of incontrovertible linguistic facts. The later stages in the composition of No. 4 show that the Mishnah serves in precisely the same way and is subjected to the same survey and analysis; there is no meaningful difference in the reading accorded to the two documents.

The same comments seem to me to apply without much variation to the following: 1:1 III.33.C; 1:1 IV.3; 1:1 V.1; 1:1 V.3.G, J; 1:1 VI.3; 1:1 IX.1-X.1 (in this case there is a substantial secondary expansion of the simple form, how do we know + a verse of Scripture); 1:2 I.1-6 (an entire talmud flowing from the simple form); 1:2 I.7-10; 1:2 II.1; 1:2 III.1; 1:2 IV.1; 1:2 V.1-2 (a matched set of the least complex variety); 1:2 VI.2.B; 1:2 VI.3-4; 1:2 VI.6-13; 1:2 VI.15-17; 1:2 VI.18.F-L; 1:2 VI.19; 1:2 VI.21; 1:2 VI. 24-25; 1:2 VI.27 (note the contrast to No. 26); 1:2 VI.37-39; 1:2 VI. 40 (if...how do we know...as it is said..., a familiar variation on the normal form); 1:2 VI.41; 1:2 VI.43; 1:2 VI.45.C; 1:2 VII.1, VIII.1-3 (I know only that....how do I know...); 1:2 VIII.5; 1:2 VIII.8-17 (No. 15 shows that, as with the

---

[1]That distinction is essential to all my analytical initiatives and is explained in *The Rules of Composition of the Talmud of Babylonia. The Cogency of the Bavli's Composite* (Atlanta, 1991: Scholars Press for South Florida Studies in the History of Judaism).

Mishnah, so with Scripture, there is no redundancy); 1:3 I.1 (how on the basis of Scripture do we know...); 1:3 IV.4; 1:3 IV.9-10; 1:3 IV.15.U-X; 1:5 I.1-VI.1; 1:7 I.3-4; 1:7 I.6, 7, 8; 1:7 I.17 (dispute on the meaning of a cited verse yields two distinct versions of the simple form at hand); 1:7 I.18, 19, 20 (variations on the simple exegetical form; 1:7 I.26; 1:7 I.27-28; 1:7 I.29-30; 1:7 II.1.C; 1:7 II.7, 8; 1:7 II.28.B, D; 1:7 II.29; 1:7 II.30-34+35, 36, 37 (Scripture says...might one say...Scripture says... – a complex composition repeating a simple form); 1:7 V.1; 1:7 VI.1; 1:7 VI.2; 1:8 I.1-VII.1; 1:8 IX.1; 1:9 I.2; 1:9 II.1-7; 1:8 II.8, 9; 1:8 II.12; 1:8 II.18; 1:10A-D I.5 (verse + for example); 1:10A-D I.7-10, 12. In all of these cases, the governing form involves citation of a verse followed by the imputation of a sense to that verse, for example, a paraphrase or an eisegesis of some other sort. The list at hand does not convey the impression that a survey of the document establishes, which is that these kinds of demonstrations form a principal component of our Talmud's repertoire, as a glance at the enormous composition at 1:2 I.1-6, 7-10 shows. Here we are dealing with the mainstay of an entire Talmud.

1:1 II.1-6. Here we find the classic form used when Scripture is asked to serve as a source of facts in the Mishnah. What I find important here is a subordinate unit, namely, II.1.C (and its numerous equivalents). There we see a process of analytical exegetical reasoning that in no important way differs from the processes of reading the Mishnah and analyzing its evidence and propositions. We propose a possibility, but then ask whether other possibilities may prove more plausible – a standard analytical initiative in the Talmud: You say this, but what about that – the opposite? That approach to a proposition governs, pertaining here to the interpretation of Scripture as much as in other passages it pertains to the interpretation of the Mishnah or the analysis of a given proposition. Scripture's paramount role here derives from the simple fact that its evidence is required, in context, for the solution to the problem at hand. The identity of hermeneutical principles pertaining to the Mishnah, Scripture, and authoritative legal sayings in general is proven beyond reasonable doubt at No. 3, a standard demonstration that a variety of facts had to be specified, since none of them can have been adduced from any of the others. Scripture does not repeat itself; neither does the Mishnah. In general, two categories we thought comparable prove otherwise, on which account Scripture, or the Mishnah, or a Tannaite formulation of law, has to make explicit the rule governing each.

1:1 III.1-5. The polemic that Scripture alone defines valid taxa is carried on here. This is not particular to the Bavli, of course, but characterizes all of Sifra and occurs also in the two Sifrés. Compositions of this classification make the same point in many ways, which is that

Scripture alone supplies reliable taxa for comparison and contrast. While the discussion is specific to its case, the polemic is general; Scripture is viewed in detail, but the point is always the same general one. The secondary expansion, denying that polythetic taxonomy solves the problem of classification, and maintaining that only Scripture guides us to valid category formations for comparison and contrast, underlines the main point. The point is not that Scripture is perceived as autonomous of the Mishnah; it is that in a conflict between two principles of taxonomy, Scripture's is sustained. The one principle is that we classify things by reference to intrinsic traits, for example, as in natural history; the other is that we classify things by appeal to the categories defined by Scripture. Argument focuses upon the latter; but the argument then is not an exegetical one, let alone a claim that the Mishnah rests on Scripture. It is an argument about taxonomy, and the point pertains as much to the Mishnah as to Scripture, namely, the Torah, and not nature, dictates the classification of things. So to see this composition as an argument that the Mishnah rests on Scripture, not on the nature of things, as I have maintained, is to state matters in a way that now appears slightly awry. The issue is not the Mishnah's classification of things as against Scripture's, it is the Torah's classification of things as against nature's.

1:1 III.12. Scripture does not generate this composition, it serves to provide a fact required for the solution of its problem. We draw information from current usage of the language and also from Scripture; the latter is privileged, but not determinative.

1:1 III.29. Let us pay close attention to this classic exegetical composition, since it defines one of the paramount ways in which the Torah enters into the Talmud. The form is simple and recurs time and again:

> 'If there be yet many years, according to them he shall give back the price of his redemption out of the money with which he was acquired' (Lev. 25:51) – he may be acquired by money, not by produce or utensils.

That is to say, we have a simple citation of a verse, followed by a paraphrase in which we say in our own words what we think the verse means. Compositions of this kind, simple or elaborate, define one principal way in which the Torah makes its way into the Talmud. What they contribute is information, facts upon which the framer of a composition or even a composite of the Talmud proposes to draw in attaining his goal. A passage of this kind rarely defines the issue or direction of a composition, but commonly exemplifies a point or validates one. Does the Talmud build sequences of such citations and glosses of verses of Scripture? Not frequently, and rarely without a purpose defined by a context other than the (mere) exposition of a verse or sequences of verses. Hence, when a verse of Scripture is subjected to analysis (for example, citation and paraphrase), it is seldom because of a free-standing interest in that verse and its meaning, but it is often because of a contingent purpose. That purpose is known to the framer of the composition (or composite) responsible for the citation of the passage.

Now that point, which readers will introduce for themselves time and again, contradicts the form of the composition. The composition is framed to highlight the verse of Scripture and to lay stress on the autonomous character of its sense and meaning: this verse means that, without regard to the issues set for us by any context that transcends the one-dimensional, exegetical task, pure and simple. So whoever made up the passage – verse, [this means:] ... – treated the task as primary, but whoever called upon the same passage regarded it as subordinate and instrumental. What this means for our larger question is, for a piece of scriptural information – verse and its paraphrase or interpretation – makes its way into a Talmud composition or composite, it has to gain admission by appeal to a purpose other than the exposition of Scripture in its own terms. So the composition on its own – this modest item, 1:1 III.29.B – presents us with a somewhat complicated literary phenomenon. In its own terms, it is a Scripture commentary; it has been written to cite and explain the meaning of a verse. It is, however, not preserved for us by the Talmud as part of a sustained commentary, for example, on Lev. 25. It has been taken over and used by the Talmud for a purpose quite distinct from the one served by its original formulation. It is the simple fact that the Torah finds its way into the Talmud on terms defined by the Talmud. But it is also a fact that the Torah has generated an exegetical process of its own, not subordinated to the purpose of Mishnah exegesis (for example). Where and how that process produced its results we cannot now say; all we have is the selection, among those results, made by those who formulated Talmud compositions and composites.

1:1 IV.1. Here the usage of Scripture is analyzed, in a manner entirely routine to the analysis of a usage of the Mishnah or a usage of everyday speech. What makes the passage noteworthy is the conclusion that rabbis sometimes do not derive from Scripture exegesis solid and incontrovertible evidence of their position, but impute to Scripture something very like the position that they wish to find there. So strict evidentiary standards govern, and facile solutions are unwelcome, in the reading of Scripture.

1:1 IV.4. A different appeal to Scripture involves finding out how advocates of conflicting positions read the relevant verses. Here we engage in not an exegesis, for example, a paraphrase of what we think

Scripture says, but an analysis of Scripture's usages. Scripture treats matters as comparable, so the conditions that pertain to the one pertain to the other. Then the dispute involves the identification of what is truly subject to comparison.

1:1 VII.10. Scripture is quoted for illustrative purposes, to endow a sentiment with authority and illustration, in the way in which people may cite a phrase of Shakespeare or a verse of Scripture today. Here the cited verse plays no role at all in the proposition of the composition. But the exposition of the illustrative verse then defines the main lines of interest of the composition.

1:1 VII:11. Time and again, the Torah is present even when a particular verse is not quoted. This item is of interest because of its playing out the theme of the law of the Torah as against the law decreed by scribes, sages, or rabbis (the terms are interchangeable in this context). The distinction is important, here as in so many other places, because a classification deemed to derive from the Torah is accorded weightier status than one not; here, if the classification of debt derives from the Torah, then certain other considerations come into play.

1:1 VIII.1. Once the Torah has defined a category, here, with a particular verse in hand, then reasoning permits us to extend or subdivide that category or to form another congruent to it. In this instance the exposition of the derivative category requires constant recourse to the mixture of Scripture and reason. If Scripture makes a given point, then that may be deemed exclusive, permitting a variety of other relationships. Where a verse of Scripture comes into play, moreover, the reading of that verse – one way rather than some other – dictates the outcome of an analytical problem.

1:1 XI.2. An inquiry into the foundations of the Mishnah's categories calls upon the logic of hierarchical classification (for example, an argument a fortiori) or a verse of Scripture, and the analysis differs not at all. Here we point out that logic can have yielded a false conclusion, and Scripture corrects it. What is of special interest is that a variety of propositions comes under examination, so that our principle of reading Scripture in the particular case at hand is tested and shown to be uniform for other cases as well. In this way what we show is the perfect consistency of not only Scripture or the Mishnah, but, of our exegetical principles in the reading of Scripture and the Mishnah. Part of perfection is avoidance of redundancy, and that, too, is demonstrated; if Scripture makes a statement, it is because that statement must be made; it makes a unique point; Scripture never repeats itself but always makes its point.

1:2 VI.26. Here the meaning of a verse of Scripture is subordinated to the problem that draws our attention to that verse. When Scripture uses a phrase, the possibilities of its meaning have to be investigated, each on its own. This requires us to compare usages in other verses of Scripture. We note that the exegesis does not define the course of argument but merely supplies facts required in context.

1:2 VI.35. The issue is whether the proposal at hand derives from Scripture or may be attained by logical deduction, in this case, an argument of hierarchical classification based on a fortiori reasoning. That proves not to be the case.

1:2 VI.46. Deriving facts from Scripture requires more than citing a verse; we have to know the rules that govern the reading of a verse, which tell us how in a consistent and objective way we may establish the facts. Scripture on its own is, while authoritative, essentially inert, and we have to know how to enter into its discipline. In the present case the issue is precisely how we establish the correct verbal analogy that will tell us the meaning of a word, hence the message of a rule. In this case there is a choice: read the verse as a statement, this, not that; or read the components of the verse in light of their meanings elsewhere. Scripture then raises questions, as much as it resolves them.

1:2 VIII.1-3. The same issue recurs. We have two distinct principles that operate, expressed as follows:

C. "You shall take" is an encompassing rule; "an awl" is an exclusionary particularization; "through his ear into the door" reverts and gives an encompassing rule. So where you have an encompassing rule, an exclusionary particularization, and another encompassing rule, you cover under the encompassing rule only what bears the traits of the exclusionary particularization; just as the exclusionary particularization states explicitly that the object must be of metal, so must anything used for the purpose be of metal.

D. *R. Yosé b. R. Judah interprets the categories of scriptural evidences of inclusionary and exclusionary usages:*

E. "You shall take" is inclusionary; "an awl" is exclusionary; "through his ear into the door" reverts and forms an inclusionary statement. Where you have an inclusionary, an exclusionary, and an inclusionary statement, the upshot is to encompass all things.

The dispute, then, is generated by the issue of which exegetical principle governs here, and the phenomena of Scripture will be adduced in evidence for both positions at hand.

1:2 VIII.6, 7. What is interesting here is that Scripture provides an allusion, which suffices in its own terms to make a point. As is commonly the case, just because a verse is not cited in so many words, that does not mean that Scripture is not in evidence. Scripture is always in evidence, and the only issue is, is Scripture at center stage or merely the backdrop. Here it is the backdrop – but also forms the defining center. The same is to be said of No. 7. We allude to Scripture, we take its facts for granted, and proceed from there to our problem.

1:2 VIII.18. Here we allude to the contents of Scripture, without a close reading of the verse at hand. How come Scripture stresses A (rather than B) – and a lesson follows. The traits of the thing about which Scripture speaks, rather than the wording of Scripture, here form the center of thought.

1:3 III.2. We derive a verbal analogy and then assign to the traits of the one the characteristics of the other.

1:3 IV.1.H. The verse here governs: the exegetical mode is, this, not that.

1:3 IV.2. Scripture is explicit on two categories; how do we know that two others fall into the same classification? We proceed to examine the traits of the categories, not the word of Scripture. The analysis shades off into an inquiry into hermeneutical principles, that is, in any case in which you have an encompassing generalization followed by a particularization, covered by the generalization is only what is contained in the particularization. So there is no boundary that distinguishes one type of inquiry into Scripture – one in which the traits of things, rather than the qualities of Scripture's wording, governs – from some other. We move easily back and forth; Scripture in no way governs the manner in which Scripture will be read, introduced, utilized, or, for that matter, ignored.

1:3 IV.15. "What is the scriptural basis..." gives way to a conflict over the governing analogy, here again shading over from exegesis to philosophy.

1:7 I.1. In interpreting a passage of the Mishnah, we propose a hypothesis and then test it against evidence deriving from various sources, including Scripture; Scripture is privileged here only because it has self-evidently valid facts to contribute:

> *What is the meaning of* For every commandment concerning the son to which the father is subject...? *Should we say, from every religious duty that the son is required to do for the father, women are exempt? But hasn't it been taught on Tannaite authority:* "Every man his mother and his father you shall fear" (Lev. 19:27) – I know only that that applies to the man. How do I know that it applies to the woman? When Scripture says, "his mother and his father you shall fear," lo, both of them are included

Without its facts beyond argument, Scripture would play no role; it does not form the foundation of the composition, only an incidental component to the solution of its problem.

1:7 I.21-25+26. The way in which words are spelled in Scripture is analyzed, with attention to the formal traits of the document, for example, its divisions, its midpoints, the spelling of its words, the number of verses here and there, and the like. This reading of Scripture is academic, and its purpose is to expound Scripture in the context of its own formal traits.

1:7 II.2. Scripture's usage forms the basis for a syllogistic argument. In stating matters in such a way, Scripture thereby establishes an analogy, and on the strength of that analogy, we are able to draw further consequences. In this way, Scripture is turned into a laboratory for the discovery of new truth.

1:7 II.10. Here the formation of Scripture yields a story with a point of its own, a "midrash" in one commonplace sense of the word. The wording of Scripture raises a question, and the question is formulated in a drama, in which opponents seize upon the wording to advance a criticism. Then the criticism is resolved by further citation of Scripture – a sequence of verses given dramatic form and controversial meaning.

1:7 II.15.C. Here we have a mere allusion to something in Scripture; this is hardly a scriptural composition.

1:7 II.44. This is a dispute about the sense of a verse of Scripture, not a propositional composition utilizing a verse in behalf of a given point. Here, the verse forms the basis for the composition, much as a dispute may form around the interpretation of a clause of the Mishnah; the form of course would be identical.

1:7 IV.1.H, 2-3. Scripture here forms a source of decisive facts, which have to be dealt with if a proposition is to stand. A sequence of verses has to be read to test a proposition. The entire, sustained and important composition depends on how Scripture is to be read, also on facts supplied by Scripture, also on the exegesis of various verses – the entire repertoire of the Talmud's analysis, in fact, responds to Scripture's entire legacy: specific statements, general themes, modes of wording, and the like.

1:8 II.16.D. This is just a routine allusion to a clause of a verse of Scripture.

1:10A-D I.2. The sense of a clause of a verse is imputed on the basis of observations of the world at large. The verse plays no paramount role in the passage.

1:10E-G I.1, 3.F, II.3. The use of Scripture is strictly illustrative; the theological discourse proceeds along its own lines. In none of these compositions does Scripture play a determinative part.

II. Generalizations?

Does Scripture define the program of the Talmud? No, except when it does.

Does Scripture supply essential facts to the Talmud? Yes, except when it doesn't.

Does Scripture form the main beam of a literary structure, or only a supporting post, or occasionally a minor detail?

All of the above.

In fact, we cannot generalize about the Torah in the Talmud. We find that the Torah defines the main lines of a composition, but only occasionally; it contributes important data, sometimes; and it forms the background of a discussion both everywhere and also only rarely. If I had to choose the single most characteristic appeal to the Torah, it is in the numerous compositions and composites, some brief, others quite formidable, that cite a verse of Scripture and paraphrase its sense so as to establish a fact. One such common form is, "how on the basis of Scripture do we know...," and another is, "Such and such is the case, as it is said...." But in these compositions, the Torah always forms a subordinated component, never defining the purpose of discourse.

A second mark that the Torah finds its way into the Talmud via the Mishnah (or other Tannaite formulations) derives from a complementary fact. Where a verse of the Torah is read, it is read in much the same way as a sentence of the Mishnah is analyzed. A single process of analytical thought – practical criticism, applied reason – governs throughout. It is rare to find analysis of a verse of Scripture that has no counterpart in analysis of a sentence of the Mishnah. The same considerations of balance, order, and formal equilibrium characteristic of the Talmudic dialectical analysis of a Mishnah passage or a legal problem govern. And what I take that fact to mean is that the Talmud reads the Torah by the same rules that dictate its reading of the Mishnah and associated statements. True, a sentence of the Torah is always set off, distinguished from the rest of its context, by citation language, for example, "as it is written" or "as it is said." But that is so when a Mishnah sentence is cited as well, for example, as we have learned in the Mishnah (TNN), or equivalent signals for other Tannaite formulations. But in the center of analytical thought, a single process functions throughout – the Talmud's. And that is so even when the exegetical media prove particular to the reading of Scripture, for example, the contrast between encompassing rule, exclusionary particularization, and encompassing rule, as against other ways of classifying precisely the same wording of a verse. The attitude of mind and the governing logic prove ubiquitous; only in details will a hermeneutic particular to Scripture, on the one side, as against one singularly relevant to the Mishnah, on the other, dictate thought.

That is not to suggest that materials upon which our framers draw, for example, compositions and even sizable composites prepared for some purpose other than that now served in the pages of the Talmud, do not focus upon Scripture and appeal to Scripture for the mainbeams of order and structure. On the contrary, a variety of compositions and composites of a narrowly exegetical character, focused upon Scripture, does make its appearance. We have sustained exercises proving that Scripture alone provides solid taxonomic guidance, the traits of things in themselves proving ambiguous. We note passages that take as their primary question the sense and implication of Scripture. But when these occur in the Talmud, they find their way in on the Talmud's sufferance, for the Talmud's purpose. Not only so, but most of the compositions and even some of the composites that do take Scripture for their focus find a more natural location in documents that center upon Scripture, for example, Sifra for proof of the priority of the Torah in the taxonomic process, Genesis Rabbah or Sifré to Deuteronomy for sustained treatments of sequential verses (of which few have passed our way in the present sample). In such instances the hypothesis presents itself that the compositions centered on a verse of Scripture, other than those that paraphrase the verse to provide information required for a Talmudic exposition, for example, of a Mishnah rule or of a law in general, or for the elaboration of an argument of the same classification, were worked out for documents other than this one.

The upshot is that the Torah's principal contribution to the Talmud comprises information, not inquiry of an abstract and speculative character, such as characterizes the type of compositions and composites in the Talmud that find no counterpart in any other rabbinic writing. When the Torah is primary, therefore, it demands a document organized around Scripture, not the Mishnah; where the Torah contributes, it contributes on terms defined outside of its own framework. And yet, that literary judgment, concerning the forms of discourse, contradicts the theological judgment, which has repeatedly come to the fore: the Talmud everywhere stands four-square on the Torah. Its authors say this in countless ways, but most eloquently when they do not say so at all.

So our result is puzzling. To repeat what I announced at the outset: in the Talmud the Torah plays an active and a passive role; it dictates the shape of inquiry and its logic, and it merely contributes inert facts to an inquiry framed in other terms altogether. In the Talmud the Torah forms the principal locus of discourse and takes up a merely tangential position. Verses of Scripture are accorded probative value and may be manipulated in an essentially formal manner. But if, as we have now seen, the Torah both determines the structure and program of a composition and even of large composites, and also plays scarcely any more than an illustrative, formal role, in a great many others, then we have to ask whether the Torah forms a valid taxic indicator in the

Talmud at all. By that I mean, if a given classification of data proves to be everything and its opposite, then something is wrong with that classification. Stated simply: we appear to have asked the wrong question. If we want to know about the Torah in the Talmud, the Talmud will not tell us. Why not?

III. Not "The Torah in the Talmud" but One Torah, Which Is the Talmud

When we speak about the Torah in the Talmud, we violate the language rules of the Talmud, and that is why our inquiry has produced hopelessly contradictory results. The framers of the Talmud did not use the word "Torah" only or mainly when they wished to refer to the Hebrew Scriptures. The word Torah bore a variety of valid meanings. And it is only in the context of that larger corpus of meanings that we shall grasp the implications of the evidence that we produce when we ask about the Torah in the Talmud. When we speak of torah, in rabbinical literature of late antiquity, we no longer denote a particular book, on the one side, or the contents of such a book, on the other. That simple fact explains why we find no evidence that the Hebrew Scriptures enjoy a privileged position in the formulation and formation of the Talmud – except as to the facts that they supply. But the one thing that the Talmud finds of only modest consequence are mere facts, out of the context of a sustained analytical argument or a complex exercise at problem solving. So far as the Torah provides facts, the document is inert, not active in the formation of the Talmud – and therefore, we have to conclude, the Torah is not active but inert in this writing. But the opposite is the case: the Torah is ubiquitous, present as often when it is not cited as when it is.

When we understand the category, "Torah," we shall find the necessary framework in which to interpret the facts at hand. For, it is clear, by "Torah," or "the Torah," the framers of the Talmud simply do not understand "the Hebrew Scripture" (a.k.a., Old Testament). They assign a privileged position to those writings, but they do not regard those writings as distinct, free-standing, autonomous. Those privileged writings – the source of the completion of all "as it is said"– and "as it is written" – sayings – form part of the Torah, the written part, the available part, the authoritative part, hence "as it is written," which only prefaces a verse of Scripture, or "as it is said," which is followed, uniquely, by a verse of Scripture. The reason the phrase, "the Torah in the Talmud," violates the language rules of the Talmud is that what we mean by "the Torah" forms part of the Torah. Hence to say "the Torah in the Talmud" is to say "the Torah in the Torah," and that is senseless. That fact underscores the absurdity of the results I have collected: top and bottom, beginning and end, fore and after, everything and its opposite. My category was wrong; there is no rule that emerges when we collect all the citations of or allusions to the Hebrew Scriptures in the Talmud, because those citations and allusions, on their own, derive from a source that is differentiated as to status but not distinct as to its structure; important in a system, but not autonomous of that system.

Before proceeding, let me briefly survey what we say when we use the word "Torah" in the Talmud. By that word, we connote a broad range of clearly distinct categories of noun and verb, concrete fact and abstract relationship alike. "Torah" stands for a kind of human being. It connotes a social status and a sort of social group. It refers to a type of social relationship. It further denotes a legal status and differentiates among legal norms. As symbolic abstraction, the word encompasses things and persons, actions and status, points of social differentiation and legal and normative standing, as well as "revealed truth." In all, the main points of insistence of the whole of Israel's life and history come to full symbolic expression in that single word. If people wanted to explain how they would be saved, they would use the word Torah. If they wished to sort out their parlous relationships with gentiles, they would use the word Torah. Torah stood for salvation and accounted for Israel's this-worldly condition and the hope, for both individual and nation alike, of life in the world to come. For the kind of Judaism under discussion, therefore, the word Torah stood for everything. The Torah symbolized the whole, at once and entire. When, therefore, we wish to describe the unfolding of the definitive doctrine of Judaism in its formative period, the first exercise consists in paying close attention to the meanings imputed to a single word.

Every detail of the religious system at hand exhibits essentially the same point of insistence, captured in the simple notion of the Torah as the generative symbol, the total, exhaustive expression of the system as a whole. That is why the definitive ritual of the Judaism under study consisted in studying the Torah as the generative symbol, the total, exhaustive expression of the system as a whole. That is why the definitive myth explained that one who studied Torah would become holy, like Moses "our rabbi," and like God, in whose image humanity was made and whose Torah provided the plan and the model for what God wanted of a humanity created in his image. As for Christians it was in Christ God made flesh, so the framers of the system of Judaism at hand found in the Torah that image of God to which Israel should aspire, and to which the sage in fact conformed.

The meaning of the several meanings of the Torah should require only brief explanation. When the Torah refers to a particular thing, it is to a scroll containing divinely revealed words. The Torah may further refer to revelation, not as an object but as a corpus of doctrine. When one "does Torah" the disciple "studies" or "learns," and the master "teaches," Torah. Hence while the word Torah never appears as a verb, it does refer to an act. The word also bears a quite separate sense, torah as category or classification or corpus of rules, for example, "the torah of driving a car" is a usage entirely acceptable to some documents. This generic usage of the word does occur. The word Torah very commonly refers to a status, distinct from and above another status, as "teachings of Torah" as against "teachings of scribes." For the two Talmuds that distinction is absolutely critical to the entire hermeneutic enterprise. But it is important even in the Mishnah. Finally, the word Torah refers to a source of salvation, often fully worked out in stories about how the individual and the nation will be saved through Torah. In general, the sense of the word "salvation" is not complicated. It is simply salvation in the way in which Deuteronomy and the Deuteronomic historians understand it: kings who do what God wants win battles, those who do not, lose. So, too, here, people who study and do Torah are saved from sickness and death, and the way Israel can save itself from its condition of degradation also is through Torah. In a word, "Torah" in the Talmud stands for "Judaism" in our language. The history of the symbolization of the Torah proceeds from its removal from the framework of material objects, even from the limitations of its own contents, to its transformation into something quite different and abstract, quite distinct from the document and its teachings.

With these facts in mind, we may state very simply that the Torah forms an important component of the Torah, or, to relinquish nonsense language, the Hebrew Scriptures in the Talmud are not "the Torah," distinct and autonomous, but a corpus of authoritative sayings, just as the Mishnah is a corpus of authoritative sayings. Then how in writing can I identify the Torah? It is, in the here and the now of the Talmud, those verses of Scripture, along with those sentences (or tractates) of the Mishnah – in neither case, the entirety of the document beginning to end – that the Talmud has selected and recast into its own statement: its Torah. It is within that framework that we make sense of the nonsense at hand. If the Talmud has formulated its (statement of) the Torah, then, quite naturally, it will draw upon received components of the Torah of Moses, according to each its proper place. Then the Torah received from Sinai in writing, a privileged corpus, will make a massive contribution of facts, settle numerous controverted questions, form a major focus of analysis. But it remains a source for this (statement of) the Torah, and not a free-standing, and autonomous document, for example, The Torah, The Written Torah, or, even "the Old Testament" for that matter. The written component, privileged though it is, forms a mere source, utilized in one way or another, as the framers of this (statement of) the Torah wish. The written component may well on occasion define the main beam of a literary structure, but that structure, whole and complete, will find a place for itself where the framers of this (statement of) the Torah choose, and nowhere else; for their purpose, and for no other purpose.

The simple fact is that the framers of the Talmud choose the verses of the Torah that they wish to utilize for their purpose, just as they choose the tractates of the Mishnah that they choose to analyze, and, within them, the sentences that they propose to identify as the mean beams of their construction. The Torah (Hebrew Scriptures, "the Old Testament") makes its way into the Talmud not whole and complete but by bits and pieces, because, so far as the framers of the Talmud are concerned, that Scripture that serves their purposes, and that part alone, is welcome, because it is useful. Otherwise, the Hebrew Scriptures bear no autonomous standing in their system and structure, and, consequently, also in their canon. The conception of a free-standing compilation, "the Holy Scriptures," or even "the Written Torah" for that matter, is alien to our document. Nothing in our survey suggests that anyone accords to "the Written Torah" the status of a complete and integral book or compilation, distinct from some other complete and integral books or compilations (for example, the Mishnah). The Christians knew that the Old Testament was distinct from, but related to, the New Testament. The framers of the Talmud knew no such thing. To them, "the Old Testament" was the written (part of) the one whole Torah of Moses our rabbi, distinguished by its medium of formulation and transmission, privileged by its authority, but in no way recognized, by reason of distinction and privilege, as other than yet another source of the Torah. But, for their part, they proposed to state that Torah. For that purpose, Scripture formed a mighty and formidable source – useful, to be sure, as the framers of the Talmud would dictate. But theirs would be the Torah: the statement of those parts of the received documents, all of them parts of the Torah in one medium or another, that they would choose to make. Privileged, paramount, preeminent in all the ways but the one that counted, in the Talmud, the Torah would emerge as contingent, instrumental, and merely useful: to be used as a dependent variable in a writing that formed an independent variable: the statement at the end.

Index

South Florida Studies in the History of Judaism

DATE DUE

Printed
in USA